Classics, Love, Revolution

POSTCLASSICAL INTERVENTIONS

General Editors: Lorna Hardwick and James I. Porter

Postclassical Interventions aims to reorient the meaning of antiquity across and beyond the humanities. Building on the success of *Classical Presences*, this complementary series features shorter-length monographs designed to provoke debate about the current and future potential of classical reception through fresh, bold, and critical thinking.

Classics, Love, Revolution

The Legacies of Luigi Settembrini

ANDREA CAPRA
and
BARBARA GRAZIOSI

Great Clarendon Street, Oxford, OX2 6DP,
United Kingdom

Oxford University Press is a department of the University of Oxford.
It furthers the University's objective of excellence in research, scholarship,
and education by publishing worldwide. Oxford is a registered trade mark of
Oxford University Press in the UK and in certain other countries

© Andrea Capra and Barbara Graziosi 2024

The moral rights of the authors have been asserted

All rights reserved. No part of this publication may be reproduced, stored in
a retrieval system, or transmitted, in any form or by any means, without the
prior permission in writing of Oxford University Press, or as expressly permitted
by law, by licence or under terms agreed with the appropriate reprographics
rights organization. Enquiries concerning reproduction outside the scope of the
above should be sent to the Rights Department, Oxford University Press, at the
address above

You must not circulate this work in any other form
and you must impose this same condition on any acquirer

Published in the United States of America by Oxford University Press
198 Madison Avenue, New York, NY 10016, United States of America

British Library Cataloguing in Publication Data
Data available

Library of Congress Control Number: 2023948679

ISBN 978-0-19-886544-5

DOI: 10.1093/oso/9780198865445.001.0001

Printed and bound in the UK by
Clays Ltd, Elcograf S.p.A.

Links to third party websites are provided by Oxford in good faith and
for information only. Oxford disclaims any responsibility for the materials
contained in any third party website referenced in this work.

To our mothers

Maria Grazia Bosi (Modena, 14 June 1938–Milano, 4 November 2021)
Marina Tarabocchia (Karachi, 30 November 1939–Trieste, 28 December 2020)

in memory of their sense of humour, spirit of irreverence, and love

Preface

This book belongs to a new series of 'Interventions': we are grateful to Lorna Hardwick and Jim Porter for their invitation to write it. Our aim is to explore the relationship between classical scholarship and revolutionary thinking, underlining the role that love *can* and—we even argue—*should* play in both. We arrive, then, at a general conclusion, even if we start from a specific encounter. The first chapter in this book focuses on a discovery, or rather a concatenated series of discoveries, that led us to consider the legacies of one man: the Neapolitan revolutionary and classical scholar Luigi Settembrini (1813–76). It is perhaps no coincidence that our discovery links back to previous ones in leaps of forty years, the span after which cultural memory generally begins to fade, as Assmann points out.[1] In our first introductory chapter, these leaps of forty years allow us to get in touch with Settembrini through the living memories of people whose cultural horizons overlapped. Our second chapter outlines the intervention we wish to make. As will be obvious from the start, in order to intervene in the way we did we needed to expand our own horizons well beyond our core areas of expertise, which are ancient Greek philosophy and literature. Colleagues working in modern European history, Italian literature, African-American studies, sociology, political theory, and gender studies have been exceptionally generous in providing feedback and encouragement.

The University Center for Human Values, Princeton University, awarded us a grant that supported archival work in Italy, for which we would like to express our gratitude. In Naples, we relied on the expertise, advice, and hospitality of Marco and Silvia Meriggi, Serena Cannavale, Gennaro Celato, Giambattista D'Alessio, Raffaele Giglio, Giulio Massimilla, Giovanni and Linda Muto, Maria Picardi, and the staff in the Rare Books

---

[1] Assmann 2011: 8.

Room at the Biblioteca Nazionale. We would also like to thank the staff of the Archivio Nazionale di Varese and the Biblioteca Vallicelliana in Rome. The Humanities Council, Princeton University, featured Settembrini at its 14th Annual Humanities Colloquium and Settembrini's legacies were also at the heart of the Gerald F. Else Lecture in the Humanities, which Barbara delivered at the University of Michigan in 2022: we are grateful for the feedback we received on those occasions and at other talks we gave in Venice, Durham, Johns Hopkins, and Stanford. At University College London, Phiroze Vasunia organized an exceptionally helpful workshop on our book manuscript: we were much energized by the attentive reading and perceptive comments provided by the respondents, Dan Orrells and Beatrice Sica, and the many participants—several of whom also followed up with email comments and suggestions.

We are lucky to belong to a thriving, international community of scholars: this book would not exist without it. Duncan Kennedy offered key insights on the conceptual framework we adopt in this book and shared early work on his own forthcoming monograph, provisionally entitled *The Emergence of Ontological Styles of Thinking in Ancient Greece*. Matt Ward went through the trouble of picking up typos, as well as offering larger comments on joy and subversion. Several other colleagues, in London and also on earlier occasions, offered crucial feedback and support: we would like to thank, in particular, Silvia Amarante, Richard Armstrong, Josh Billings, Connie Bloomfield, Rachel Bowlby, George Boys-Stones, Omar Brino, Fabrizio Buccigrossi, Alberto Camerotto, Eva Cantarella, Carlo Capra, Giovanna Ceserani, Domenico Conoscenti, Sandra Cuocolo, Antonino De Francesco, Catharine Edwards, Marco Fantuzzi, Meg Foster, Elena Giusti, Eddie Glaude, Emily Greenwood, Constanze Güthenke, Johannes Haubold, Brooke Holmes, Maurizio Isabella, Maddalena Italia, Jack Kelleher, Jhumpa Lahiri, Melissa Lane, Miriam Leonard, Artemis Leontis, Nick Lowe, Fiona MacIntosh, Justine McConnell, Katie McHugh, Sebastian Matzner, Valentina Monateri, Sheila Murnaghan, Dan-el Padilla Peralta, Aglae Pizzone, Enrico Prodi, Anna Rau, Jonathan Ready, Matteo Residori, Lucy Riall, Antonio Sennis, Michael Silk, Oliver Taplin, and Phiroze Vasunia. At Oxford University Press Charlotte Loveridge and Nadine Kolz have been wonderful in their care and support. We would also like to thank our production manager,

Manimegalai Devi, and copy editor, Kim Richardson. Last but not least, we would like to thank Luigi Settembrini himself. We worked on this book rather slowly, in a period of isolation and bereavement: he kept us company, offered a humbling example of productivity and good cheer under harsh conditions—and often made us smile.

Contents

List of Illustrations   xiii

INTRODUCTION: TRUTH AND FAKERY

1. The Discovery   3
2. The Intervention   23

PART I: AUTOBIOGRAPHY AND REVOLUTION

3. Luigi Settembrini, According to Himself   37
4. Luigi Settembrini, According to His Wife   54
5. Revolutionary Heroes and Italian Men   80

PART II: PLATONIC FICTIONS

6. The *Dialogue on Women*   97
7. *The Neoplatonists*   114
8. How to Live and How to Read   136

PART III: *THE NEOPLATONISTS*: ENGLISH TRANSLATION AND NOTES

9. *The Neoplatonists* by Aristaeus of Megara   149

   Epilogue   184

Bibliography   185
Index   193

List of Illustrations

1.1 L. Settembrini, *The Neoplatonists*, autograph, p. 1 (Pessina archive, XVI A 66, National Library, Naples)   5

1.2 L. Settembrini, *Memoirs of My Life*, autograph, p. 1 (Pessina archive, XVI A 65, National Library, Naples)   6

1.3 E. Fabietti, *Luigi Settembrini*. La Centuria di ferro: la pattuglia dei precursori, vol. 9, Milan, 1936: book cover   9

1.4 R. Cantarella, ed., *I Neoplatonici*. By Luigi Settembrini. Milan, 1977. book cover   13

4.1 A recent picture of the Panopticon's central courtyard, Wikimedia Commons   61

4.2 Cork model of the Panopticon, made by an inmate, Museum of San Martino, Naples   62

4.3 Pasquale Mattei, 'Scoglio di Santo Stefano', 1850 (Mattei archive, II 2, Biblioteca Vallicelliana, Rome)   64

4.4 Vincenzo Montefusco, *Settembrini Reading to Inmates in the Panopticon*, Museum of San Martino, Naples   71

4.5 Nautical map with annotations by Giuseppe Garibaldi, outlining the route he was planning to sail to rescue Settembrini and other political prisoners (taken from Capasso 1908: 27)   76

5.1 'Arrival of Neapolitan Exiles at Paddington Station', *Illustrated London News*, 2 April 1859, p. 321, Mary Evans Picture Library   82

INTRODUCTION
Truth and Fakery

You need a little fakery in all enterprises in this world: it is like salt which, in small measure, adds to the flavour, but in excess ruins everything.

Luigi Settembrini[1]

---

[1] Settembrini 1971: 91, for context and discussion see p. 47.

1
The Discovery

It can happen, in scholarship as in life, that you discover something you never wanted to know. The reaction is the same, either way: you feel betrayed. What you held dear, what gave you comfort and made you feel secure, no longer makes sense. Or perhaps it does make sense, but along lines you had rather not imagine. When something like this happens, it is tempting to pretend nothing happened at all.

Naples, 1937

Between the years of 1929 and 1937, Professor Raffaele Cantarella worked in the National Library of Naples as director of the Officina dei Papiri: in that capacity, he was responsible for the preservation, decipherment, and publication of several hundred charred papyri retrieved from the ancient city of Herculaneum—an enormous task, which carries on to this day. For Cantarella, making new discoveries was a matter of routine—and yet he long failed to acknowledge what was arguably his greatest find.[1] Towards the end of his tenure, in 1937, while looking for a Byzantine manuscript, he happened upon a small, handwritten, modern-looking paper booklet. It attracted his attention because it seemed 'recent and quite flimsy among the grand, solidly bound ancient codices'.[2] The cover (Figure 1.1) bore these words:

---

[1] For Cantarella's contributions to papyrology, see, for example, his edition of P.Herc. 1413, a fragment of Epicurus' book *On Time*: Cantarella and Arrighetti 1972.
[2] Cantarella 1977: 21.

Classics, Love, Revolution: The Legacies of Luigi Settembrini. Andrea Capra and Barbara Graziosi,
Oxford University Press. © Andrea Capra and Barbara Graziosi 2024.
DOI: 10.1093/oso/9780198865445.003.0001

The Neoplatonists
by
Aristaeus of Megara.
Translation from the Greek.

This piqued Cantarella's curiosity: despite his vast knowledge of ancient literature, he had never heard of an author called Aristaeus of Megara, or a text entitled *The Neoplatonists*. He read the whole manuscript there and then: compared to the challenges posed by charred papyri bearing faint traces of ancient Greek it was, as he put it himself, 'not hard to read'.[3] The hand was clear and elegant, the Italian prose attractively cultivated, with touches of vernacular colour. The content, however, seemed to him disturbing.

Cantarella quickly established that he was dealing with a fake: some anachronisms pointed to a modern forgery.[4] He vaguely decided he would try to discover, at some point in the future, the date and origin of the 'strange text' he had encountered and then put it back where he had found it. It was that very act of shelving that provided him with immediate answers to his questions. Next to the booklet he noticed another, much thicker manuscript (Figure 1.2):

Memoirs of My Life
1.
Childhood

In the top left-hand corner, a more recent hand had added: 'Autograph by Luigi Settembrini'.

Now this volume was no fake—and Cantarella immediately saw that it was written in the same hand and on the same kind of paper as *The Neoplatonists*. The manuscript he now held in his hands was the autograph copy of a famous book, written by a man who, especially in the 1930s, was even more famous. Luigi Settembrini, a revolutionary hero of

---

[3] Cantarella 1977: 22.
[4] He knew, for example, that 'Neoplatonists' was a neologism, even if he failed to appreciate its significance (on which see pp. 29–30) and noticed other minor anachronistic details too. On anachronism as a mode of relating to the past which allows for affective investment, Holmes 2020.

THE DISCOVERY 5

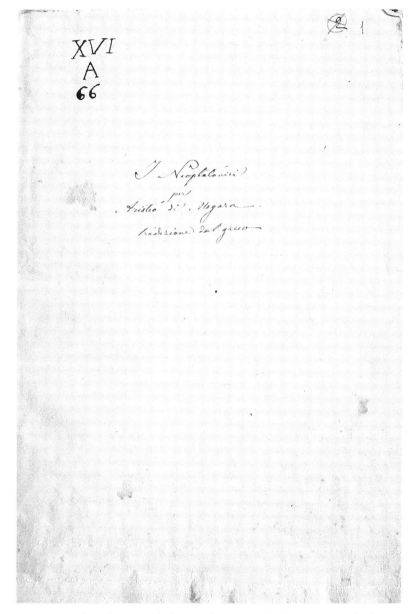

Figure 1.1 The title page of *The Neoplatonists*, clearly written in the hand of Luigi Settembrini.

6 CLASSICS, LOVE, REVOLUTION

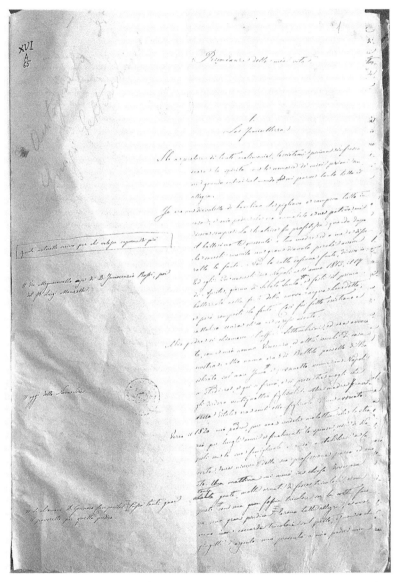

Figure 1.2 The first page of Settembrini's celebrated *Memoirs*, autograph copy.

the nineteenth-century Risorgimento, the movement that freed Italy from foreign rule and unified the country, was held up as an example to all. Every major Italian city had (and still has) a street or school named after him. Every child was expected to know the basic facts of his life: martyr of the Bourbons, condemned to death for his role in the 1848 revolution, pardoned, imprisoned for life in the Panopticon (a notorious island prison off the coast of Naples), exiled—and then, finally, after mutiny, poverty, displacement, and distress, returned to his country in the company of Garibaldi's men, in a rare moment of national pride. The problem confronting Cantarella was this. Settembrini was not only the author of his celebrated *Memoirs* but, it now turned out, a forger of Greek tales. Worse. He had committed to paper a story of joyous, unbridled sexual pleasure and homoeroticism: 'to Platonize', in the idiom of his tale, meant having anal sex.

Cantarella quickly replaced *The Neoplatonists* where he had found it. Thousands of charred papyri demanded his attention, after all, and they were actual remains of genuine Greek philosophy, not fake-ancient, 'Platonizing' obscenities. Later, he explained that he 'had work to do which seemed more urgent' and that he 'was embarrassed by the content of the tale and the strange personality of its author'.[5] That may be all that Professor Cantarella was prepared to admit, even forty years after the fact. But at the time, in 1937, there were other, rather compelling reasons to shelve *The Neoplatonists*.

The fascists were at the height of their power: it would have been damaging, if not downright dangerous, to reveal the national hero Settembrini as the author of sodomitic fantasies. The problem went deep, because the fascists saw themselves as heirs of a virile ancient Roman empire and an equally virile Italian nation created by men like Garibaldi and, indeed, Settembrini himself. The revolutionaries and romantics who had freed the nation in the nineteenth century were held up as examples of virility—not least in an attempt to disprove northern European clichés about Italian sensuality and effeminate weakness. As Patriarca compellingly argues, those clichés were routinely used to keep the nation divided and dominated by foreign interests.[6] The fascists took inspiration from the Risorgimento and replayed its heroism as farce.[7] In 1930, a new type of submarine, the pride of the fascist navy,

---

[5] Cantarella 1977: 23.   [6] Patriarca 2005.
[7] Marx 2013: 9, first published in 1852. Marx draws a contrast between the French Revolution of 1799 and the coup of 1851, when Napoleon III assumed dictatorial powers.

was named 'Luigi Settembrini'. In 1936, he was described as an 'iron centurion' of the Italian nation, in a new biography that bore little resemblance to his own *Memoirs*: the fascist symbols of power surrounding his portrait, on the cover, were somewhat undermined by the quizzical, gentle expression of the man himself (Figure 1.3).

Mussolini presented his vision of the future by drawing strength from Roman antiquity and the Italian Risorgimento: on 4 June 1932, for example, he stood atop the Janiculum, one the seven hills of Rome, and delivered a mighty speech to the effect that his 'black-shirt' militias were the descendants of Garibaldi's 'red-shirt' volunteers, the brave men who had liberated Sicily and the Italian south from the Bourbons, thus uniting Italy. Mussolini added, from his position next to an effigy of Garibaldi himself, that he wished the statue could open its eyes and see what Mussolini had accomplished—for there, before them, shone the city of Rome, 'luminous, vast, and pacified', once *caput mundi*, head of the Roman empire, now capital of a glorious Italian nation.[8]

How could Professor Cantarella, patient editor of Greek papyri, put himself in the way of such exalted visions of history? Who was he to march against armies of Roman legionaries, Italian revolutionaries, and fascist thugs? And, anyway, why publish *The Neoplatonists*? Cantarella had, as he put it himself, more urgent things to do.[9] Still, a doubt lingered in his mind. It had nothing to do with the content of Settembrini's tale, which he did not much like. It was a doubt about editorial duty.

Milan, 1977

Forty years later, shortly before dying, Cantarella returned to *The Neoplatonists* and began preparing a scholarly edition of the text. Over the years, he had made tactful enquiries about his discovery and established that he was by no means the only scholar aware of the tale's existence. Benedetto Croce (1866–1952), the most powerful intellectual

---

[8] See Fogu 2001.
[9] That said, Cantarella frequently hosted and helped various opponents of the fascist regime: Alfieri 1986: 264–7.

Figure 1.3 A biography of Settembrini by Ettore Fabietti, published in 1936: surrounded by fascist symbols, he is presented as a 'centurion' and a 'precursor' of Mussolini's regime, in one of the most bizarre attempts to claim his legacy.

in Italy between the late nineteenth century and the 1950s, knew all about it. When asked what he thought of it, he answered with a 'broad smile' and a 'gesture of indulgence', suggesting that Settembrini had spent too much time translating the ancient author Lucian and that he had been infected by his obscenities.[10] Francesco Torraca, another prominent man of letters (and pupil of Settembrini) considered *The Neoplatonists* 'a mistake', best kept 'in the shadows of the library, accessible only to infrequent scholars'.[11] Emidio Piermarini, the librarian responsible for cataloguing the manuscript, was prepared to praise the novella for its 'freshness', 'grace', and effective portrait of 'the brave and joyous lifestyle of the ancient Greeks'; indeed, he was unusual in recognizing its literary merit and moral intent—yet he too, in the 1930s, thought it simply had to be kept in the shadows of the library.[12] By the 1950s, he was no longer so sure: as he pointed out in a letter to Cantarella, 'these days an André Gide can win the Nobel Prize'.[13]

And yet it took another two decades before the tale was finally published. That delay needs to be seen as part of larger clashes in Italian attitudes towards the national past and, simultaneously, towards homosexuality. The Risorgimento, which had been so forcefully claimed by the fascists, was equally important for the antifascists. Already in the 1930s, Italian volunteers fighting against Franco in the Spanish Civil War organized themselves into 'Garibaldi brigades'. A few years later, after the military collapse of fascist Italy in 1943, the 'Second Risorgimento' (1943–5) saw the same communist brigades fight in both Italy and Yugoslavia.[14] When the Second World War was finally over, a constitutional referendum, held on 2 June 1946, asked the Italian people whether the country was to remain a monarchy or become a republic. The interest

---

[10] Cantarella 1977: 26f., see also Manganelli's comments on p. 11: censorship of *The Neoplatonists* allowed Croce to present Settembrini to the public as having had 'the purest life, entirely consecrated to the ideal of the fatherland, enlivened by love for his family—a mild yet unbending life, quiet, and brave: the life of a good man, which is at the same time a lesser life and a greater than that of a hero'. Manganelli's point is somewhat misleading, however, in that Croce had no active role in hindering the publication of the *Neoplatonists*: see Fubini 1977, who exposes Manganelli's gross misrepresentation of the evidence. Croce did, however, hedge his bets, just in case *The Neoplatonists* was to be discovered, by adding that being a hero involved having 'faults, tempestuous passions, sharpness, errors', but also 'greatness, which is all the greater as great are the battles fought within one's own chest'. As a curiosity, we may also mention that Croce assumed that Thomas Mann's Settembrini, a prominent character in *The Magic Mountain*, was inspired by Luigi. Mann denied this, but in his exchanges with Croce he came to believe that there was a strong resemblance between the fictional and the real Settembrini, only to change his mind at a later point, when he learnt more about Luigi: see Zapperi 2014.
[11] Cantarella 1977: 27.   [12] Cantarella 1977: 25–7.   [13] Cantarella 1977: 27.
[14] Isnenghi 1997: 41–3; Grévy, Heyriès, and Maltone 2001: 212–18.

of the Allied forces in this referendum is easy to trace: predictably, Britain favoured retention of the monarchy, whereas the USA wanted to see the birth of an Italian republic. The republican side won by a narrow majority. Great efforts were made, at that point, to present the result as the culmination of an Italian story that had its roots in the Risorgimento itself, rather than a reflection of foreign interests. Giuseppe Mazzini, the main ideologue of the Italian revolutionary movement in the nineteenth century, believed that Italy needed to be 'united, free, independent, republican' (*una, libera, indipendente, repubblicana*, as the much-repeated phrase went). The abolition of the monarchy and the establishment of the Italian Republic were presented as the fulfilment of his revolutionary vision.[15]

In post-war Italy, the Risorgimento proved useful: it could be mobilized to bring together a country that had been torn apart not just by war, but by a civil conflict and an ensuing constitutional crisis. Great energy went into turning the heroes of the Risorgimento into consensual figures, a manoeuvre which eventually reduced them to 'apolitical banalities', to quote Lucy Riall's apt description.[16] Many of their more controversial and interesting aspects (such as the extreme anticlericalism of Garibaldi—and of Settembrini himself) were successfully hidden from view, in the long decades of Christian Democrat rule after 1948. As personal links and memories of the nineteenth century receded, the Risorgimento became a repository of traditional virtues—unity, patriotism, military courage—which soon began to sound like empty rhetoric. By the 1960s and 70s, young people had had enough. They were ready for their own student revolution.

In Milan, where Cantarella now lived, protesters were taking to the streets daily, marching against the patriarchy, misogyny, homophobia, war, colonialism, economic inequality, and political oppression. With their long hair, bell-bottom trousers, and eskimo jackets, it was sometimes difficult to tell men and women apart. Cantarella, at this point, came to think it was perhaps time to publish Settembrini's tale. He began

---

[15] See Mack Smith 1994: 218–21 on how Mazzini was claimed for the antifascist cause and (with greater difficulty, it must be said) by the fascists too.
[16] Riall 2007: 7.

to prepare an edition, documenting his find, attempting to date *The Neoplatonists*,[17] identifying the ancient sources that had inspired it, and explaining his own motivations: 'if, today, after so many years, I have decided to make known to the public this short work by Settembrini regardless [of its content], it is also because—quite apart from its historical and literary interest—it cannot in any way tarnish the figure of this man, and patriot, so worthy of our admiration and respect'.[18] How wrong he was.

Cantarella died before he could complete his edition. The publishers, Rizzoli, decided to print *The Neoplatonists* anyway—and without much respect for either editor or author.[19] Now that Cantarella could no longer control the terms in which the tale was to be presented to the public, Rizzoli turned the whole discovery into a scandal. The cover featured an explicit scene of sex between a man and a boy (Figure 1.4).[20] The strapline read: 'A literary sensation: the erotic tale written by a hero of the Risorgimento and kept secret until now.' A new preface, provided by the avant-garde controversialist Giorgio Manganelli, took pride of place before Cantarella's scrupulous and timid introduction. It began with a grim allegory of the 'father of the fatherland':

At the head of the table sits a man. The table is vast, yet this man is visible to all, and at all times: his face is sombre, unsmiling. His manners are noble and he is obviously disgusted by the company he has to keep. He eats slowly, looking around the table, examining his companions one by one, following their gestures and the movement of their mouths. He dislikes them all. Under his gaze, each guest feels uncomfortable, becomes unattractive, and falters.[21]

Manganelli depicted the whole history of the Italian nation, from the Risorgimento to the 1970s, as an oppressive family meal. The younger generations ate avidly, without manners, yet felt inhibited by the patriarch

---

[17] See p. 13.   [18] Cantarella 1977: 27f.
[19] See Fubini 1977. An outstanding scholar of Italian literature, Fubini was Cantarella's colleague at the University of Milan: he outlived him by under two months, and yet made it his priority to make that point.
[20] On Settembrini's condemnation of pederasty, see, pp. 30f.   [21] Cantarella 1977: 5.

THE DISCOVERY 13

Figure 1.4 The sensationalist cover of the first edition of *The Neoplatonists* (1977).

watching over them. 'We all know who he is,' continued Manganelli, 'and we do not love him: he is the Father of the Fatherland, an archaic rhetorical figure, known under many different names, with whom we share no language.'[22] Liberation, he further suggested, was to be found in the tale discovered by Cantarella, and kept hidden for so long:

> We have long waited for a miracle, an event that would allow us to talk to this man without incurring his rightful anger—this man who seems ever more distant, more menacing, more disappointed in us. A simple and absurd event would be enough, an act of childish iconoclasm; for example, see that boy, that freckled boy right over there, who is now standing up and asking with respect, in fact even some friendly complicity: 'Daddy, is it true that you are a pederast?'[23]

Settembrini was exposed. His forged ancient tale was read as documentary evidence for his life—evidence that was suddenly considered more reliable than the self-portrait he had offered in his *Memoirs* and letters.[24] It was conjectured, in particular, that Settembrini had experienced homosexuality while serving his life sentence in the Panopticon.[25] On the basis of a curtailed and misunderstood passage in Cantarella's own Introduction, it was also suggested that Settembrini had written *The Neoplatonists* specifically for his wife, as a form of coded truth-telling from prison.[26] This biographical fiction based on Settembrini's own fictional tale proved popular. As people took to the streets in a new period of deep civil conflict, the so-called *anni di piombo* ('years of lead'), Settembrini was discarded as a founding father of the Italian nation and rediscovered as a closet homosexual.

---

[22] Cantarella 1977: 6.   [23] Cantarella 1977: 7.
[24] See Conoscenti 2019: 212f. for a list of the main reactions in the press immediately following publication.
[25] Cantarella 1977: 30.
[26] Manganelli (in Cantarella 1977: 13f.) was the first to suggest this hypothesis, which continues to be repeated as fact, see, for example, https://nonsologay.blogspot.com/2013/08/i-neoplatonici-di-luigi-settembrini-e.html (accessed 30 November 2023). Conoscenti 2019: 34–5 shows how Manganelli's interpretation was based on a misreading of Cantarella 1977: 28f. (itself less clear than an earlier version of the same paragraph). We believe, in agreement with Conoscenti 2010, but on the basis of further evidence, that the version of *The Neoplatonists* we have dates to a later period in his life. For discussion see pp. 25–7.

A few errors were made in the course of this manoeuvre. For example, Settembrini was turned into 'a pederast',[27] although we read in *The Neoplatonists* that lovers should be of equal or similar age and, if both male, switch roles.[28] This and other misrepresentations were symptoms of a larger problem. When *The Neoplatonists* was published, nobody thought to ask how the tale related to Settembrini's political commitments.[29] And although Settembrini's work as a classicist was sometimes used to explain—or rather, excuse—his decision to write *The Neoplatonists*,[30] his views as a *critic* of ancient Greek culture were never considered in relation to the tale.[31] In short, *The Neoplatonists* was used to drive a wedge between two versions of Settembrini: the maker of Italy on the one hand, and the champion of Greek love on the other. One element of continuity remained. In the 1970s as in the 1930s, Settembrini was to be *either* a father of the fatherland *or* the author of homosexual fantasies.

Durham, 2017

Forty years since the publication of *The Neoplatonists*, and eighty since Cantarella's first discovery, we decided that the text needed a reassessment—also in relation to what was happening in contemporary politics and in our own field of classics. When the novella first came up in conversation between us, we were having coffee on Andrea's terrace, overlooking the rooftops of Chinatown, Milan.[32] At the time, Andrea was working on *The Neoplatonists* for a paper on the reception of the ancient

---

[27] See Figure 1.4, Manganelli in Cantarella 1977: 7, and Cantarella himself at p. 107. Of course, distinctions that are important in contemporary discourse, for example about consent and the age of consent, were less clear-cut in the 1970s, when 'homosexuality' and 'pederasty' were often used as near synonyms.

[28] See, pp. 30 and 118f.

[29] The trend to treat *The Neoplatonists* in isolation continues. A popular survey of the main actors in the Risorgimento (Sconocchia 2019) recounts at length the life of Settembrini, making no reference to *The Neoplatonists* at all.

[30] Gigante 1977.

[31] For further discussion of Settembrini's stance as a critic of ancient literature—and the importance of that stance for the interpretation of his legacies—see, p. 134.

[32] At the time we did not know that the publishing house La Vita Felice was reissuing Cantarella's edition of *The Neoplatonists*.

novel and was much taken by its style:[33] 'You should translate it into English, Barbara. It deserves to be better known. Besides, you would enjoy the challenge: his classical allusions, gentle humour, and sheer sense of physical pleasure are easily lost in translation.' 'Right, Andrea, let me see. Settembrini. Who was he, again?' Initially, we left it at that. Just like Cantarella, we also thought we had better things to do.

Andrea was in the process of moving from Milan to the north of England, to take up a professorship at Durham, while Barbara was preparing to leave Durham for Princeton, New Jersey. These personal signs of restlessness were indirectly, yet unmistakably, linked to wider political shifts. The British people had just voted to leave the European Union, to the chants of 'we want our country back'. In Italy, Salvini was preparing a campaign directed against poor migrants from the south and privileged European Unionists from the north. Meanwhile, in the United States, Donald Trump had just been elected on the promise that he would 'make America great again'. What these different movements had in common was a vague nostalgia for a past of national unity, when life was supposedly simpler and more secure, when men were men, women served their needs, and foreigners lived abroad. We asked ourselves what we were doing, moving so far from home to teach classics in foreign lands. The ancient civilizations of Greece and Rome had, through the centuries, often inspired a deep longing for the past. Classics, as a discipline, was often nostalgic in orientation, for all that its relationship to nationalism was not, on the whole, straightforward.[34] Greeks and Italians took inspiration from antiquity when fighting for the unity and independence of their nations—but they knew that German, British, French, Russian, American, and other interlocutors considered themselves more worthy heirs of Greco-Roman legacies.[35] In Italy, moreover, some thinkers (Settembrini included) cast the Romans as conquerors of older, local Italian populations, while associating the

---

[33] Capra 2018.
[34] We are, of course, aware of the nostalgic strain in our own project here—our own return, that is, to nineteenth-century nationalisms and classicisms, as a means of thinking about the present and future.
[35] On Greece, Güthenke 2008; on Italy, De Francesco 2013; on classics and nationalism more generally, Stephens and Vasunia 2010.

Greeks with progressive political positions, a valorization of the south, and a multiethnic vision of a united Italy.[36]

While leaving behind our old academic jobs and accepting new positions—and in between packing, moving, and resettling—we focused our conversations on a few basic facts. First, that Italy, as a nation, was created by revolutionaries who spent some, or most, of their adult lives abroad: Garibaldi, Mazzini, and Settembrini himself were all cases in point—a point now conveniently forgotten both in Italy and in the countries that offered refuge to those men.[37] Second, that the cultures of Greece and Rome enabled conversations across large divides not only of nationality, but also of class, race, and sexual orientation: a fact again often forgotten, especially in light of a growing discourse that tends to equate the field of classics with the systemic oppressions of white supremacy.[38] Third, and relatedly, that the history of classics as a discipline was often told from a narrow Anglo-German perspective, which in turn meant that the history of homosexuality often suffered from similar limitations in perspective.[39] It seemed to us that Settembrini could offer a new and helpful focus of attention—both in terms of his biography and in light of his work. At a biographical level, he personally owed his liberty (and possibly his life) to a motley crew manning a US schooner headed for New York in 1859: two Black sailors, in particular, had sided with their cargo of Neapolitan prisoners and threatened their own captain, in a gesture that involved common commitments to

---

[36] For further discussion, see pp. 92f. and 104f. on Vincenzo Cuoco (1770–1823), an important influence on Settembrini. A full exploration of Settembrini's commitment to the Greeks (and the more general association, in Italy, between studying the Greeks and championing progressive, left-leaning politics) goes beyond the scope of this book. In the case of Settembrini, it would involve distinguishing his attitudes from those of other major figures of the Risorgimento, who placed greater emphasis on Rome as the future capital of Italy and the ancient capital of a non-Christian empire. On Mazzini, Garibaldi, Rome, and the ancient Romans, see Springer 1987: 136–57

[37] The contribution of 'expatriates and exiles', from the Middle Ages onwards, is clearly articulated in Duggan's brief introduction to 'Italy' as a concept: 1994: 1–8.

[38] Attention to Black classicisms is important here, see Greenwood 2009.

[39] Dan Orrells's *Classical Culture and Modern Masculinity* (2011), for example, focuses exclusively on German and English intellectuals active between 1750 and 1910. Within those constraints, the discussion he offers is excellent: we wish we had more space, within the limitations of our own short book, to explore Settembrini's ideas about love and antiquity more fully in relation to those of his northern European contemporaries. A broader investigation of that kind would also profit from Shane Butler's *The Passions of John Addington Symonds* (2022).

self-determination and effective solidarity among different and differently oppressed groups.[40] In his work, Settembrini explicitly argued in favour of strict equality between people in general and lovers in particular (in both homo- and heterosexual relationships); he also repeatedly offered a multiethnic vision of classical antiquity, matching his aspirations for the future of Italy and clashing with other, dominant (and domineering) visions of the ancient world. Such visions, it might be useful to point out, were often imposed on Italy by superior foreign powers, but were also internalized.[41] In Settembrini's account, the Romans were a northern people who had violently subjugated other, earlier, and more varied Italic populations, the Etruscans and the Greeks of southern Italy.[42] Settembrini had no patience at all for arguments about the racial superiority of 'Indo-European' ancestors: he made fun of the Germans for the pride they took in claiming to be 'close relatives of the Indians', as he put it, typically exposing a will to power by cracking a joke.[43] These considerations led to our third observation: that the study of ancient Greece and Rome was (and arguably always is) directed towards the future.[44] We wondered, then, what kind of future we ourselves were envisaging, as classical scholars. And here we entered into a discussion of method.

One of the most remarkable developments in the field of classics is a surge of interest in reception studies stemming, in part, from the belief that 'all meaning is constituted or actualized at the point of reception', to quote a phrase by Charles Martindale that has, by now, been repeated countless times.[45] One reason why this assertion has proven influential is that, as Sheila Murnaghan points out, it 'offers an alternative to traditional, positivistic views of classics as the quest for unmediated knowledge of an exemplary past. With the idea of an essential, knowable past under pressure from various forms of postmodernism, it is a relief to

---

[40] See pp. 103f. [41] See esp. pp. 91–3.
[42] See pp. 104f. [43] Settembrini 1964: 1176.
[44] See Settis 2006, with Graziosi 2005. In making the case for the value of anachronism, Holmes 2020: 69 argues that 'in time's folds lies the possibility of a surprise that shifts the conditions of our ethical orientation towards the next "now" and indeed transforms our understanding of what *is* now'. Alarmingly, this description fits the affective and anachronistic nostalgia of powerful political movements in the present, as well as the kind of enabling case study in reorientation she proposes.
[45] Martindale 1993: 14.

highlight instead the partiality and particularity of any attempt to grasp antiquity. As classicists give up the struggle to defend antiquity's privileged place in history, there is considerable appeal in focusing on what others have made of that cultural moment'—without, as it were, having to make the case for ancient Greece and Rome ourselves.[46]

Of course, in this crisis of positivist approaches to history, it is all too easy to trace a line between postmodernist and 'post-truth' attitudes to what used to be called historical 'fact'.[47] If meaning is realized at the point of reception, then one obvious question is 'whether all instances of reception have an equal status, as witnesses to their ancient sources or in other terms, or whether we can and should discriminate among them'.[48] To put it bluntly: do some acts of reception get it right, while others do not? And by what criteria can we establish the difference? Specifically, in our case: are we better placed to assess Settembrini's *The Neoplatonists* (itself an act of reception, or forgery, of the classical past) than Cantarella in 1937, or Manganelli in 1977?

Some steps can be taken towards providing (we hope) an honest answer. First of all, rather than work with binary oppositions between true/false and right/wrong, we ask what is 'better', mobilizing what Barbara Cassin calls the 'dedicated comparative'. Relativism, in her account, does not lead to the conclusion that 'all opinions have the same value', but rather becomes a precondition for collective self-determination, politics as the 'differential aid to choose the better', not in absolute terms, but rather in terms of what is 'better for' something.[49] And this, in turn, implies an affective shift towards care and, indeed, love. The generation of our students asks us 'not to judge': the point, we gather, is not to insist that all views are equally valid, but rather to express the need for care. Discriminating between true and false suggests objectivity; asking which is better implies involvement.

The dedicated comparative offers a useful theoretical framework for this book, given our interest in classics, love, and revolution. It also allows us to articulate the different value we assign to previous

---

[46] Murnaghan 2007.
[47] Latour 2004 traces precisely that line, see further pp. 28 and 142f.
[48] Murnaghan 2007.   [49] Cassin 2014: 315–16.

discoveries and discussions of *The Neoplatonists*. Cantarella cared about Settembrini: he wanted to give a reliable account of his work and legacies even if, as he put it, he felt 'embarrassed...by his strange personality'.[50] Manganelli was not especially interested in giving Settembrini a fair hearing; he was more concerned with exposing some oppressive banalities associated with Risorgimento figures in general. This can be seen, for example, in the way he handled Settembrini's smile. Indeed, the way *we* handle that smile may be taken as an illustration of the more general approach we plan to take.

Now, it goes without saying that we can no longer know whether Settembrini was prone to smiling by direct, face-to-face observation. We can, however, observe that those who knew him often remarked on his smiling appearance.[51] We can also note that, for his part, Settembrini frequently recollected the smiles of others, particularly when facing situations of extreme danger or despair.[52] More importantly, he considered fair weather in the land and a bright clarity in the people as typical traits of Italy and Greece, and saw them reflected in both ancient and modern literature emanating from these countries.[53] In fact, he made it clear that he *wanted* to see them there. Thus, for example, when advising a young scholar who had sent him a rather gloomy essay, he wrote: 'I would like to see you happy, pleasant, good humoured, affectionate—in other words, young and Sicilian, just as you are. There you have it: my honest opinion. Please do send me some more writings of yours, but let them be cheerful.'[54] Settembrini's smile was, then, not just a biographical trait but an ideological position.[55]

---

[50] Cantarella 1977: 23.

[51] Francesco De Sanctis 1876: 6, for example, wrote about how he visited Settembrini three days before his death, and found him 'cheerful and with a bright expression'; see also De Sanctis's preface to Settembrini 1892: xv: 'that smiling face of his'.

[52] Recollections of smiles while waiting to be executed (Settembrini 1961: 268f.); the smile of Settembrini's wife (Settembrini 1971: 95, quoted below, p. 175, n. 4.); Settembrini's father also seemed to remember pivotal moments in his life in terms of the encouragement offered by the smiles of others (Settembrini 1961: 4).

[53] See, for example, his chapter on the 'character of Italian literature', Settembrini 1964: 17–19.

[54] Settembrini 1971: 840.

[55] Cf. his observations on 'pagan' Catholicism and the smile as a national characteristic of Italians, quoted on p. 153, n. 15.

Despite this, in his preface to *The Neoplatonists* Manganelli described the father of the fatherland as 'sombre, unsmiling', constantly disapproving of others. Now, it seems that Manganelli knew his description did not fit Settembrini in his biographical and ideological specificity—and that is one reason why he presented his portrait as an 'imprecise image... an archaic rhetorical figure'.[56] Still, his account was certain to mislead readers by suggesting that the *joie de vivre* emanating from *The Neoplatonists* was to be understood in contrast to, rather than in line with, the rest of Settembrini's life and work.

As a result of this (misre)presentation, Settembrini was neatly divided into two. His public (heterosexual) *Memoirs* were severed from his private (homosexual) fiction—and this despite the fact that *The Neoplatonists* insists on the importance of symmetry in heterosexual relationships as well as homosexual ones, while many passages in the *Memoirs* speak movingly of love between men. The dichotomies established in the 1970s have not been overcome.[57] In fact, they manifest themselves today in the widening gap between nationalist and other kinds of identity politics—not only in Italy, but in many other countries, including Great Britain and the United States, where we currently live and work. On the one hand, there are those who insist on the value of equality and diversity; on the other, a growing electorate longs for a past (and future) of greater national unity and uniformity. One reason, then, why we decided to write this book is that we would like to gain a better understanding of how the classical past shaped both modern nationalisms and modern sexual identities. The legacies of Luigi Settembrini seem interesting in this respect, precisely because they are sharply divided between the nationalist revolutions of 1848 and the sexual revolutions of the 1970s.

The question is whether our need to shed light on nationalist and other kinds of identity politics today will lead to our own forgeries, our own fake creations of the past. One way to acknowledge that risk is to be

---

[56] Manganelli in Cantarella 1977: 6.
[57] Conoscenti 2019 offers an excellent study of *The Neoplatonists* without, however, considering it in relation to Settembrini's political legacies. The most convincing attempt to put the various versions of Settembrini together is, in our view, Minniti 2022. It is a work of historical imagination and, for that reason, difficult to integrate fully in our more scholarly reconstruction, but it is highly recommended reading.

explicit about our own situatedness, our motivations and commitments, which we have tried to be. Another and perhaps even more important move is to trust what remains of the past in the present. This too is a form of care and it demands that we take a stance in another raging debate in reception studies. To quote Sheila Murnaghan one more time, we can ask 'whether the privileging of reception means that reception gets sole credit for determining meaning, with no contribution from the ancient object being received'.[58] We argue, in this book, for the authentic presence of classical antiquity in our world—even in the case of an anachronistic fake such as Settembrini's *The Neoplatonists*.[59]

---

[58] Murnhagan 2007. [59] For the value of anachronism, see Holmes 2020.

2
The Intervention

> The notions of importance, necessity, interest, are a thousand times more determining than the notion of truth. Not because they replace truth but because they measure the truth of what I am saying.
>
> Gilles Deleuze, *Negotiations* (our translation, inspired by Barbara Cassin's modification of the version made by Martin Joughin)[1]

This book stems from our discovery of *The Neoplatonists* coupled with a growing sense of its relevance to the present moment. It is also, as we mentioned, our response to a specific invitation on the part of Lorna Hardwick and Jim Porter. Just as we were considering the implications of our interest in Settembrini, they wrote to solicit an 'extended essay' that would set 'recent and contemporary issues against the background of classical antiquity'. We offered to respond by letting antiquity speak through Settembrini—and Settembrini speak through us. This, we would like to insist at the outset, does not involve abdicating responsibility, or abandoning our own commitment to the study of ancient Greece and Rome. We aim, in this book, to demonstrate the positive contribution of the classical past in relation to the present and future—and, for this particular project, we aim to do so in the company of Settembrini. At the end of this short book we chart a way forward—for living and reading—that emerges in conversation with him, but answers to our own current (personal as well as political) needs.

We begin, in Part I, by investigating the relationship between autobiography and revolution, as a means of reflecting on individual identity

---
[1] Deleuze 1995: 131; Cassin 2014: 310.

Classics, Love, Revolution: The Legacies of Luigi Settembrini. Andrea Capra and Barbara Graziosi, Oxford University Press. © Andrea Capra and Barbara Graziosi 2024.
DOI: 10.1093/oso/9780198865445.003.0002

and larger political enterprises. We introduce Settembrini as he appears in his *Memoirs* (which he left incomplete, a point to which we return), supplemented by his letters, political pamphlets, translations, and works of scholarship. We likewise introduce his wife, Raffaella ('Gigia') Faucitano, an effective political operator and letter writer in her own right, who played a crucial role in establishing Settembrini's public persona. We consider their relationship and offer a brief sketch of how they, in turn, interacted with a wide range of other actors: revolutionaries, sailors, priests, Piedmontese aristocrats, common criminals, classical scholars, and British statesmen. Settembrini's connection to William Ewart Gladstone, in particular, is crucial—also in relation to current debates in postcolonial criticism. Settembrini, Faucitano, and other subaltern figures affected shifts in imperial British politics, at a level of power very far removed from their conditions.[2] We place autobiographical writing within this complex network and show how it was used for the purposes of revolution and, later, nation-building.[3]

Settembrini's *Memoirs* were meant to entertain as well as instruct—as did his letters. To this day, they read like a gripping adventure tale, featuring daring plans to escape from the Panopticon (coordinated by Faucitano, with support from Britain), shipwreck, mutiny, messages hidden in wine bottles, and the creation of a secret language, based on ancient Greek, to communicate between political prisoners and fellow conspirators. All these features are, in part, generic: the account Settembrini gives of himself bears comparison with the lives of other revolutionaries and romantic heroes, as well as fictional characters populating novels such as Walter Scott's *Ivanhoe* (1819) and Dumas's *The Count of Montecristo* (1844). There are, however, some specific qualities to his writing—a gentleness of tone, an unusual patience, elegance, and humour—that are not so easily matched in other revolutionary autobiographies and go some way towards explaining Settembrini's love for the ancient author Lucian. They also help to illuminate the life-long, loving bond of trust between him and his beloved wife, 'Gigia' Faucitano, well

---

[2] Sahlins 1995 remains important reading on the agency of the subaltern.
[3] Riall 2007: 25.

documented in both the *Memoirs* and the letters they exchanged.[4] Our aim, for the first part of the book, is to show how autobiography was used to redefine Italian masculinity and unify the nation. We also explore how Settembrini and Faucitano fit (or did not fit) within that broader enterprise.

The interaction between revolutionary politics, autobiographical writing, and lived experience becomes more complicated—and interesting—when *The Neoplatonists* is brought into play. The second part of this book focuses on this tale, approached by way of an earlier Platonic fiction, Settembrini's brief *Dialogue on Women*. The reasons for considering these two works together are, we hope, obvious: they are both works of Platonic inspiration and both attempt to leverage the classical past in order to open up possibilities for new bonds of equality, justice, and love in the future. They deal with related concerns (most obviously the intellectual education of women and the sexual education of men) and help to shed new light on the relationship between fiction and lived experience—a key issue in Settembrini's reception of classical literature and, in turn, a key issue in our own reception of his work.

Unlike *The Neoplatonists*, whose circumstances of composition cannot be established with certainty, we know that Settembrini wrote the *Dialogue on Women* during his first incarceration and thinking specifically of his wife. In a private dedication of the work (which he planned to publish anonymously from prison) he offered this comment on fiction, autobiographical experience, and authorship: 'In many parts [of the *Dialogue*], I talked about you, even without mentioning you by name; and many of the things I wrote I learnt from you. For this reason, this dialogue is also your work.'[5] In the *Memoirs* he adds that although he never managed to publish the dialogue, he chose not to destroy it, as he did with 'many other writings', because it reminded him of a relatively happy time spent in the prison's infirmary, writing under bearable conditions.[6] For *The Neoplatonists*, we have no clear information about the circumstances of composition, but we do know that he chose, in the

---

[4] It is a pity that Riall 2015 does not include Settembrini in her study 'The Sex Lives of Italian Patriots', since his example does not conform to the patterns she describes.
[5] Gigante 1977: 138.   [6] See further on pp. 50f.

case of this text too, not to destroy it. Indeed, it seems he made more than one copy.[7] Already the fact that he preserved *The Neoplatonists* allows us to suppose that his attitude was similar to the regard in which he held the *Dialogue on Women*: perhaps he associated *The Neoplatonists* too with pleasant memories of the time in which he wrote it, or first conceived it;[8] and perhaps he silently recognized the contribution of a real person (or people) dear to him, also in the case of this text. As for the fact that he copied out this love story more than once, it suggests that he wanted the *Neoplatonists* not only to be preserved but distributed and read.[9]

We can perhaps go further: Conoscenti rightly argues that some aspects of *The Neoplatonists* closely recall the language and style of *Quattrocento* literature, Masuccio in particular, as well as the earlier Boccaccio, and points out that Settembrini was reading those authors between 1864 and 1876, while working on his *Lectures on Italian Literature*, and that those authors had not made much impact on his style before then. On the basis of those considerations, Conoscenti concludes that our version of *The Neoplatonists* was probably written in that late period, shortly before Settembrini's death in 1876. He concedes, however, that 'no reference to this work has been found in the quite considerable mass of private writings'.[10] On that, we may have made some progress: a private letter dated 21 August 1872 seems to us to confirm Conoscenti's argument, both in terms of date and in relation to the stylistic considerations he brings to bear on the issue of dating. This is what Settembrini writes to his colleague Raffaele Masi:

'I am copying out Masuccio—a beastly effort. A German effort. And moreover Masuccio puts into my head some quite fanciful thoughts and makes me write crazy things – and right here, at the desk of the Rector of the University of Naples.'[11]

---

[7] Conoscenti 2019: 42 mentions the existence of an (allegedly earlier) version, seen by Professor Raffaele Giglio in the 1970s and belonging to a private collection: this version has not been sighted since, though Professor Giglio confirmed his memory of its existence to us *viva voce*. Apparently, it is still in the hands of Settembrini's descendants.

[8] For further discussion, see below, p. 135.

[9] Here we part company with the many scholars who have argued, in print and orally, that the text was a private affair not meant to be read.

[10] Conoscenti 2010: 150.   [11] Settembrini 1990: 97.

There is a good chance that these 'crazy things' he was writing, while serving as Rector and working on Masuccio's *Novellino*, are something close to the version of *The Neoplatonists* we now have—even if, as often happens with sexual fantasies, there may have been an earlier, recurrent core to this tale, as well as possible later reworkings.[12] Elements of the story will no doubt have been shaped by earlier experiences as well as fantasies, including earlier scholarly works, or 'beastly efforts' (to use his idiom), most obviously the translation of Lucian. In any case, the relationship between fictional creation and lived experience, which has shaped the interpretation of *The Neoplatonists*, should be considered in light of the many pages Settembrini himself devoted to the issue. Imagined pleasure in the past and the future is often introduced, in his writings, as a powerful antidote to political defeat and physical pain in the present.[13] Memories of his first night in prison, for example, lead to a more general reflection on his ability to draw strength from remembered (or imagined) pleasure:

> I do not know why this is, but I do know that whenever fortune inflicted on me the worst suffering and sank me into the deepest abyss of pain, the rare moments of happiness in my life came right back to me. In that prison cell and on those hard stones, I dreamt that I was returning home after a long journey and that my young child, used as he was to recognizing the way I rang the doorbell, would cry from inside, 'Daddy, daddy!' and would run towards me, leaping into my arms and giving me those kisses that only a father knows how sweet they are. And it seemed that he was holding on so tight with his arms and legs that my right shoulder and hip hurt and I had to tell my Gigia, 'Please, take this boy off me because he's hurting me'; but she could not get him off, because he would hold on even tighter. The noise of the lock and key then woke me up, the prison guard came in, and I got to my feet, my bones aching. 'Is there a chance I could be given a mattress?' I asked.

We also read in the *Memoirs* how, just over a decade later, Settembrini managed to withdraw to a place of relative peace, and even some kind of

---

[12] On recurrence see, for example, Leitenberg and Henning 1995.
[13] For pleasure as an antidote to political defeat in contemporary discourse, see pp. 145f.

reverie, on the night before his planned execution, despite the pain caused by heavy chains constricting his feet and ankles.[14]

Now, it is easy to recognize, also in *The Neoplatonists*, a tendency towards a dreamlike escapism leading to scenarios of imagined pleasure. Those scenarios belong, for Settembrini, simultaneously to the Greek past and the Italian future. They help with the business of living (that is to say: they make life more bearable in the painful present) and simultaneously demonstrate the pleasures of literature. The second part of this book ends, accordingly, with a chapter on the relationship between living and reading, in light of current debates on the value of classics as an academic discipline but also, more generally, as a reflection on pleasure, joy, and political activism.

If there is one hope that motivates this book, then, it is this: considering 'contemporary issues against the background of classical antiquity', as our editors ask us to do, is supposed to lead to 'new resources for living' in the present. Nostalgic longing for the past is, indeed, a resource for living: current politics confirms it, as do several studies in experimental psychology.[15] Settembrini's own sexual fantasy, set in ancient Greece, provides concrete evidence—but also makes us confront the issue of fake and wishful recreations. What are the ethics of inventing the past as best suits the present? And how can we even distinguish between historical fact and fiction? As Bruno Latour puts it, 'entire Ph.D. programs...make sure that good American kids are learning the hard way that facts are made up, that there is no such thing as natural, unmediated, unbiased access to truth, that we are always prisoners of language, that we always speak from a particular standpoint, and so on, while dangerous extremists are using the very same argument of social construction to destroy hard-won evidence that could save our life'.[16] He is writing about climate change. This book, by contrast, focuses on other issues. The difficulty, however, is the same.

Settembrini insisted that criticism was not to be used as a demolition tool but as a means of increasing pleasure. In his *Lectures on Italian Literature*, he identified two critical stances:

---

[14] Settembrini 1961: 268–70.
[15] See, for example, Newman, Sachs, Stone, and Schwarz 2020.   [16] Latour 2004: 227.

...one aimed at pinpointing faults, the other at revealing what is beautiful. I prefer the second, because it springs from love, and wants to inspire love—and love is the father of art. The other type of criticism seems to me akin to arrogance and, while flying the flag of looking for truth, destroys everything, leaving our soul barren.[17]

This statement of principle informs Settembrini's practice of criticism throughout his oeuvre and, we argue, has problematic consequences for the later criticism of his own work. Because of his emphasis on beauty, and his disregard for 'pinpointing faults', his work has been misunderstood—both in its critical stance towards antiquity and in its legacy for the future.

We offer here three illustrations of what we mean by this, taken from the three moments in the reception of *The Neoplatonists* we have already described. Our first example is provided by Cantarella, who read *The Neoplatonists* in 1937 and was puzzled by its title, given the spiritual and even ascetic character of Neoplatonic philosophy. He attempted to solve the problem by taking it as a vague designation meaning simply 'philosophers'.[18] We argue, by contrast, that Settembrini chose the title critically and with precision: it expressed his downright rejection of Neoplatonism, particularly in its Catholic revival, and its rejection of physical pleasure. We demonstrate, on the basis of his other works, that Settembrini used the term 'Neoplatonism' very much as it is defined today—and not simply as a synonym for 'philosophy'. He took the term to describe an ancient system of thought inspired by Plato, which argued for the priority of mind over matter, the insignificance of the body, and the need to elevate the soul towards the 'One' or 'God'. It is also clear that Settembrini condemned Neoplatonism as an especially nefarious influence on Catholic thought.[19] The protagonists of his tale—two boys who love each other—are to be understood as the true Neoplatonists, that is 'young followers of Plato', in opposition to those who usually claimed that title and who, in Settembrini's view, wilfully and hypocritically misrepresented Plato's true legacy.[20] Right at the start of *The Neoplatonists*, in his

---

[17] Settembrini 1964: 619.   [18] Cantarella 1977: 107.   [19] See pp. 121f.
[20] Settembrini's assessment of Plato's legacies is in line with much more recent studies, most obviously Reeser 2015.

'translator's warning', Settembrini suggests that Platonic love is nothing but a clever ruse, invented by some *furbi*, some 'clever types', in order to hide their love affairs with other men.[21] The title of Settembrini's tale is, then, a radical and pointed attempt to redefine what it means to be a Neoplatonist, a new follower of Plato. It should not be misunderstood as a vague or imprecise reference to classical philosophy, *pace* Cantarella.

Our second example is Manganelli's presentation of Settembrini as 'a pederast'.[22] Contrary to that description, *The Neoplatonists* tells the story of two young boys growing up together and gradually discovering the pleasures of sex. We are explicitly told that love is best enjoyed by 'people of the same age and, second best, by those who are not too distant in age from each other'.[23] The tale admits the possibility of love between men, and between men and women, of radically different ages: in that case, however, the suggestion is that the younger partner is motivated more by kindness than attraction, and that s/he is likely to be less in love than the older partner.[24] Equality between lovers is important to Settembrini—not just in the bedroom but in the siblinghood of the nation too. Even more important than age, however, is a reciprocity of roles and a focus on mutual pleasure: there is a great insistence, in the *Neoplatonists*, that male partners should take turns in penetrating and being penetrated, and that men should never demand of women 'what they do not enjoy and brings no advantage to them',[25] but rather enjoy the greatest and most intense explosion of pleasure mutually available to human beings, as 'each body part meets and mates', between a man and a woman, on equal terms.[26]

Early on in the tale, one of the two boys wonders how it is that 'many criticize this kind of love [i.e. love between men]; and even more people find fault with the law of reciprocity [i.e. the switching of roles]'.[27] This is best taken as an acknowledgement that, in ancient discourse, sex between male partners was accepted, but on the basis of a strict separation between 'lover' and 'beloved' (that is to say an older, 'active' partner

---

[21] See p. 150, n. 8.   [22] See p. 14.
[23] *The Neoplatonists*, ch. 2. On the importance of this point for Settembrini, and his implicit criticism of ancient homoeroticism, see further Conoscenti 2010.
[24] *The Neoplatonists*, ch. 2 and ch. 5.   [25] *The Neoplatonists*, ch. 6.
[26] *The Neoplatonists*, ch. 5. Cf. p. 116.   [27] *The Neoplatonists*, ch. 2.

and younger, 'passive' one). Where ancient practices fall short of Settembrini's ideal, he resorts to ancient political discourse and applies it to what, in his view, should happen in the bedroom: to be Greek, we read at one point in the tale, entails a commitment to equality—you should be able to do to your lover what your lover does to you, rather than think of sex as a means of 'overwhelming' a partner.[28] Political equality and sexual 'reciprocity', *reciprocanza* in his idiom, are closely aligned. This ideological position matches Settembrini's accounts of lived experience, for example his horror when recounting how an inmate in the Panopticon once managed to isolate and rape the young son of a prison guard.[29] That Manganelli turned Settembrini into 'a pederast' must be denounced not just as an interpretative error, as in the case of Cantarella's views on the title of the tale, but as wilful misrepresentation—something that was designed to shock his readers rather than inform them.

Our third example is taken from the latest major publication on *The Neoplatonists*, a monograph published in 2019. In the preface, Maya De Leo argues that, according to Settembrini, love between men is superior to love between men and women, since the latter is intoxicating and irrational.[30] In *The Neoplatonists*, this view is ascribed to a character named Codrus, an old teacher of Platonic philosophy whom De Leo takes to be the mouthpiece of Settembrini himself. The difficulty with this interpretation is that, in *The Neoplatonists*, Codrus does not know best.[31] Although he sets out to teach the young protagonists in the tale, it is the two boys who end up giving him a lesson in reciprocity—in a hilarious scene of *sexe à trois*. As for Codrus' own views on the inferiority of heterosexual love, the two boys never openly contradict him but, on the basis of their own experiences, reach different conclusions: both types

---

[28] The statement is attributed to Codrus, in *The Neoplatonists*, ch. 2. As we have argued, this does not guarantee they represent Settembrini's own views, though here we can match them with views expressed in his own voice. On Codrus as a semi-, but never fully, autobiographical figure, see below, p. 135. As well as being influenced by the democratic legacies of Greece, Settembrini was also thinking about the ancient novel, as we argue in chapter 7. In emphasizing equality and reciprocity between lovers, the Greek romances were unusual in the ancient world: this is something that Settembrini noticed already in the nineteenth century but has, otherwise, become the object of systematic attention only recently; see Konstan 1994.
[29] Settembrini 1971: 475.   [30] De Leo in Conoscenti 2019: 13f.
[31] See Conoscenti 2019: 122–35, who however overstates Codrus' incompetence, cf. our discussion at pp. 118f.

of love are wonderful, they agree in a private conversation when the 'teacher' is not listening, and there is no need to adjudicate between them. The main difference, in their view, is not between sex with men or sex with women, but sex for physical pleasure alone and 'sex together with love'.[32] It seems to us that the way the boys deal with their teacher Codrus parallels Settembrini's own attitude towards antiquity. The two boys treat their teacher kindly, even with indulgence: they take from him what he has to offer, appreciate his wisdom and even his beauty, but then go their own way, forming their own views, which do not tally with his.[33]

Recent approaches to classics could not be more different from Settembrini's stance towards antiquity. What we see is a widening gap between a celebratory, acritical stance towards the classical past and a tendency to sit in harsh judgement and denounce it as sexist, imperialist, hegemonic.[34] This has, as a result, produced a climate in which the legacy of 'dead white men' is alternatively decried or defended.[35] If, in this book, we focus on the legacy of one dead white classicist, it is because we find value in what Settembrini wrote and how he lived. We are convinced, in other words, that his legacy is useful for the present and the future too, particularly in showing how his revolutionary commitments interacted with a radical rethinking of masculinity, based not on domination of women and younger men, but on equality and reciprocity. This does not mean that we agree with everything Settembrini had to say.[36] We have already shown how his views on the purpose of criticism, his insistence on 'revealing what is beautiful' rather than 'pinpointing faults', contributed to some serious and recurrent misunderstandings on the part of

---

[32] *The Neoplatonists*, ch. 3.

[33] This is stated explicitly: *The Neoplatonists*, ch. 6: 'whatever the philosopher might opine'.

[34] Louis MacNeice, classics professor and poet, captured the mood as early as 1939, in 'Autumn Journal' (*Collected Poems*, 1967: 30), when he thought of the Greeks in terms of crooks, adventurers, opportunists, careless athletes, fancy boys, hair-splitters, pedants, hard-boiled sceptics, demagogues, quacks, women pouring libations and 'lastly...the slaves'. Since then, there have been impressive scholarly attempts to 'imagine oneself' among ancient slaves; see, for example, Padilla Peralta 2017 and Forsdyke 2021: 4, whose book sets out to give 'the reader a sense of the rich diversity of experiences of individual slaves'.

[35] For two influential and radically different statements on 'dead white men' see Knox 1994 and Zuckerberg 2018. In Italy, the discussion was long deemed irrelevant or dismissed as unsophisticated. It is however now gaining traction in academic discourse: see Borgna 2022, Traina 2023, and Bettini 2023. It may not be coincidental that all three scholars have lived and worked abroad.

[36] See especially chapter 4.

later readers, who failed to recognize his ironic 'pinpointing of faults' in relation to antiquity.[37] Because he treated classical culture with gentleness, even when he disagreed with its legacies, and because he sometimes made up the past so as to match what he wished it had been, later readers have supposed that he never disagreed with the classics, which, in his words, 'lightened [his] sadness'—and yet he did disagree with them, just as the boys in *The Neoplatonists* dismiss the views of their teacher, even while treating him kindly.[38] As for our own stance, we admire Settembrini and are grateful for his work and his example. However, we plan to be explicit in our criticism, in our 'pinpointing' of Settembrini's faults, and shall avoid engaging in deliberate 'fakery' ourselves.[39]

---

[37] This is another instance of how past literature shapes its own reception, to return to our discussion above, p. 22.

[38] Settembrini 1961: xli.

[39] For all that we insist on the value of criticism, we also recognize the limits of critique (a phrase we borrow from Felski 2015): we return to the issue in the final chapter of this book.

PART I
AUTOBIOGRAPHY AND REVOLUTION

It is four years now that I sleep inside this prison: I resemble the dormouse who sleeps in winter, feeding himself on the juices and blood he built up in summer. I live that way too, feeding my mind on memories of the past.

       Luigi Settembrini, diary entry, 23 January 1855[1]

---

[1] In Settembrini 1971: 474. The specific (and somewhat unusual) word he uses for 'memories', *ricordanze*, is also the title of his autobiography. After this statement, Settembrini goes on to say that he is reading Humboldt's *Kosmos*, the latest installment of which his wife has managed to have delivered to him in prison. This suggests a keen interest in the latest and most important publications of the period: Settembrini's self-portrait as a slumbering dormouse may, therefore, be a little inaccurate. Still, the absence of comfort and intellectual stimulation was a problem for him in the Panopticon and recourse to personal and classical memories helped him build a degree of resilience.

3
Luigi Settembrini, According to Himself

I must speak of many miseries: let me first refresh my spirit by remembering my first years, when I came into the world and it seemed to me so beautiful and joyous. I was a little devil of a boy; I would touch and break everything at home, and my father, who was ill and found this difficult, would say: 'The midwife was a prophet when she gave you to your mother and me after your baptism and said you would become a great big devil because you had broken the font.' 'I did not break any font!' I would reply. And he, 'You were born in Naples, in the year 1813, on April 17th, on Holy Saturday, and you were the first to be christened in the font filled with new Holy Water: in that sense you broke it into use.' And so it was that I was made into a Christian and a Catholic, without my knowing anything about it.[1]

So begin Luigi Settembrini's *Memoirs*. The opening sentences may explicitly recall how he was 'made into a Christian and a Catholic', but also imply that he was born a pagan. By comparing this passage with descriptions of ancient Greece strewn across his scholarly works, this becomes clear. Here, for example, is a statement taken from Settembrini's *Disquisition on the Life and Works of Lucian*:

The religion of the ancient Hellenes was the virgin and serene sentiment that the soul enjoys in its first youth, at the time when we first

[1] Settembrini 1971: 35.

Classics, Love, Revolution: The Legacies of Luigi Settembrini. Andrea Capra and Barbara Graziosi,
Oxford University Press. © Andrea Capra and Barbara Graziosi 2024.
DOI: 10.1093/oso/9780198865445.003.0003

entered into this world and it seemed to us full of so much beauty, and so many marvels, and so much love.[2]

The past, then, is a source of happiness, a place where recollections of early childhood and memories of ancient Greece blend into one uncorrupted sense of wonder and wellbeing. Catholicism turns out to be antithetical not only to this childlike, pagan sense of beauty, but also to patriotic duty, as the next pages in the *Memoirs* go on to suggest.

What we are offered, after this opening, is a family portrait.[3] Settembrini's father, a lawyer much inspired by the Neapolitan Enlightenment, is huddling around the brazier with likeminded friends, while his wife, 'a woman', we learn later in the *Memoirs*, 'with a head as good as Napoleon's, capable of anything, and always a winner',[4] sews at a table nearby. Settembrini, the eldest of what would eventually be six children, sits on a little stool next to his mother, listening quietly as the men talk politics: they remember the short-lived Neapolitan Republic of 1799 and recall the street violence that followed, when the king was restored. On that occasion, we discover, Settembrini's father almost lost his life in a lynching and, after surviving the mob, ended up in the Panopticon, on the island of Santo Stefano, for fourteen months. His health, we are told, never quite recovered after his incarceration. The conversation, in Settembrini's family home, then moves on to current attempts to conspire against the Bourbon king and the young Settembrini suddenly pipes up, in opposition to discouraged statements that nothing can be done, that a lot can surely be achieved; in fact, he has seen one of his father's friends at a different gathering, wearing a *tricolore* armband in support of a united Italy. Suddenly, his mother marches the boy out of the room. 'But I told the truth!' he insists. 'Keep quiet, my son, or you'll get the poor man hanged!'[5]

A few months later, Settembrini's parents send him off to a Jesuit boarding school: his interjection that evening, we are told, precipitated

---

[2] Settembrini 1988: 1080.
[3] This paragraph summarizes the first chapter of the *Memoirs*: Settembrini 1971: 35–40.
[4] Francesca Vitale (1877–25) died in childbirth when Luigi Settembrini, her eldest son, was only eleven: this is how her sisters-in-law described her to him. It is a portrait that gives some insight into his family background in terms of both gender and politics: Settembrini 1971: 45.
[5] Settembrini 1971: 40.

his parents' decision to send him there. And so it is that the Catholic education he receives at the Collegio di Maddaloni is motivated, in the *Memoirs*, by patriotic rather than religious concerns. The school itself, we go on to read, was terrible: 'education in that place was meant to break the spirit and reduce the boys to a stupid and friar-like obedience'.[6] After their time there, they would leave the school with 'no knowledge and, in total exasperation, no true faith either'.[7] Despite this damning assessment, the *Memoirs* are full of happy memories from his time in school. Two people, in particular, had a lasting influence on the young Settembrini: one was Vincenzo Amarelli, a lay teacher of history, geography, and Latin, whose liberal convictions later forced him into exile (and who was appointed Professor of Classics at the University of Pennsylvania in 1851). The other and even more influential figure was Luigi De Silva, a boy 'of great intelligence and already more advanced in his studies'.[8] The friendship between the two boys is described at length:

> We were forever discussing ancient stories... and felt we were born too late, in an age that was lazy and servile. Our schoolmates, annoyed with our grand statements, would tease us and call us *the little doctors*. I could not swallow the insult and felt provoked, not so much on my behalf, as on account of my De Silva, who was only small but had a great mind; so one day I lost my temper, used my fists and got hit in return. I was punished for that, of course, but afterwards nobody called us names to our face again. De Silva often read out to me some translations of his, rendering Horace's most beautiful odes, and passages from Livy, and Latin verses which he composed with great ease. I listened to him full of wonder and came to realize that sometimes we learn more from a schoolmate than from a teacher.[9]

Unsurprisingly, given the context of their friendship, the two boys soon became interested in God. An archpriest, who visited the school during

---

[6] Settembrini 1971: 40.   [7] Settembrini 1971: 40.   [8] Settembrini 1971: 44.
[9] Settembrini 1971: 44. Note the similarity between this statement and the limited pedagogical impact of Codrus on the two boys in *The Neoplatonists*: they learn a lot more from each other.

the Catholic Jubilee of 1825 and spoke 'with much simplicity',[10] inspired them to sudden and fervent devotion:

> Every star we saw shining above our heads seemed to us the face of an angel or of a virgin smiling down at us, and it would summon us upwards, to contemplate the beauties of heaven and sing the praises of God. We abandoned ourselves to the most fiery devotions: no more fooling around, no more games, no dancing, no fencing. All these things seemed to us profane; even our lessons seemed but worldly obligations, to which we submitted until we could go and read the lives of saints, together with sermons, psalms, and prayers. I always wanted to be the one to say the rosary, in order to recite it most slowly; and, after the litanies, I would invoke some twenty saints, not caring at all that some of my schoolmates were twisting and whispering, 'Get on with it, you fool, my knees are hurting!' Every night, before going to bed, I would spend at least one hour with my head touching the floor, reciting my various Paternosters, Ave Marias and Salve Reginas. Now the other boys started calling us *the two monks*...[11]

The Catholic devotion of the boys had obvious pagan and, indeed, Neoplatonist overtones.[12] It also clearly involved much devotion to each other: we read that the two boys were soon placed in separate bedrooms. They nevertheless continued to exchange letters, using their schoolmates as postmen: 'He often sent me epigrams and odes in Latin about I do not know which obscure saints; for my part, I was not so strong in verse composition and, because I did not want to look bad, I would just answer *oremus*' (i.e. 'let us pray').[13]

Worried about his son's passions, Settembrini's father (by then a widower) arranged for the boy to return to the family home in Caserta, a sleepy town 25 miles north of Naples, where the Bourbon king resided in a palace built to surpass Versailles. As well as enrolling him in a local

---

[10] Settembrini 1971: 45, where he presents his interest in God also as a reaction to the sudden death of his mother; cf. above, n. 4.
[11] Settembrini 1971: 46.
[12] On Neoplatonism, ascesis, and the search for higher beauty, see pp. 121f.
[13] Settembrini 1971: 46.

school, his father now personally oversaw the boy's education, making him read 'great books' and suggesting new models of behaviour: 'Tell me, would you rather be a friar or Markos Botzaris?' The heroes of the Greek revolution had enormous attraction for the young Settembrini, who saw in his mind's eye 'Botzaris in a battlefield full of Turks' and heard the cry of Konstantinos Kanaris ring in his ears, as he sank the flagship of Kara-Ali Pasha, 'Victory to the Cross!'[14]

Now that he was back home, Settembrini forged a close friendship with a different boy: the two spent much time together in the *bosco reale*, the wooded park that surrounded the royal palace, discussing what they were reading (Virgil, Ariosto, Chateaubriand), and letting their surroundings fire up their imagination. Settembrini saw before his eyes 'the virgin forests of America' and once, confronted with a row of trees neatly cut into a topiary wall, declared to his friend that there was a 'whole book' to be written about those trees, which were not allowed to grow as nature intended. 'This is tyranny,' he insisted: 'men and trees cut down to size!' A few days later, Settembrini's father summoned his son and warned him about writing 'books about trees'. Anyone in the *bosco reale* could have heard him and denounced him to the authorities. Indeed, his own friend had reported his speech to his parents. 'That boy', Settembrini adds in the *Memoirs*, 'later became a police inspector with the darkest reputation, working in the service of the last Bourbon king.'[15]

It is surprising that the first pages of *The Neoplatonists* have not been systematically compared to the opening chapters of the *Memoirs* because the themes, atmospheres, and friendships match closely—except for one detail. The Catholic devotion described in the *Memoirs* is replaced, in the *Neoplatonists*, with homosexual love. The 'ancient' love story speaks of two boys who go to school together, share the same room, and go for walks in a lovely grove surrounding, in this case, not the royal palace in Caserta, but the temple of Apollo in Athens.[16] Both accounts, moreover, move from male friendships to a sudden interest in girls. Just as, in *The Neoplatonists*, Callicles meets Hymnis in the street and is captivated by her lively looks, so in the *Memoirs* we read of this encounter:

---

[14] Settembrini 1971: 48.   [15] Settembrini 1971: 48–9.   [16] *The Neoplatonists*, ch. 2.

When I started living at home again, I went to church every morning before school and always walked there with lowered eyes. Except that, one day, I don't know how, I lifted my gaze and met the eyes of a lovely girl, a neighbour of ours, who was staring at me intently. And so it was that—one glance today, another tomorrow—I started to care about her and stopped writing *oremus*. Then, one day, I don't know how, I wrote down a love sonnet and, after that one, many more. The eyes of that girl de-monked me and brought me back to the crazy boy I was by nature. But do you want to know what happened, meanwhile, to my friend De Silva? When he left the Jesuit boarding school, he dressed up as priest and studied theology but, because he was prone to arguing, he was taken for an atheist and caused great scandal; then he ripped off his collar, became a lawyer, did many crazy things, and the last of them was that he truly became a monk, in the monastery of Saint Teresa; then he de-monked himself; and now again dresses as a priest and has become a teacher. Of fiery spirit, restless, kind-hearted, full of talent, and generous, he was always, and remains to this very day, my dearest friend.[17]

The story of Settembrini's first moment of heterosexual interest in the *Memoirs* immediately takes him back to De Silva, his closest male friend in boarding school, and inspires a breathless summary of his life, culminating in a declaration of everlasting friendship. Again, the parallels with *The Neoplatonists* are straightforward: in the ancient tale, the two protagonists remain close throughout their lives, even after they fall in love with, and marry, two young women. In that tale, heterosexual promiscuity (as preached in the *Republic* and practised by the boys in the first half of the story) is replaced *not* by monogamous heterosexuality, but by lifelong, stable bisexual relationships:

> The two friends no longer followed Plato's teaching, according to whom women should be held in common,[18] but rather followed the

---

[17] Settembrini 1971: 46–7.
[18] Plato, *Republic* 5, 457b–458d and 461e–462e. For further discussion of Settembrini's engagement with Plato and Neoplatonism, see chapters 6 and 7.

laws of their fatherland and those of love. Each of them loved and honoured his own wife. And yet, they always continued to love each other too and, even in old age, if they happened to share a bed for any reason, they would entangle their feet and embrace as they did long ago, in the first years of their youth.

The mixture of ancient Greek fiction and personal recollection marks not only Settembrini's first moment of birth, then, as described in the *Memoirs*, but carries on throughout life, as the conclusion of *The Neoplatonists* makes clear.

The method of reading we have adopted so far, in this chapter, involves a straightforward comparison between autobiography and fiction—thus already moving our discussion beyond current scholarly positions on Settembrini's life and work. Rather than posit a radical break between official autobiography and erotic fiction it is possible, we believe, to establish close parallels between the two. Lived experience, and specifically the experience of love, colours Settembrini's approach to antiquity and also, as we argue below, his revolutionary commitments. After an extended account of childhood, the *Memoirs* tell the story of how Settembrini met his wife. Here too we note some parallels with *The Neoplatonists*, though the *Memoirs* lend greater weight to heterosexual love and marriage—as do the copious letters Settembrini and Faucitano exchanged through their long enforced periods of separation, when he was in prison and later in exile. Once hailed as 'one of the most beautiful love stories in nineteenth-century epistolary literature',[19] the extraordinary relationship between Settembrini and Faucitano has been sidelined since the discovery of *The Neoplatonists*.[20] The reason we pay attention to it here is that, yet again, it reveals a strong connection between

---

[19] De Rienzo in Settembrini 1979/1: 26; he collects many of Settembrini's letters to Faucitano in that edition. Her own letters, meanwhile, remain largely unpublished.

[20] The relationship of love between Settembrini and Faucitano made a great impression on those who could observe it at close quarters. Most revealing is the testimony of Silvio Spaventa, who was long imprisoned with Settembrini in the Panopticon, and who tried to imitate, in his own epistolary exchange with Felicetta Ulisse, what he could see of the love between Settembrini and his wife. It was, clearly, a relationship he admired and, some might say, envied: Spaventa 1977.

Settembrini's work as a classical scholar, his experience of love, and his revolutionary fervour.

According to his own account in the *Memoirs*, Settembrini became a classical scholar very precisely *because* he fell in love with Faucitano. The two met in the street, when Settembrini was a student at the University of Naples and Faucitano was a shy fifteen-year-old girl, preparing to enter a convent.[21] There were some obstacles to their romance, since the plan to become a nun was not only a reflection of Faucitano's own wishes, and those of her parents, but a matter of economic need: the family was too poor to provide her with a dowry. Despite this, Settembrini was eventually admitted to Faucitano's home and, as he talked to her parents, he remembers how she 'lifted her eyes from her embroidery and fixed her gaze on me with a smile that made me tremble'.[22] This account yet again finds close correspondence in *The Neoplatonists*, when Callicles meets his future wife.[23]

Faucitano's parents agreed to their daughter's engagement, on condition that Settembrini find a steady job. After trying and failing to become a lawyer (he had left his legal apprenticeship in disgust, after two hungry men he was representing were punished harshly for stealing bread), he decided to take the qualifying exams to become a classics teacher. He knew that a position had opened up in one of the four classical high schools in the Kingdom of the Two Sicilies, the *liceo classico* of Catanzaro, a city of some twenty thousand inhabitants in the mountains of Calabria. And so he put his mind to the task of securing that job: 'I wasted no time at all and, even while walking in the streets, would read Homer and rehearse his lines; and then suddenly my thoughts would run to her and I would forget all about Homer. Ah, who can give me back those years, those studies, those days of love and hope? Only once in life we truly study well and only once we truly love.'[24]

Settembrini's recollections of the exam leading to his appointment in Catanzaro are surprisingly detailed, suggesting not only his romantic side but also his intellectual desire to prove himself:

---

[21] When writing a first version of these pages, Settembrini confided to his wife that he wanted her to read them and wondered what she would think of them; see p. 86.
[22] Settembrini 1971: 95. [23] *The Neoplatonists*, ch. 6. [24] Settembrini 1971: 95.

The professors [at the University of Naples] opened up their books and gave us our tasks: Homer fell open, and we were asked to turn into Latin the first ten lines of the second book of the *Iliad*, accompanied by a philological commentary. Next, Cicero's *De oratore* fell open and we were asked to write, in Latin, a dissertation on rhetorical action. Horace was opened and we were asked to write a poem in praise of Augustus in Latin hexameters and then to compose a Sapphic stanza, in Italian, on the same subject. As soon as I heard the tasks, I breathed again and stopped trembling—actually, I even approached my battle for the post with a certain boldness... I wrote with vigour, presenting my philological commentary in Greek, which made a great impression: the professors thought I was some valiant Hellenist, a new Henricus Stephanus,[25] whereas I was only a cocky little parrot, able to memorize even commas and full stops: and now all that Greek is gone, anyway. Eight days later... the faculty gave their verdict and, after praising the runner-up, offered the post to me.... I went straight to my girl and she welcomed me in great high spirits. In fact, she gave me her first kiss. I am an old man now, sixty-two years of age: forty years have passed since that kiss, but I remember it as the one true moment of sweetness in my life. That sacred kiss fired up a light that I have kept always and still keep now before my eyes, and shall keep until my final day.[26]

The young couple made their journey to Catanzaro in 1835, on a rickety wagon: 'a road suitable for wheels had only just been opened, otherwise we would have had to travel on a jagged path among the rocks, difficult even for mules'.[27]

In Calabria, the situation was dire, worse even than the young couple had imagined. Landowners ruled over the peasants 'with ancient ignorance and neglect'.[28] 'The women were illiterate, almost without exception'.[29] There was no industry, and only minimal manufacturing,

---

[25] Henri Estienne, or Henricus Stephanus in the Latin version of his name, was a sixteenth-century editor of Plato. His pagination numbers are used to this day.

[26] Settembrini 1971: 97. Settembrini's age at the time of writing dates this part to 1875, when he resumed work on the *Memoirs* after interrupting it in December 1859: see p. 88 for discussion.

[27] Settembrini 1971: 101.   [28] Settembrini 1971: 100.   [29] Settembrini 1971: 102.

'The single art that everyone mastered, from the richest to the poorest man, was that of handling a gun.'[30] The cholera epidemic that raged across Europe in 1835 reached southern Italy a year later, in 1836, and the local people immediately concluded that the government was out to kill them.[31] Popular uprisings, fuelled by ignorance, were repressed with cruelty. 'Then the cholera abated and the oppressive government remained', we read, 'for many years yet.'[32]

Settembrini began to conspire against the Bourbon regime as soon as he arrived in Catanzaro—though he had little infrastructure and less support.[33] As a student, he had wanted to join Young Italy, the revolutionary organization led by Mazzini in London, but repression was so extreme, in the south of Italy, that he had no access to printed materials, let alone revolutionary cells. Eventually, he had managed to make contact with one like-minded student, Benedetto Musolino, who claimed to know all about Young Italy, because of revolutionary contacts he had established during a trip to Malta:

> I kept asking whether he had received the 'catechism' [i.e. Mazzini's writings] ... He made me wait for a long time until, at long last, he gave me a handwritten notebook which, he claimed, he had copied from a printed original ... I greatly praised this book in conversation with him and my friend let me elaborate at length, taking up various points with me. Then he confessed: 'Well, I am the author of this book.' 'What? You? This is not Young Italy, founded by Giuseppe Mazzini?' 'No: I gave it a name that is already known, because if I chose another name, and founded a new movement, who would follow me?'[34]

---

[30] Settembrini 1971: 100.
[31] Settembrini compares these events to Thucydides' description of the plague and to Manzoni's famous description of contagion followed by fanciful accusations of poisoning in *The Betrothed* (1827), a nation-building novel influenced, like Settembrini's *The Neoplatonists*, by the ancient Greek romance.
[32] Settembrini 1961: 95.
[33] This may help explain why he resorted to Greek and Roman literature to articulate his revolutionary thoughts. In Catanzaro, he penned an incomplete and still unpublished draft of an essay on Italian literature, in which he uses the classical world to expose the reactionary elements in romanticism as well as, implicitly, the reactionary nature of Bourbon regime. See Themelly 1994.
[34] Settembrini 1971: 89–90.

Settembrini decided that Musolino's Young Italy, fake as it was, nevertheless deserved support:

> Once alone, I considered various issues: 'So we are just two! And how are we to start such a great movement? And with what means, and with what friends, we two unknown youngsters? We are going to have to lie when somebody asks whether the movement has many recruits... But you need a little fakery in all enterprises in this world...'[35]

The kind of fakery described here should once again, we think, be compared with Settembrini's fake translation from the Greek: *The Neoplatonists*, far from being an empty, stylistic exercise imitating ancient Greek models (as some have tried to present it) or simply a personal statement of Settembrini's own sexual preferences (which is how it is often read today) is a *political* fake—or so we argue in chapter 7. For now, we note that faking revolutionary activity continued in Catanzaro, where Settembrini managed to recruit a few friends to the counterfeit Young Italy invented by Musolino. Soon enough, though, a priest infiltrated Settembrini's circle—and betrayed him.[36]

The *Memoirs*, despite the serious consequences of Settembrini's early efforts at conspiracy, insist in presenting his revolutionary activities as child's play: 'all that foolishness was the making of Italy; without that faith, that high fever, that enthusiasm, wise men would still be quibbling over the details'.[37] The *Memoirs*, despite the backwardness of Calabria, likewise present life in Catanzaro as an idyll of young love: 'Gigia and I were constantly revolving around our baby, who was growing stronger and more lively every day. We talked about him all the time and my wife's acquaintances would come and see how he splashed about in his cold bath water' (cold baths being an enlightened novelty in Calabria).[38] Both tone and content reveal the distortions of hindsight: in writing his

---

[35] Settembrini 1971: 91.
[36] We read that Faucitano had suspected the priest from the start: 'my wife, with that fine sense women have, feared him like the enemy' (Settembrini 1971: 111). Settembrini's own judgement, by contrast, was clouded by the fact that the priest had some kind of disability or physical defect, which made Settembrini work hard to overcome his own revulsion and distrust.
[37] Settembrini 1971: 91. On the use of invisible ink: Settembrini 1971: 111.
[38] Settembrini 1971: 110.

Memoirs, Settembrini was clearly trying to 'refresh his spirit' with 'beautiful and joyous' memories of the past, to paraphrase his own opening statement. He was also attempting to minimize the secrecy and radicalism of his own earlier activities: 'today nobody wants to hear about conspiracies—and fair enough' we read in the *Memoirs*.[39] Meanwhile, an unpublished play he wrote in Catanzaro (the autograph of which we read in the Pessina archives) gives a better sense of the danger and foreboding he felt at the time—even if the play itself turned out less dramatic than what was about to happen in real life.[40]

On the night of 8 May 1839, the police surrounded Settembrini's house, entered, confiscated papers and books, and—in a typical show of corruption—stole all valuables ('my wife's earrings, whose diamonds seemed real', he points out, with his typical sense of fun).[41] Then they marched the young family into the street, locked the door, and took away the key. Faucitano and the baby found temporary shelter with neighbours. Settembrini was taken to Naples under arrest, on unknown charges. On the way there, he made friends with the guard in charge of delivering him to prison—to the point that, once in Naples, the 'good man' briefly left Settembrini alone, while tending to some personal family business in the capital, and even handed him his gun for safe keeping. The episode later became a celebrated example of Risorgimento high-mindedness: 'at that late hour, in a city whose every narrow alley I knew so well, and where nobody had heard I was under arrest, I felt tempted to bolt and run, dropping the gun somewhere—but then I thought this amounted to betraying a man who trusted me: I would have ruined him, for he would then have been the one to be arrested and destroyed'.[42] Apart from setting a high-minded example, the episode illustrates the extreme ease with which Settembrini tended to make friends and inspire trust—even in the most unlikely circumstances. But there is also something more specific in this episode that deserves attention: the emphasis on symmetry and reciprocity is, as we argue in chapter 7, a central concern also in the *Neoplatonists*.

---

[39] Settembrini 1971: 89.
[40] *La donna del proscritto*, Biblioteca Nazionale di Napoli, carte Pessina, 2, C1, 71–2.
[41] Settembrini 1971: 112.   [42] Settembrini 1971: 113.

After failing to 'bolt', Settembrini spent almost four years in prison, without conviction. For the first two, he awaited trial. After his acquittal for lack of evidence, he was kept indefinitely, 'at the disposal of the police'.[43] On the strength of the priest's denunciation, the Bourbons had immediately announced the discovery of a vast international conspiracy, led by Mazzini in London—and were now at some pains to prove its existence. Europe, meanwhile, was watching. Mazzini himself, when he eventually learned of the fake Young Italy invented by Musolino, was horrified—especially by its secular and anticlerical stance.[44] The situation, however, was no joke: held in prison, Settembrini lived in fear of torture. He kept thinking of the mangled hands of an acquaintance of his, who had been interrogated by the police a few years before his own incarceration and had been maimed for life. Food was scarce and rotten. The water malodorous. It was impossible to wash. Still, Settembrini soon began 'to withstand the prison air and understand a few things'.[45] He learnt to pace his cell, for example, 'nine steps diagonally across, then along the wall, once to the right, once the left, to avoid vertigo...same as all prisoners, as I later realized'.[46]

Imagination helped with survival. From a slit high up on the wall, he could see a house on a hill, a pergola, and the young family who lived there: the image became a recurrent motif in his later writings, including *The Neoplatonists*.[47] Literary memories were simultaneously put to practical use: he soon began to communicate with other political prisoners (including Musolino) using a mixture of mock prayers in Latin, items of ancient Greek vocabulary, and personal code names taken from Sir Walter Scott's nation-building novel *Quentin Durward* (1823).[48] When Settembrini was finally allowed to have books, he requested Homer's *Iliad* and read it out to his neighbour, across the prison wall between their cells: a 'man of limited culture but great intelligence, generous, impatient', he took to the ancient poem, Settembrini remembered that he 'especially liked the similes...but found Hector's death undignified,

---

[43] Settembrini 1971: 149. [44] See Alatri 1982.
[45] Settembrini 1971: 120. [46] Settembrini 1971: 119.
[47] For the house seen from the prison window, Settembrini 1971: 131–2; the house in *The Neoplatonists* features in ch. 8 of that work.
[48] Settembrini 1971: 129.

saying it was like that of a hunted fox running round and round a tree trunk'—a convincing Homeric simile in its own right.[49] Experiences in prison, such as this one, profoundly shaped his efforts to translate the classics into accessible, modern versions.

While Settembrini made himself at home in prison, Faucitano was facing different problems. At the age of twenty-two, in sole charge of a toddler, pregnant, and without income, she sold everything she could ('except the books') and left Catanzaro for Naples, travelling partly on a wagon, but mostly on foot, 'with a little boy who wanted to be carried all the way'.[50] After an eight-day journey that, as she put it in her own recollections, almost killed her, she moved in with her parents and found new purpose. As soon as she was allowed to supplement Settembrini's rations with parcels of food, she hid, inside a wine bottle, pencil and paper, wrapped up in fig leaves for insulation. This system of communication served the two spouses for years to come: 'the guards never thought to look inside those bottles, which were always of the darkest glass'.[51] Some of Settembrini's messages can still be seen in the Museo di San Martino in Naples; Faucitano's were, of course, destroyed on receipt.

When Faucitano was eventually allowed to visit her husband, she made a great impression on Settembrini, insisting he needed to keep up his spirits and make her proud:

> I had never heard my wife talk like that before. Misfortune had transformed her, developing her character into something strong and strict, yet loving and active at the same time. Her words lifted my spirits and did me great good. I started to get to know this woman better, and respect her, and love her much more than before.[52]

That respect inspired a new engagement with the legacies of Greek antiquity—Plato in particular, as we argue in chapter 6—since it is in this period that Settembrini wrote his *Dialogue on Women*. The *Memoirs* offer a detailed account of the circumstances: Settembrini had already

---

[49] Settembrini 1971: 133–4: 'for a few weeks, this man did not feel the anxieties of prison life'.
[50] Settembrini 1971: 124.   [51] Settembrini 1971: 125.   [52] Settembrini 1971: 124.

been acquitted, but was still being kept indefinitely in prison, at the orders of Francesco del Carretto, minister of (so-called) justice:

> The wine bottle continued to convey my wife's letters: 'I have been to see the minister of justice and he was as spiky as a porcupine. He said your release did not depend on him, but on the king. I'll ask for an audience with the king.' 'You do that.'... In other letters, Gigia gave news of Raffaele, who was already going to school, and Giulia, who was extremely ill.... A constant worry burnt my heart: that my wife and children were in great need and that I, who could have supported them with my work, was languishing and unable to do anything—and this not because of any law, or any sentence in court, but because of the will of a single man [del Carretto], who kept me there. I was desperate for work, so I told my brother Peppino to find me any job, even just as a copyist. My brother, who was in touch with architects and constructors, found me some *Measures* to copy out. I was happy about that and would copy these for days on end until my hands ached. When I had nothing to copy, I worked on a dialogue entitled *Women*; I also translated Horace's *Ars Poetica* and wrote an extensive commentary on it: I did not destroy those writings, as I did many others, because they reminded me of the prison's infirmary, and the inmates who were busy sewing soldiers' uniforms in there, while I sat among them on a bench, wielding my pen.[53]

Settembrini and Faucitano planned to publish the *Dialogue on Women* anonymously. In fact, they had already secured a publisher and had made complicated arrangements to ensure the proofs would be corrected, when Settembrini was suddenly released.[54]

---

[53] Settembrini 1971: 153–5.
[54] Settembrini 1971: 512. Immediately after his release, Settembrini was too frightened to pursue publication and later he turned his attention to more important (and far more inflammatory) anonymous publications. As a result, the *Dialogue* was only published in 1977, as an appendix to Gigante's attempt to mitigate the scandal caused by *The Neoplatonists* earlier that same year. The *Dialogue* made almost no impression at the time and has received no critical attention since. Guidi, writing about Settembrini's views on women's education, thinks the *Dialogue* is still unpublished ('un documento inedito', Guidi, Russo, and Varriale 2011: 55).

On 14 October 1842, on a rainy evening, he was summoned from his cell and told to leave. He was handed his few possessions, and shown to the door: the *Memoirs* give a powerful impression of his stunned surprise, as he walked home in the falling light. A neighbour guessed who he was and cried out to Faucitano. Little Raffaele ran into his father's arms and held him tight, in a real-life version of the dream that had consoled Settembrini on his first night in prison.[55] A few moments later he was sitting down, with his son and daughter on his knee and his wife by his side, enjoying a meal of 'bread and lettuce... what she could put together for our feast'.[56] This touching scene of domestic reunion concludes Settembrini's self-portrait in his *Memoirs*: now, he thought, their 'troubles would be over'; now he would be 'able to work'.[57]

From this moment onwards, in the *Memoirs*, Settembrini all but disappears from view, except as a seemingly inactive observer of the main events, debates, and atmospheres leading up to the revolution of 1848. We may well ask how it is that the *Memoirs* reveal almost nothing about how he began to conspire in earnest—how he started to work with men intending to throw bombs and take up arms,[58] and how he conceived of providing written ammunition in the form of his decisive *Protest of the People of the Two Sicilies*. A Tacitean indictment of Bourbonic abuse, mixed with Neapolitan vignettes of injustice, the *Protest* circulated widely, if illegally, doing much to inspire insurrection in the south and in Sicily, leading the authorities to begin a veritable hunt for its anonymous author.[59]

The main reason for Settembrini's failure to give a detailed account of his revolutionary activities is, we believe, that he wrote his *Memoirs* after

---

[55] See p. 27.
[56] This detail of 'bread and lettuce' does not make it into the final version of *Memoirs* (which gives a more dignified family portrait) but belongs to an earlier account written in 1852: Settembrini 1971: 390.
[57] Settembrini 1971: 158.
[58] As Themelly points out in his introduction to Settembrini 1961: xix, very little is known about Settembrini's activities between 1841 and 1848; though De Sanctis in his preface to Settembrini 1892: xiv–xv offers a portrait of clandestine meetings, when the possibility of bombing the Royal Palace was discussed, we read nothing of this in the *Memoirs*.
[59] De Sanctis, in his introduction to Settembrini 1892: xii, is eloquent about the immense popularity of the *Protest* and, after 1860, of Settembrini as its author: 'had Luigi been ambitious he would have held the top positions in government: he, the author of the *Protest*, and extremely popular as he was'.

Italian unification, when his priorities had changed: the image of a simple family meal and a desire to work (for all that he was banned from teaching in public school again, after his prison sentence, despite acquittal on no charge) have greater unifying power than a detailed account of conspiracy and instigation to violence: in short, the heroes of the Risorgimento started to become 'apolitical banalities' in their own writings—and long before the process reached its completion in postwar Italy.[60] To the challenge first of unifying Italy, and then keeping it united, we may add a psychological consideration. As Halberstam points out in the introduction to *The Undercommons*, 'what we want after "the break" will be different from what we think we want before the break and both are necessarily different from the desire that issues from being in the break'.[61] This is a point to which we return in chapter 8, where we also explore a third line of thought, concerned specifically with resilience: an important reason why, in our view, Settembrini failed to detail his revolutionary activities between 1842 and 1848 is that reading and writing were for him means of escaping the present to reach into a past and future of shared pleasure—and this despite the fact that he did also write the *Protest*, an unflinching account of what were, for him, present horrors.[62]

---

[60] Riall 2007: 7.   [61] Harney and Moten 2013: 6.
[62] The same could be said about his attitude to teaching. After his arrest and despite his acquittal, Settembrini was no longer allowed to teach in public schools, and so between 1842 and 1848 he became a private tutor, offering his lessons 'door to door, like a bagpiper who comes, plays his tune, and leaves' (Settembrini 1971: 159). In an effort to disguise his revolutionary activities in the period, he claims in the *Memoirs* that 'to teach was to conspire...because it meant letting the young fall in love with truth and beauty' (Settembrini 1971: 159).

4
Luigi Settembrini, According to His Wife

The revolutions of 1848, which swept across Europe in the course of a brief few months, began in Sicily—inspired, not least, by Settembrini's *Protest of the People of the Two Sicilies*. On 12 January 1848, the Sicilians rose up against the Bourbons. A few weeks later, a second revolution broke out in Paris. Within the year, rebellion had spread to over fifty countries across Europe. There was little coordination between different revolutionary outbreaks, yet people fought in pursuit of similar goals: the end of absolute monarchy, republican rule, a constitution, universal male suffrage, freedom of the press, a civilian army, free education, increased worker control of the means of production, and, especially in the south of Italy, peasant liberation from feudal forms of bondage. These demands were sometimes expressed through an appeal to national self-determination, though in practice revolutionary outbreaks were often more local: the Sicilian uprising offers a telling example in this regard, since it sought to establish the independence of the island from the Kingdom of the Two Sicilies (then the largest state on the Italian peninsula) while asserting only a vague commitment to a future Italian federation.

As unrest spread from Sicily to Naples and armed revolutionaries declared independence in Calabria, King Ferdinand II reluctantly granted a constitution, swore to uphold it before God, and called elections by limited suffrage. Settembrini returned home (after fleeing to Malta, in fear of being identified as the author of the *Protest*). Fellow revolutionary Carlo Poerio was elected to parliament and briefly served as minister of education in the aftermath of the revolution; Settembrini took up a position in his ministerial office. The *Memoirs* communicate his disorientation at the noise, petulance, corruption, and general chaos he experienced while working there.[1] A few months after taking up the post he resigned, refusing a state pension to which he was entitled but which he thought he had not earned: 'I achieved little with my service and did not deserve one.'[2] The king, meanwhile, declared the elections null and void. New ones, held in June 1848, yielded a more conservative chamber of deputies, who quickly agreed with the Bourbon king that the Sicilians, at any rate, needed to be brought back under Neapolitan control. At that, Ferdinand II prorogued parliament to focus on military action, bombed Messina (gaining the nickname of *Re Bomba*), and began to rule as an absolute monarch again. He never formally revoked the constitution (he was too superstitious to do so, after swearing before God to uphold it), but found other ways to mark the end of his constitutional experiment. The main one was this: on 23 June 1849, forty-three noted revolutionaries were arrested. Settembrini was among them.

The last events recorded in Settembrini's *Memoirs* date to a few months before he was sentenced to death after that arrest. There are many other autobiographical accounts of his life—treatises he wrote about prison conditions, defence speeches delivered in court, diary entries, letters to his wife and other correspondents—but these were never reworked into the *Memoirs*. That he originally intended to use those materials as a basis for his autobiography emerges from a letter to his wife, written from exile on 14 March 1859, in which he asks her to send 'all the writings about incarceration, the description of the Vicaria prison, the *Three Days of Waiting in the Chapel*, your own letter, the description of the Panopticon, and the diaries. You know why I need them—and quickly.'[3] The explanation generally given as to why the *Memoirs* do not incorporate those materials and stop before his scheduled hanging (and last-minute pardon) is that he died before he could complete the book: a note at the end of the manuscript, added by his son Raffaele, reads as follows: 'Here, on 3 November, my poor father stopped writing.'[4] By this he meant 3 November 1876, thus suggesting that

---

[1] Settembrini 1971: 198.   [2] Settembrini 1971: 28.   [3] Settembrini 1971: 783–4.
[4] This is reported in all the major editions of the *Memoirs* and is still clearly legible in the manuscript.

Settembrini's death interrupted his writing. This explanation for why the *Memoirs* remained incomplete, however, does not hold.

Settembrini had the time to copy out *The Neoplatonists* more than once before dying, one version on the same paper and at the same time as he was working on his *Memoirs*. More importantly, he had begun working on his autobiography in 1859, so he had almost two decades to complete the work before his death. That he stopped his *Memoirs* where he did needs, in short, a better explanation than his biographers (following his son's note) have been able to offer—particularly since it was only after his second arrest that his life began to fit into the conventions of the heroic revolutionary autobiography that most readily appealed to the public. Why Settembrini could not find the time to write a riveting story complete with near hanging, island incarceration, escape plot, exile, mutiny, and a final triumphant return home (especially when he wrote so much else in that period) is an issue that opens up broader considerations about revolution, autobiography, and homosexuality. Indeed, it is a useful way for us to approach the relationship between Italian masculinity and Greek love.

The content of 'the chapters Settembrini never wrote' can be pieced together from the materials his wife collected, organized, and preserved—as well as from her own accounts (many of which remain unpublished—despite the precision and liveliness that characterize her own writing).[5] From the time of Settembrini's second incarceration, she emerges as the main conduit between him and the rest of the world: in that role, we see her make crucial decisions about the future course of his life and about how that life might be best presented to the public. This chapter, then, follows the life of Settembrini from the revolution of 1848

---

[5] On the authorship of the 'account of my wife' (*racconto di mia moglie*, Settembrini 1971: 369–84), see Themelly's comments in Settembrini 1961: lxi. Faucitano's account of the days leading up to Settembrini's planned execution is so well written that some suspected Settembrini himself of being its true author, a view with no foundation in fact. A letter Settembrini wrote to his wife from prison on 29 March 1851 includes this brief statement: 'I send back to you herewith only your beautiful narrative, while I keep the letters'; Settembrini 1961: lix. It is regrettable that most of Faucitano's letters remain unpublished to this day and that the 'account of my wife' is published exclusively in collections of Settembrini's own work.

until his exile, in full awareness that it was told, retold, and shaped to suit different aims—and always through the mediation of his wife.[6]

Arrested for the second time on 23 June 1849, Settembrini was initially incarcerated in the Vicaria prison, accused of plotting against the king. He awaited trial in that prison for almost two years. His description of the place began to circulate internationally in the early 1850s and was instrumental in accelerating the demise of the Bourbons not only in the eyes of foreign observers but also in Italy where it accelerated the process of unification:

> After going through the visiting hall, you entered the first dungeon: a dark, huge, cavernous space, with only some light filtering from a window across the other side. You could see nothing and, unless somebody took you by the hand, you were in danger of breaking a leg. After your eyes got adjusted to the darkness, you saw men moving around with strange, distorted faces, in rags, or almost naked, speaking in strange idioms. Against the walls there were beds, or kennels, together with rolled-up mats that were moved into the middle of the room at night, when people slept obscenely naked in summer and covered in rags in winter—in total filth always.... This was the noble prison, where about four hundred men suffered the stench, darkness and insects, all mixed together—the guilty with those awaiting trial, the student who was late to apply for his residence permit and the man who had hacked his wife to pieces... You could not go near the only window at the back, because the most awful stench rose up from below. For beneath our floor there was the common prison, where men were pressed together like beasts—naked, filthy, without even a mat to sleep on, constantly begging for alms through the grates.... Those alms, given by passers-by in the street, were considerable, because Neapolitans immediately feel pity and give of their own when they see misfortune. The money, however, did not help provide food or

---

[6] Soper 2020 goes some way towards recognizing the role of Faucitano and he outlines a broader network of wives of prisoners, working relentlessly to publicize their plight, but much more work remains to be done on Faucitano: she would, in fact, deserve biographical treatment herself.

clothes for the desperate, but went straight into the hands of the *camorristi* [organized criminals].[7]

Settembrini remained in the Vicaria, awaiting trial, for twenty months, the last three in the lower prison. While he was there, the future prime minister of Great Britain, William Ewart Gladstone, was vacationing in Naples. A classical scholar, High Tory, and vocal champion of slavery in his student years (when his father owned thousands of slaves across nine plantations in the Caribbean), he had already served as member of parliament and colonial secretary under the Conservative government of Robert Peel, and was now enjoying his stay in Naples in 'circumstances purely domestic':[8] he hoped that the mild climate would benefit his daughter's ailing eyes, and was meanwhile taking the opportunity to visit various classical sites.

Antonio Panizzi, an exiled revolutionary in London who had established himself as an authority on classical antiquity and was soon to become 'principal librarian' (i.e. director) of the British Museum, saw in this Neapolitan vacation an opportunity—and insisted that Gladstone go visit Poerio and Settembrini in prison: they were classical scholars, after all, and he would find their conversation interesting.[9] Gladstone was horrified by what he saw in the Vicaria and Nisida (where he met Poerio). On his return to London, and via the constant advocacy of Panizzi, he addressed two letters to Lord Aberdeen, describing what he had witnessed in the Vicaria as 'the negation of God erected into a system of government'.[10] His letters proved influential, also because they came from an unexpected source: Gladstone was no revolutionary, indeed he firmly believed that all governments deserved full respect, 'whether they be absolute, constitutional, or republican'.[11] The reason why he denounced conditions in the Neapolitan prison was that the arbitrary and harsh treatment of 'real or supposed political offenders' was, in his

---

[7] Settembrini 1971: 149–53.   [8] Gladstone 1859: 3.
[9] Gladstone's own classical learning included excellent knowledge of Italian. This can be assessed, for example, on the basis of some stanzas in Italian comic verse he tossed out in a letter to Panizzi, when he was afraid his friend might resign from the British Museum. At the end of the letter he apologized for possible metrical errors, half in Latin and half in Italian: '*Erroribus innumerabilibus exceptis: d'arrezione e di surrezione, e che so io*'; quoted in Foot 1979: 53.
[10] Gladstone 1859: 7.   [11] Gladstone 1859: 3.

view, 'certainly, and even rapidly, doing the work of republicanism in that country: a political creed', he added, which had 'little natural or habitual root in the character of the people'.[12] The Bourbon king, in his view, was doing Mazzini's revolutionary work for him—and, indeed, more effectively. Apart from making this argument, the two letters to Lord Aberdeen are famous today because they mark a change in Gladstone's own views and career, 'smoothing his transition from High Tory to Liberal in British politics'.[13] Here, then, we have a case in which we can track the influence of a subaltern figure like Settembrini on developments at the heart of British imperial politics.[14] As for improving prison conditions in Naples, the letters achieved nothing at all. What they did do was create a new, international readership for Settembrini himself—and this proved crucial in avoiding the gallows.[15]

After almost two years awaiting trial in the Vicaria, Settembrini was sentenced to death on 1 February 1851, together with two other revolutionaries, Filippo Agresti and Salvatore Faucitano (no relation of his wife). It was a Friday, and it was therefore necessary to wait until Monday to carry out the execution: no hangings took place at the weekends. That Friday, Settembrini wrote a moving letter to his wife, which circulated to influential interlocutors mere hours after it got into her hands and was published in the *Edinburgh Review* a few months later.[16] On the Saturday, shackled and already dressed in rough black hemp, ready for hanging, he wrote her a second letter, which also drew

---

[12] Gladstone 1859: 4.   [13] Riall 2007: 144.

[14] Soper 2020: 97 rightly insists on this aspect: 'we should not view the events of the 1850s as a one-sided tale of "humanitarian intervention," carried out by the British (and French) to the surprise of a fortunate but passive group of prisoners in Naples. In fact, the prisoners played an active and important role in the process leading to their release.'

[15] Settembrini himself later translated Gladstone's first letter into Italian; Pessina Archive, II. C1.78.

[16] Faucitano immediately sent the letter to Antonio Panizzi in London, who inserted it into a much longer piece on Neapolitan justice published that same year in the *Edinburgh Review*, vol. 94, July–October 1851, with the following, hero-making introduction at p. 515: 'On the morning of the 1st of February, whilst the judges were still deliberating, Settembrini, who fully expected to be condemned to death, as he eventually was, addressed to his wife the most touching, noble, and manly letter that we can conceive it possible to write under such circumstances. It breathes the serenity of mind of innocence, the resignation of a Christian, and the affection of an attached husband and father, as well as the calm reliance on truth of a martyr. Conscious of our inability to render all the feeling, the delicacy and graceful elegance of the original, we lay it before our readers...'. Faucitano became increasingly aware that her husband's letters could be used to his advantage: a letter dated 20 September 1853 clearly documents this: Settembrini 1971: 581.

international attention. On Sunday morning, the main guard, don Ciccio, brought coffee to the prisoners, together with some news: Gigia Faucitano had received the first letter and was now leading a delegation of wives and children to Caserta, to visit the royal court and beg the king for mercy. On Monday, the prisoners smelled incense and concluded that the *bianchi*, the white-robed friars who accompanied the condemned to the gallows, had arrived. Contrary to expectation, however, Settembrini and Agresti were unshackled, taken out of the chapel, and asked to wait for an announcement. The third prisoner, Salvatore Faucitano, remained in the chapel, while the gallows were being erected outside.[17] Nothing happened in the course of that whole day. After midnight, the prosecutor announced that the king had pardoned all three men, commuting their sentences to life imprisonment in the Panopticon on the island of Santo Stefano. Gigia Faucitano had succeeded in mobilizing the relevant authorities and let the king understand that the executions were likely to cause an international uproar.

On Tuesday morning, the families were allowed to visit the pardoned prisoners. Gigia Faucitano appeared to Settembrini 'pale, with a stony face, silent, with eyes that darted everywhere, as if offended'.[18] Another wife had, by contrast, entirely lost her mind: she kept asking to be taken to her husband, while he was in front of her. After short goodbyes, the prisoners were added to a mass of other sentenced men, handcuffed in pairs, and paraded through the streets of Naples for public mocking. After that, they were stowed tightly into the hull of a ship, 'in the same way as negroes', in the words of Settembrini.[19] Those condemned to irons, including Poerio, were taken to the island of Nisida; those sentenced to life imprisonment arrived, two days later, at Santo Stefano.

The Panopticon was designed to make an impression on the incoming prisoner: planned by Francesco Carpi and built by convicts between 1793 and 1797, its circular structure enabled total surveillance of all cells from a single guardhouse in its central courtyard (Figure 4.1). 'Imagine a vast

---

[17] Though Settembrini said nothing about this in his Memoirs, Faucitano had been involved in secret discussions to murder the king—discussions at which Settembrini had also been present: see further p. 66 n. 58.
[18] Settembrini 1971: 363.
[19] Settembrini 1971: 367. For the crucial intervention of Black supporters later in Settembrini's life, and their recognition of important commonalities, see pp. 17f. and 78f.

Figure 4.1 A recent photograph of the Panopticon, which was used as a prison until 1965 and was subsequently abandoned. As well as several heroes of the Risorgimento, the prison later housed antifascist objectors, including Sandro Pertini, who later became president of the Italian Republic. A new plan to turn the Panopticon into an academy for the next generation of European leaders was approved by the Italian government in 2022.

theatre', wrote Settembrini, 'and a guard looking and dominating this theatre all round.'[20] It is likely that the building was directly influenced by the theories and designs of Jeremy Bentham, who published *Panopticon or The Inspection House* in 1791, though we are not certain of this.[21] What we can say without doubt is that long before Michael Foucault placed the Panopticon at the centre of his investigation of state control, common prisoners understood the building on Santo Stefano as a structure that itself needed to be 'watched back', as an act of resistance to its architecture of surveillance.[22] While Settembrini wrote about its Dantesque organization on three levels, each of which comprised thirty-three communal cells, illiterate prisoners crafted detailed models of the

---

[20] Settembrini 1971: 403.   [21] Parente 1998: 36.
[22] Foucault 1995 focused on the Maison centrale at Rennes. It is a pity that he did not consider the Panopticon on Santo Stefano, because there is a rich record of reactions to the architectural structure on the part of inmates.

Figure 4.2 A cork model of the Panopticon, Museum of San Martino, Naples. The building's architecture of surveillance inspired keen observation by inmates in return. Settembrini's memorable description of the building can be compared with this and many other models made by illiterate prisoners during his time there.

building out of cork (see Figure 4.2). It seems to us that this kind of activity stemmed from the need to control a building that was controlling them. We know that Settembrini later kept one such model of the Panopticon at home.[23] This is a subject for a different book, but we note here the rich and untapped materials provided by prisoners: Foucault's analysis focuses entirely on the accounts provided by those who had the power to imprison, but it is our assertion here that the subaltern can indeed 'write back'—or rather, in this case, respond to oppressive architecture by architectural modelling.[24]

Once in the Panopticon, Settembrini continued to write and Faucitano ensured that his writings reached an international readership. His *Three Days in the Chapel* offers a detailed account of the time spent shackled, in black hemp sack, awaiting execution: we experience, through reading, his

---

[23] That model is now also in San Martino, see Parente 2008: 45.
[24] We borrow the phrase 'write back' from postcolonial theory (see Ashton, Griffth, and Tiffin 1989) and adapt it for our illiterate context.

hypervigilance, the ebb and flow of his despair, the minute perception of tiny sounds and smells, the disjointed conversations exchanged with the other two prisoners, the disproportionate relief at the sudden kindness of a guard, the memories of past domestic happiness—all mingled with physical pain.[25] It makes sense, as we argue in chapters 7 and 8, to compare this description, which he wrote mere weeks after avoiding execution, with his later works of Platonic fiction and, specifically, his handling of Socrates' execution.

After receiving *Three Days in the Chapel*, Faucitano answered with an account of her own recollections of the same three days; her 'beautiful narrative', as Settembrini later called it, gives a sense of swiftly paced, determined action: we read about how, within hours of hearing the sentence, she had gathered the women and children of the other condemned men; sought legal advice; dealt with false rumours; made sure Settembrini's letter was read and reported as broadly as possible; then taken everyone to Caserta late at night. There she failed to secure a hotel room for her disgraced party; worried about mounting exhaustion and incipient insanity among the women and children in her charge; realized that the king would not receive them; and went straight to the bishop of Caserta, asking him to intercede with the king on their behalf: 'the more my suffering and fear increased, the more I felt impelled to act'.[26]

In the same month of April 1851, while Settembrini and his wife were exchanging accounts, Gladstone was penning his first letter to Lord Aberdeen. Conditions in the Panopticon and the Nisida prison, where Poerio was kept in irons, were hard to reconcile with his vivid memories of 'those lonely islands scattered along the coast, whose picturesque and romantic forms delight the eye of the passing voyager, ignorant what huge and festering masses of human suffering they conceal' (see Figure 4.3)[27] The fact that the prisoners belonged to a land of great beauty and antiquity, and were themselves classical scholars, affected Gladstone to the point that he felt compelled to elevate the convicts to the rank of honorary Englishmen: 'Carlo Poerio...is himself a refined and accomplished gentleman, a copious and eloquent speaker, a

---

[25] Settembrini 1971: 337–68.   [26] Published in Settembrini 1971: 369–84.
[27] Gladstone 1859: 14.

Figure 4.3 Pasquale Mattei (1813–79) depicted the island of Santo Stefano shortly before Settembrini, an exact contemporary, was sentenced to life imprisonment there. Mattei included the Latin inscription that stood at the entrance to the prison: *Donec sancta Themis scelerum tot monstra catenis victa tenet, stat res, stat tibi tuta domus* ('As long as blessed Themis will keep so many monsters shackled, the State and your house will be safe').

respected and blameless character... strictly a Constitutionalist... his pattern is England, rather than America or France... I must say, after a pretty full examination of his case, that the condemnation of such a man for treason is... as gross an outrage... as would be a like condemnation in this country of any of our best known public men, Lord John Russell, or Lord Landsdowne, or Sir James Graham, or yourself.'[28] He also reported that Settembrini, a man 'with a character quite as pure and fair', had been condemned to 'double irons for life, upon a remote and sea-girt rock: nay, there may even be reason to fear that he is directly subjected to physical torture. The mode of it, which was specified to me upon respectable though not certain authority, was the thrusting of sharp instruments under the finger-nails.'[29]

The information concerning Settembrini's torture was inaccurate and, a few months later, Gladstone publicly retracted it: 'I have learned nothing to confirm the statement, which I reported as probably though not certainly true, that Settembrini has been tortured. I therefore think it

[28] Gladstone 1859: 15.   [29] Gladstone 1859: 15–16.

my duty to withdraw it, although it is not met by the Neapolitan Government with an explicit denial.'[30] He then went on to point out that there were nevertheless reasons for concern: 'while stating that Settembrini is not in double irons, I do not mean to mitigate the general idea I have given of his cruel and wicked punishment. He is confined, with eight more prisoners, at San Stefano, in a room sixteen *palmi* square [i.e. about 2.5 metres, or 8 feet], which they are never allowed to leave: one of them is a man named Cajazzo, who was condemned for murder forty-nine years ago and boasts of having at different times murdered thirty-five people. Several of these exploits he has committed in the prison upon his companions... What kind of protection, I want to know, is thus afforded to the life of Settembrini?'[31] The details of these later statements are clearly based on Settembrini's own description of the Panopticon (written in the spring of 1851), which include an account of Cajazzo that, in our view, displays subtle but significant differences in emphasis, when compared with Gladstone's peroration: 'Cajazzo... from Calabria, seventy-five years old, thirty-five murders: slim, tall, straight, he speaks little and with very good sense: he says he committed the first murder in the fire of youth, and the others out of necessity.'[32]

Settembrini's revolutionary and republican convictions can be contrasted with Gladstone's anti-revolutionary, monarchic, and imperialist politics at the level of ideology, of course. But our argument here is that they are also reflected in how each of our two men described an illiterate criminal like Cajazzo. It is our belief that Settembrini's ability to see in him not just a serial killer but a man of 'good sense' goes some way towards explaining how, in fact, he managed to survive in a prison where inmates frequently murdered one another. It was the way in which Settembrini related to others that afforded him the protection the government denied him.

Differences notwithstanding, Settembrini and Gladstone agreed on one point: the Panopticon was a mirror of the state. Some months after his incarceration, Settembrini managed to persuade the director of the prison to let him see the archives—perhaps, we venture to speculate, on the excuse that he wanted to check the entry for his own father, who had

[30] Gladstone 1859: 58. [31] Gladstone 1859: 60. [32] Settembrini 1971: 414.

served time there in 1799–1800. Whatever the pretext, Settembrini was able to gather and publish, via Faucitano, some eye-opening statistics. In the period between January 1848 and 30 June 1852, he counted fifty-one violent deaths: forty-five inmates killed by other inmates, two guards killed by inmates, and four suicides.[33] He also compiled statistics about crimes, convictions, and punishments, professions and regions of origin of the inmates, ethnicities (he was interested in the high number of Albanians serving life sentences in the Panopticon), and percentage of prisoners in the Bourbon penal system overall (the archives contained numbers for the other prisons too): 'if France had the same percentage of prisoners sentenced for life as we have in our Kingdom, instead of the 6,780 currently serving a life sentence there, their number would be 60,000'.[34]

These factual reports, compiled in the context of broader international and diplomatic exchanges, are important when it comes to assessing Settembrini's relationship to truth, fiction, and forgery: he knew when to be accurate. They also show that Faucitano was, as ever, resourceful in smuggling written communications in and out of prison, despite harsh but unimaginative censorship: archival material and published letters reveal that she used parcels of food, baskets sent with changes of clothes and books, open letters they were allowed to exchange, which often contained coded allusions and abbreviations, and ample use of invisible ink. What was different, compared to her earlier system of wine bottles, was that she was now in a position to divulge—through her international contacts—crucial information that the Neapolitan authorities were intent on keeping hidden. She was also able to rely on those same contacts to solve other problems, such as that of securing a future for their fourteen-year-old son Raffaele, who, because of his father's incarceration, was not allowed to attend school and could not even secure a private teacher.

The man who came to her aid, in solving that specific problem, was none other than Antonio Panizzi. The naturalized British 'Sir Anthony' is remembered today primarily as the director of the British Museum

---

[33] Settembrini 1971: 429.   [34] Settembrini 1971: 428–9.

who commissioned its famous Round Reading Room (according to a design not unlike the Panopticon, in fact—with the difference that it placed books, rather than a prison guard, at the centre of institutional operations). He is also remembered for enforcing the Copyright Act of 1848 ('I want a poor student to have the same means of indulging his learned curiosity...as the richest man in the kingdom'[35]) and for devising the system known today as International Standard Bibliographic Description. What is less well known about Panizzi is his hands-on support for revolutionaries fallen on hard times. While Gladstone enjoyed Naples 'in circumstances purely domestic', Panizzi himself had also travelled there, attempting to intercede with the king on behalf of the prisoners and ensuring, at the very least, that the British statesman would visit them in prison. A few months later, Gladstone and Panizzi were sitting together, in the comfortable reading rooms of the British Museum, drafting the first letter to Lord Aberdeen.

Panizzi, then, looked after individuals who needed help, while keeping in mind broader political opportunities. This is what he wrote to a friend about Faucitano, for example: 'You may recollect the name of Settembrini among those of the persons condemned to death, and then to an *Ergastolo* for life, of whom Gladstone spoke in his publications, and I myself more at length in my article in the *Edinburgh Review*, in which I inserted the letter which he (Settembrini) wrote to his wife whilst the judges were deliberating on his fate. When at Naples, I became acquainted with Settembrini's wife and his two children—a boy and a girl. The persecutions to which that poor woman and those children have been subjected are incredible. Among other things, no tutor dared give instruction to the boy for fear of losing the permission which every teacher must obtain from the Government to be allowed to follow his profession.'[36]

Panizzi then arranged for Raffaele to be placed in a boarding school in England—even if the displaced Neapolitan boy, disregarding his father's wishes that he apply himself to the study of ancient Greek and draw

---

[35] As he stated in 1836 to the members of the Parliamentary Commission on the British Museum, see Gambari and Guerrini 2018: 547.
[36] Later dated 20 March 1852, published in Fagan 1881, vol. 2: 127.

68   CLASSICS, LOVE, REVOLUTION

inspiration from the wise words of Pindar,[37] soon quit school and joined the merchant navy. Partly in order to discuss the conduct of his son, Panizzi now began to correspond, via Faucitano, with Settembrini himself: their exchanges had important consequences, practically, politically, and intellectually—not just for revolutionary politics but also for the history of classical scholarship.

Inside the prison, Settembrini had time to think about the history of captivity on the small islands surrounding Naples, including the one where he was now serving his life sentence: he requested that a copy of Tacitus, in Latin, be sent to the prison,[38] and wrote about 'the cold cruelty of the man who killed the fatherland and his own daughter, that *furbo* and *fortunato*, whom flatterers called Augustus'.[39] While assessing Roman imperial history, Settembrini also took time to observe his fellow prisoners: 'in this fierce communal life, you find all the hatred, the envy, the plotting, the gossip, the cunning, and the lasciviousness that you may expect in a convent of friars'. While striking his characteristic note of anticlericalism, he could see that there were differences between a monastery and that prison: 'everyone gets irritated and angry for the smallest reason: a look, a word, nothing at all; and then the issue gets settled with weapons... It may seem impossible that men locked up for life on a remote island, who are strictly guarded and constantly threatened with the most severe punishments, can get hold of so many weapons—but they buy them from the guards... they fashion them from door hinges... they hide them inside the prison walls, or under flagstones, or inside carefully hollowed-out wooden tools; some thin blades, wrapped up in rags, inside their own anuses... these men kill each other for no reason, but do not touch their oppressors; only once a prisoner killed a sergeant, and was immediately stabbed to death by his own mates. The stupidity of the weak is always the same. The most common reasons for violence here are wine and gambling... feuds carry on from one killing to the next, until in the end the wounded go to the infirmary, the dead are buried, and the rest get punished. This is the

---

[37] Settembrini in a letter to Raffaele dated 16 January 1852: 'Do not ever neglect to study Greek and Latin... Pindar's saying is beautiful *"the gods sell us everything in exchange for hard work"; learn it: πάντα ἡμὶν οἱ θεοὶ πωλοῦσι τῶι πόνωι'*", Settembrini 1971: 554–5.
[38] Settembrini 1971: 527–8.   [39] Settembrini 1971: 397.

manner: they are placed face-down on a table in the central courtyard and lashed with ropes dipped in tar and then water, while the other prisoners are made to look on... after the lashes, they are tied with a chain to a ring fixed to the wall for months on end.'[40]

Settembrini listened attentively to the stories prisoners told him and observed how feuds and killings followed loyalties of origin—something that did not bode well for the unification of Italy: even within this one gaol in the southern Kingdom of the Two Sicilies, Calabrians stuck to Calabrians, Neapolitans to Neapolitans, Lucanians to Lucanians, and Sicilians to Sicilians. Settembrini nevertheless attempted to find ways to assert the dignity of all prisoners, as well as his own. A few months after arriving in the Panopticon, he organized a fundraiser among the prisoners, collecting meagre funds for the victims of an earthquake that had just devastated the southern region of Lucania. He hoped that their efforts would be reported in the press. He wanted to honour the prisoners and lift their sense of civic duty, to be sure—but he also aimed to increase pressure on the government by commanding public attention.[41]

It is possible to detect a shift of attitude in Settembrini's diary and letters during his time in the Panopticon: after a few months of incarceration, his writing moves away from the horrors of the factual report towards a greater sense of calm, affection, and even dreamy reverie. He attempts to reassure his wife about his own safety: 'Among murderers, whom I pity but do not despise, I sleep all safe—indeed, well loved! And you, without a man by your side offering his assistance and support, are well respected yourself! Is this not the work of Divine Providence? Not everyone sleeps and enjoys his dreams as peacefully. Not all women are as respected as you are. Let us give thanks to God for this.'[42] He also writes about his physical wellbeing and torpor of mind: 'I feel fine in my body and my mind is calm; many hours of the day go by in a stupor... if I am to remain here for many years, I will become quite stupid.'[43]

As well as writing about his own physical conditions, he insists, obsessively, on the importance of Faucitano's own health. This is a theme that features in almost every letter, over the span of decades,

---

[40] Settembrini 1971: 408–11. [41] Settembrini 1971: 545–6.
[42] Settembrini 1971: 567. [43] Settembrini 1971: 531.

and which is of some relevance when it comes to assessing his attitudes to the body in his polemical attacks on ascetic Neoplatonism: 'I hear that you and the boy are curing yourselves with figs and gaining weight: great!';[44] 'Do go for walks because they do you good, you used to walk a long way to visit me in that other prison';[45] 'I beg you to look after your health, when I bid you farewell before coming here you scared me; write to me and tell me, in every detail, about your health';[46] 'when I know that you are in good health, I live';[47] 'I heard you are very ill; it would be better if I died, I am of no use to anyone, but you are essential to our children... spend everything you can put together on your health.'[48] These passages express Settembrini's utter dependence on his wife, of course, but also reveal an attention to physical wellbeing that bears comparison with what he has to say in many of his other works, *The Neoplatonists* included.[49]

As for the dangers of intellectual atrophy, in August 1853, Settembrini started to work on what he insisted would become a complete translation of the works of Lucian. He tested the effectiveness of his version on his illiterate cellmates, checking whether his Italian idiom worked well for them, despite the fact they spoke a variety of dialects (see Figure 4.4). The enormity of the task he took on is staggering—it would be a daunting enterprise even today, for professional scholars enjoying full institutional, domestic, and library support. In a diary entry, he joked about it, 'true hard labour, suitable for a convict', then reviewed his reasons for undertaking it: 'not to lose the ability to write Italian and practise some Greek', but also out of a 'certain sympathy I have always felt for the most graceful Lucian'.[50] After a few years, when he realized the translation was indeed taking shape, he added yet one more reason for completing it: the proceeds from publication would provide a dowry for his daughter.[51]

---

[44] Settembrini 1971: 504.   [45] Settembrini 1971: 520.
[46] Settembrini 1971: 526–7.   [47] Settembrini 1971: 533.
[48] Settembrini 1971: 584.
[49] See also his insistence on physical exercise for women, p. 103.
[50] Settembrini 1971: 446.
[51] In a diary entry dated 22 August 1855, Settembrini 1971: 487: 'But what dowry can I provide for my darling daughter? I had a thought: to give her my translation of Lucian, cede copyright to her: this thought has rekindled my life, cleared my head, and increased my strength. I do not think, I do not read, and I do not write anything else but that: it seems so beautiful and sweet to work now, whereas before it made me tired and bored.'

Figure 4.4 Vincenzo Montefusco (1852–1912), *Settembrini Reading to Inmates in the Panopticon*, Museum of San Martino, Naples. The painting is based on a detailed reading of Settembrini's diaries. The man on the far right, for example, is clearly 'the shoemaker, born in a small village in the mountains north of Naples, with the blood, pride, and toughness of an ancient Samnite ... he tells us the varied and whimsical events of his life in a rough, poetic language that I cannot imitate' (Settembrini 1971: 444).

We know from Settembrini's diaries and letters that he kept a routine which involved some hours of translation every morning. Unsurprisingly, though, he ran into difficulties and interruptions: there were times when he felt too despondent to work, particularly as he questioned the utility of what he was trying to do: 'Even assuming I manage to make a good version, what is the value of fashioning some Italian clothes for a Greek man who believed in nothing and laughed about everything?' There were also other, more gruesome interruptions. On 23 January 1855, for example, he complained in his diary about 'screams which would make even Archimedes lose his concentration: a prisoner has stolen and raped a chicken, and has therefore been given fifty lashes in the courtyard, while the dead chicken is held over his face.'[52] And yet, page after page, the translation grew. Not even a year

---

[52] Settembrini 1971: 475–6.

after beginning, he was ready to send half of it—the equivalent of a thick, single-spaced printed volume of some five hundred pages, to Panizzi in London. As to the possibility of sending it to another prominent supporter, Lady Holland, he asked his wife for advice:

> I cannot send it to her directly. Since there are some obscenities, it is not prudent to send it to a woman, who could take offence, or form of me a less than wholesome impression. Once Mr P. has read it and given his opinion, then some of it can be given to her too, and some also to others. She can read it all, of course, but it is best for me not to send her everything. You will say: and how did you get it into your head to translate a writer capable of obscenities? Well, there you have it, my Gigia: this was what happened in antiquity, because of the times and the voluptuousness of the people; the best works are full of obscenities. We Italians actually suffer from the same thing. The works of Boccaccio and Firenzuola are most beautiful, but smeared with the same tar. Even the strict Machiavelli is infected with obscenity in his comedies. Were I to write something myself, I would stay clear of the smut, but when I translate I can do nothing about it. Still, I do not know whether a woman, living in our time and in such a country, may not take offence. It seems prudent not to present the translation to her. And, even were she not to be offended by it, I would look shameless for not acting with some tact. Enough: please read it yourself and tell me what you think.[53]

Some scholars have wrongly taken a few decontextualized sentences from this letter to refer to *The Neoplatonists*: the genesis and effects of this error have now been painstakingly reconstructed.[54] That important correction notwithstanding, it seems to us that the letter remains relevant to an interpretation of Settembrini's own fake (and smutty) 'translation from the Greek'. For one thing, it shows that Settembrini was well aware that, as a translator, he could hide behind an ancient author (whether real, as in the case of Lucian, or invented, as in that of Aristaeus of Megara). Moreover, the letter betrays an interesting perspective on sex:

[53] Settembrini 1971: 588. [54] Conoscenti 2019: 32–5.

the assertion that ancient Greek and modern Italian literature differ little when it comes to sexual content holds true only if the differences between homosexual and heterosexual obscenities are deemed of no account. Lucian, after all, writes about sex between men in a manner that cannot be paralleled in Boccaccio, Machiavelli, or any other Italian author who influenced Settembrini—and yet that difference is entirely elided in the letter to his wife. This is, we argue, in line with the way he treats heterosexual and homosexual relationships in *The Neoplatonists*: there is essentially little difference between them in that text too.

Beyond these two points, there is a third detail that seems to us of interest. A little earlier in the same letter, Settembrini tells his wife that he is sending her two copies of his Lucian translation, one written in his own elegant hand and a rougher version made by another inmate, Gennaro Placco. This means that Settembrini had shared Lucian's obscenities with at least one other man in his cell. Several diary entries confirm that Settembrini and Placco loved each other and show how their real-life experience in prison coloured Settembrini's apprehension of ancient Greece. Here is a description of Placco that explicitly compares him to Alcibiades—or rather: here is Settembrini imagining that Alcibiades talked like a nineteenth-century Albanian peasant from the south of Italy:[55]

> A young Albanian from Calabria... with a Greek face, sparkling eyes, a certain Albanian emphasis in his words, and the 'r' pronounced like Alcibiades.... It is four years now, that this brave and unlucky young man is my friend: I love him with brotherly tenderness and I am certain that I am loved back.... In the evenings while the others walk, or sleep, or talk at random, I lie down silently on the planks that make up my bed, and he comes companionably to lie next to me, and for long hours he tells me about his family with such affection that he almost makes me cry,... Take courage, my Gennarino, dear and unlucky friend. God

---

[55] Altimari 2014 outlines the growing connections between Italian revolutionaries and members of the Albanian minority in the Kingdom of the Two Sicilies, without however considering the well-documented (and moving) relationship between Settembrini and Placco. It would fit his discussion of southern Italian Hellenisms in relation to both the Greek and the Albanian communities living there.

will surely not want such a fine mind and heart, and such a clear soul, to perish in this prison. *Non si male nunc et olim sic erit.*[56] It is not without reason that you have this confidence, this cheerfulness in your heart—it is an omen for a future far less evil. And if our fate is written otherwise, if we have to suffer here for many more years, and perhaps die here too, then take comfort from the affection and admiration of a friend who, because he is as ill-fated as you, does not ask for anything other than to be loved in return.[57]

...

Now next to my bed there is the bed of my kind Gennarino, who cannot fall asleep in the evening unless he first tells me about his family and his village, and a thousand other pleasant things, after which he suddenly takes the attitude of a young boy, puts his hand under his cheek and falls asleep: in the morning, before day breaks, we place a plank on my bed or his and we make some coffee on it, which we drink together.[58]

Settembrini shared Lucian's 'occasional obscenities' not only with his wife, then, whose opinion of them he wanted to know, but also with Gennaro Placco. She, for her part, thought that Settembrini loved Placco 'too much'[59] and yet carefully preserved letters and diaries that bear witness to that love, and to the quasi-domestic arrangements that the two men shared in prison. The whole set-up again bears comparison with *The Neoplatonists*.

Faucitano's own accounts suggest that, apart from supporting and acting as a conduit between the world and 'that poor convict of mine

---

[56] A quotation from Horace, *Odes* 2.10: 'if it's bad now, it will not be thus forever'.
[57] Diary entry dated 17 September 1854, Settembrini 1971: 455–61. Settembrini gave these pages to Placco, together with a note: 'In my memoirs, where I have the habit of writing my thoughts and pour out the suffering of my tormented soul, I have written a few pages about myself, my Gennarino. You have already read many unhappy words of mine that I have thrown down desperately into these pages. Read these two which I copy out for you and which I beg you to keep in memory of our friendship and our misfortune. A painter made your portrait on canvas and I have painted an image of your soul in a few words. One day you may show them to somebody else and say: this is how somebody—a man who valued only truth and virtue—valued and loved me.' For a collection of writings by Settembrini and Placco, see Tocci 1892.
[58] Diary entry dated 15 December 1854, Settembrini 1971: 463.
[59] Settembrini 1971: 594.

in prison', she had other concerns. Her son Raffaele, after a stint as a merchant sailor, had joined the military navy of the northern Italian kingdom of Piedmont and had fought in the Crimean War against Russia. In 1856, news reached Faucitano that her son had made it back from the war and was now dying in a hospital in Genoa. Within a few days, and despite government obstruction, she managed to secure a travel permit with the help of her British contacts, sailed to Genoa, nursed her son in the first stages of his unlikely recovery, then rushed back to Naples, because she needed to assist her husband in a daring new plan.

Constant international pressure ensured that Settembrini and the other political prisoners were eventually housed together in a separate cell within the Panopticon. Away from the eyes of random prisoners and potential spies, they decided they would try to dig themselves out of prison and climb down the walls of the Panopticon to a secluded beach. There they hoped they would be met by a rescue party that would take them to England (see Figure 4.5). Panizzi, in London, soon collected enough funds to hire a vessel and a crew in Newcastle. Garibaldi agreed to board the ship in Genoa, pilot it to the island of Ventotene, near Santo Stefano, and send a skiff to pick up the prisoners from a designated cove near the prison. Faucitano returned to Naples in order to smuggle digging tools into the prison and give the inmates 'at least four days of warning'[60] (as Settembrini obsessively kept reminding her in his coded letters) to dig the hole before the arrival of the vessel. Initially, all went well: Faucitano hid the tools in a laundry chest with a double bottom; the ship departed from the north of England; the prisoners started digging. Unfortunately, though, the vessel went down in a storm, only a few miles south of Newcastle. The anguish and disappointment at the shipwreck reached the prisoners at an advanced stage of digging and radiated out to revolutionary circles across Europe.[61]

Now Faucitano faced new problems. Various revolutionaries and adventurers were keen to provide their services and revive plans of escape, but their offers needed careful vetting. Meanwhile, Raffaele was in trouble again. After allowing him to serve in the military navy in the Crimean War, the administration of Piedmont would not grant him a

[60] Settembrini 1971: 624.   [61] See Reidy 2005.

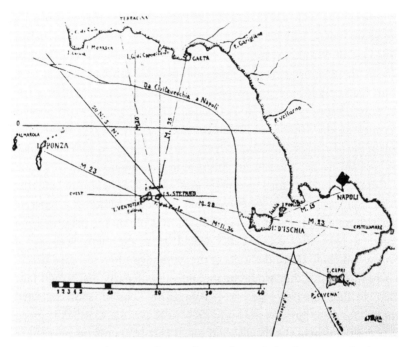

Figure 4.5 Settembrini tried to explain to his wife (and to Panizzi) what he could see from his cell and where he should be picked up, should he manage to dig himself out of prison: based on that information, Garibaldi planned the route he was going to sail, as seen on the annotations he left on this map.

permit to enrol in the merchant navy, declaring him a Neapolitan from the south and, therefore, 'a foreigner'. Faucitano again travelled to the north, this time to Turin; managed to secure an audience with Count Cavour (who will feature more prominently in our next chapter);[62] falsely suggested that her imprisoned husband was a constitutional monarchist, rather than a staunch republican; and eventually managed to secure papers for her son in the name of a future Italian nation. She then found herself unable to return to Naples. Spies had reported on her meeting with Cavour, the Bourbon administration feared an alliance between southern revolutionaries and liberal northern aristocrats, and

---

[62] For the briefest summary of Cavour's role in the unification of Italy, see pp. 83–6.

immediately revoked her passport. Her account of how she smuggled herself back into the Kingdom of the Two Sicilies makes for picaresque reading: she had not only extraordinary courage, but an eye for the absurd situation.[63]

As for her political acumen, it emerges from the judgements she needed to make in the following months. The balance of power was shifting rapidly in Europe, after the Crimean War, and political developments were increasingly difficult to predict. Plans of escape needed to be weighed against rumours that political prisoners would soon be released and sent into exile—perhaps to Argentina or, according to other whispers, the United States. Prisoners were encouraged to ask the king for a pardon; some did, but Settembrini and others refused to do so, on the ground that they had not committed any crime. Faucitano corresponded and negotiated widely, trying to settle on the best course of action. Settembrini articulated his political principles from inside the prison but left matters of action very much to her judgement: 'I will do nothing except what you tell me to do, I cannot judge better than you, and you have excellent judgement.'[64]

On 17 January 1859, Luigi Settembrini and other political prisoners were suddenly released into exile and made to embark on a Neapolitan ship that took them to the bay of Cadiz. Eight years after their trial, Settembrini met the revolutionaries who had been condemned to irons in the nearby prison of Nisida: 'I saw and embraced my Carlo [Poerio] again, who was very ill and broken... we were treated with Neapolitan kindness by the captain'.[65] The prisoners waited for over a month at

---

[63] The account is published in Settembrini 1971: 489–95, with only a note indicating her authorship. To mention just one episode: Faucitano returns in disguise and ends up almost face to face with the king himself in the woods near Gaeta: he is on an outing with his son and needs to leave his carriage to relieve himself. While her female travel companions are all excited at the sight of the king—'what a beautiful man!' 'Oh, we would like kiss his hand!'—she thinks 'with a certain self-satisfaction, "You condemned me to exile and here I am, looking at you, and coming to challenge you..."'. The whole account is so vivid and so in tune with Settembrini's own sense of fun that some have suspected him of ghost-writing it. We discuss the issue on p. 56, n. 5.
[64] Settembrini 1971: 625. Settembrini deferred to his wife also on many other occasions, for example during a cholera epidemic (1971: 602): 'I hope it does not reach the prison; as for you, I give you no advice; you have good sense'; or, again, in the early stages of plotting the escape: 'Enough! You know what needs to be done' (1971: 617).
[65] Settembrini 1971: 770.

anchor, in the bay of Cadiz, for the arrival of a ship that was due to deliver a cargo of tobacco from Baltimore and had been hired by the Bourbon government to take the exiles to New York. Poerio wrote to the Spanish authorities, arguing that he and the other former prisoners were now free men, and that they wanted to disembark in Spain. There was no reply on the part of the Spanish crown.

Meanwhile, Settembrini's son, Raffaele, had read in the international press that his father, among other Neapolitan prisoners, was waiting to be taken to the United States. He made his way to the bay of Cadiz as fast as he could and managed to get hired, incognito, on the relevant American vessel when it arrived from Baltimore, hiding two pistols in his luggage. Careful plans were made to manage Settembrini's surprise, on realizing his son Raffaele, whom he had not seen in years, was on board. Once at sea, after reuniting with his father and plotting with him, Raffaele tried to reason with the captain on behalf of the prisoners, but with no success: the captain insisted that he had to deliver his cargo, unless the prisoners were in a position to pay the fee he was due on arrival in New York. The prisoners had no money. The captain was then given some evidence that there were weapons on board, but not about how few were actually in possession of the prisoners and their accomplice Raffaele. Mutiny, in other words, was raised as a possibility, for all the political dangers and bad press the manoeuvre was likely to entail.

There were sixty-six Neapolitan prisoners on board. Raffaele Settembrini knew how to sail a ship. The crew comprised seventeen sailors. Some were Black and made it known they would side with the revolutionaries who were now being transported across the Atlantic against their will.[66] The captain reconsidered his answer:

> Fear proved more persuasive than profit: the captain assembled his crew, explained that we did not want to go to America and that he was setting course for Cork, in Ireland. As soon as the crew heard this they shouted 'Hooray!' and two negro sailors insisted on hugging 'captain

---

[66] On sailors, slaves, and commoners and their contributions to the revolutionary Atlantic, see Linebaugh and Rediker 2012. For a good discussion of the Black/black distinction, also in relation to classical antiquity, see Derbew 2022.

Raphael'. They could not get enough of looking at him and smiling, and nodding their heads.[67]

A few weeks later Settembrini was in London, hoping his wife's letters might include news of Gennaro Placco, who was still serving his life sentence in the Panopticon. Unlike the intimate, family meal of 'bread and lettuce' that had marked the end of his first incarceration, this time he was feted like a hero by the highest authorities in England.[68]

> My Gigia, on Thursday I have been invited to lunch with Member of Parliament Milers, who says Mr Gladstone will also be in attendance. I have had to get a black suit made for me, because here they have lunch according to strict etiquette. The meal, the hour, the manner, everything is new to me and feels oppressive; if this goes on, I will not be able to bear the yoke. Ah, our simple life and the freedom it afforded! Raffaele laughs at me and says that you kept saying the exact same thing when you assisted him in Genoa.[69]

Then he added, by way of postscript, a request that she send him 'all the writings about incarceration, the description of the Vicaria prison, the *Three Days of Waiting in the Chapel*, your own letter, the description of the Panopticon, and the diaries', so that he may begin to write his *Memoirs*.

---

[67] The extract is taken from *Information about the Life of Raffaele Settembrini*, written by his father in 1861; Settembrini 1971: 500.
[68] On the enthusiastic reception of the Neapolitan prisoners in London and the unifying effect they had across divisions of class, see Isabella 2003: 78.
[69] Settembrini 1971: 783.

5
Revolutionary Heroes and Italian Men

Historians have generally been harsh in their judgements of the 1848 revolutions. Starting from Karl Marx's view that, in France, the revolution was fought 'once as tragedy, and then again as farce',[1] and taking on board the even dimmer views he expressed about Italian revolutionary activities in this period,[2] many have dismissed the uprisings of 1848–9 as incompetent, romantic, and, in short, too poetic to be taken seriously. As Sperber points out, the 1848 revolutions suffered by comparison with 'the real business of 1789 and 1917'.[3] Settembrini himself wrote about the events in which he almost lost his life as a 'revolution of schoolteachers who, not used to the task, made a few errors'.[4] In this deceptively modest statement, as in many other aspects of his thought, he proved to anticipate intellectual developments that took shape long after his lifetime: 'I say that the great European revolution was made by the people—and those who educated and trained the people brought it on.'[5]

His position, once considered naïve, fits for example with Benedict Anderson's insistence that the spread of literacy brought about the 1848 revolutions and, more generally, that printed literature was a crucial factor in the rise of nationalism, allowing for the conception of the nation as an 'imagined community'.[6] The role of 'schoolteachers', to adopt Settembrini's modest terminology, should not be underestimated, in other words. Alberto Banti has shown that the preferred literature of young Italians in the mid-nineteenth century was patriotic in orientation: a common canon of novels and poems fostered a new sense of

---

[1] Marx 2013: 9.
[2] On Marx's plea to Engels to 'tackle the rotten Italians along with their revolution', see Claeys 1989: 253. More generally, Marx loathed Mazzini (who lived a few streets away from him in London) and despised Garibaldi: Macks 1994: 199.
[3] Sperber 1994: 1.   [4] Settembrini 1961: 154.
[5] Settembrini 1961: 154.   [6] Anderson 1991.

Classics, Love, Revolution: The Legacies of Luigi Settembrini. Andrea Capra and Barbara Graziosi, Oxford University Press. © Andrea Capra and Barbara Graziosi 2024.
DOI: 10.1093/oso/9780198865445.003.0005

national belonging.[7] Building on his insights, Riall offers a clear assessment of the period in her magisterial biography of Garibaldi: 'the failure of the 1848–9 revolutions—the practical reversals suffered as a result of internal divisions, military weakness and conservative counter-attack between the summer of 1848 and the summer of 1849—has tended to overshadow its more lasting achievement in politicising the people'.[8] She goes on to point out that autobiography was especially important in Risorgimento literature, because it offered charismatic new models of behaviour.

Luigi Settembrini understood all this. More specifically, he realized that stories about the gruesome treatment of political prisoners in the various gaols of Italy were popular in England. His own case had been put to good political use by Panizzi, Gladstone, and others, as we have seen.[9] And his arrival, together with the other Neapolitan revolutionaries, caused a sensation (see Figure 5.1). More generally, Settembrini was aware of a longer tradition of political insurrection and writing within which he could develop his own autobiographical portrait. Silvio Pellico had already established the genre of Italian revolutionary writing with *Le mie prigioni* (1833), a book of lasting popularity in England—as well as an early influence on Settembrini.[10] The revolutionary Felice Orsini, after accomplishing a daring escape from an Austrian prison in the northern Italian city of Mantua, arrived in England in 1856 and immediately went on a lecture tour, to sell-out success. In the same year, Orsini also published a sensational account of his experiences, *The Austrian Dungeons of Italy*, which immediately sold some 35,000 copies.[11] A second edition came out in 1859, just as Settembrini was beginning to write his own memoirs. In that same year, Alexandre Dumas, author of *The Count of Montecristo*, was busy reworking the autobiography of Garibaldi, so as to turn it into a better written and more exciting book.[12]

---

[7] Banti 2000: 37–53.   [8] Riall 2007: 75
[9] Just how large Neapolitan prisons loomed in the British imagination emerges, for example, from a novel published just two years before Settembrini's arrival in London: C. G. Hamilton, *The Exiles of Italy* (1857: 3).
[10] For Pellico's influence on Settembrini and fellow students in Naples in the 1830s, see Settembrini 1971: 72; for the lasting popularity of his book in England, see Isabella 2003: 62.
[11] See Isabella 2003: 76.   [12] Riall 2007: 154–63.

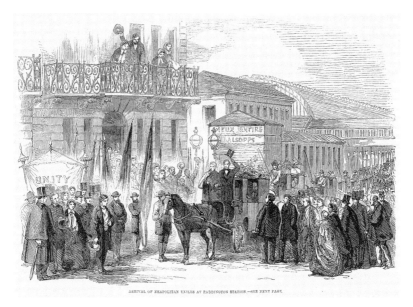

Figure 5.1 'Arrival of Neapolitan Exiles at Paddington Station', *Illustrated London News*, 2 April 1859. Gruesome stories of incarceration in the gaols of southern Italy were popular with the British public. Settembrini knew his *Memoirs* would greatly consolidate his fame (and provide a much-needed source of income) and yet he could not bring himself to write them to the end. This fact deserves attention, particularly given that he was otherwise well able to complete his writing projects.

It is not surprising, given the general popularity of Italian revolutionaries as subjects of biographical representation (and Settembrini's own urgent need of money), that mere weeks after arriving in London he settled into damp, cramped quarters and began to write. The reasons why he did not complete his *Memoirs* are more surprising than his initial decision to write them.

In broad terms, it is possible to offer three kinds of explanation for Settembrini's unusual lack of perseverance when it came to completing his *Memoirs*. Our first line of argument is historical and, indeed, biographical in orientation: various events intervened and interrupted Settembrini's writing of his *Memoirs* and he, in turn, responded to what was happening by prioritizing different kinds of work. We also offer a second set of considerations, arguing that Settembrini's choices should be understood by reference to dominant, and emerging, models of Italian masculinity (and here consideration of other major figures in the period, most obviously Giuseppe Garibaldi and King Victor Emmanuel, proves useful). Finally, and most importantly for our purposes, we argue that Settembrini's autobiographical project needs to be set in dialogue with his approach to ancient Greece as a source of alternative values and models of behaviour. We know, for example, that rather than finish his *Memoirs*, he spent the last months of his life rereading his beloved 'Greek and Roman classics'.[13]

The revolutions of 1848–9 ended in sweeping repression: of all the constitutions that were granted in those years, the only Italian state that still had one in 1850 was Piedmont. Its king, Victor Emmanuel, was not enthusiastic about upholding it, but deferred to his advisors, who correctly maintained he would be stronger with a constitution than without one. Meanwhile, as one historian put it, the Piedmontese king 'kept up his self-respect by boasting of his physical courage (which was not inconsiderable) and of his sexual prowess—which was rather less than he liked others to imagine but sufficient for a joke to circulate that no sovereign had been a more successful "father of his subjects"'.[14] The Piedmontese constitution was a deeply conservative document, hardly concerned with protecting the rights of citizens. It was primarily through the steady and careful work of successive governments, between 1849 and 1860, that the powers of King Victor Emmanuel were gradually curtailed. The most influential figure in this process was a man who has already made a cameo appearance in our chapter 4: Count Camillo Benso di Cavour.[15] Politically liberal, socially conservative, resolutely monarchic, and intensely opposed to revolution, he believed that progress could only be achieved through what he called (in French, his strongest language) *le tact des choses possibles*.[16] He was by no means a fervent Italian nationalist but, in the late 1850s, unification of the peninsula under the rule of Victor Emmanuel suddenly seemed indeed

---

[13] See below, n. 35.   [14] Duggan 1994: 121.   [15] See p. 76.
[16] In a diary entry dated 26 August 1836: 'pour être un homme d'état utile, il faut avant tout avoir *le tact des choses possibles*', https://www.camillocavour.com/archivio/diari/26-agosto-1834-26-agosto-1834/, accessed 4 August 2020.

possible: Cavour had the ability and, indeed, *tact* to recognize this—for all that he could not unite the country on his own. A deeply fraught collaboration with the revolutionary republican patriot (and by then international celebrity) Giuseppe Garibaldi proved crucial in the enterprise.

After returning to Italy from exile, Garibaldi had joined the Piedmontese army as major general and fought with Piedmont and France against Austria in 1859. After the war, in 1860, Cavour ceded the culturally Italian city of Nice to France, in a complicated manoeuvre that involved the Piedmontese annexation of Tuscany and some cities in Lombardy. Garibaldi, who was a native of Nice, flew into a grandiose rage and concluded (rather accurately, it must be said) that Cavour did not care much about Italy and was mainly interested in the 'aggrandizement of Piedmont'.[17] And so it was that, on the back of yet a new peasant revolt against the Bourbons in Sicily, Garibaldi gathered an army of one thousand volunteers (many of them students with no military experience), seized two steamships from the port of Genoa, and had his ramshackle troops sail to Sicily—to liberate the south from the Bourbon king and unite the Italian nation. It was a desperate course of action. Garibaldi himself saw it as a final, fatal gesture: 'Everything crushes and humiliates me', he wrote before setting sail. 'I will never ask if an expedition is possible or not... For me it is enough that it should be an Italian expedition... I have only one remaining desire: *To Die for Italy*.'[18]

As Riall points out, his words suggest that he was reverting to the romantic and impractical patriotism that had guided the revolutions of 1848 and, indeed, his earlier revolutionary exploits in South America.[19] In any case, the expedition of the Thousand was marked by symbolic gestures rather than sober planning. Before setting sail, Garibaldi ditched his Piedmontese uniform and presented himself to his men in a red shirt, a silk handkerchief tied round his neck, a poncho slung over his shoulder, and a black felt hat planted, at a jaunty angle, on his head—the very

---

[17] Duggan 1994: 129.   [18] Garibaldi 1973–2002 (vol. 5): 73–4.
[19] Riall 2007: 183: 'the expedition, in other words, followed an established Mazzinian tradition of committing acts of martyrdom for symbolic purposes. Once again, it reminds us of how much Garibaldi's political outlook and practice continued to be determined by romantic tropes and Mazzinian assumptions.'

image of the romantic revolutionary, with more than a hint of the South American gaucho.[20]

What Garibaldi did, in shaping both his image and his actions, was probably the result of sexual as well as political frustration. In the summer of 1859, he had fallen violently in love with Giuseppina Raimondi, an eighteen-year-old aristocrat; a few months later he had proposed marriage to an older marchioness; meanwhile he was writing passionate letters to the sister of a fellow soldier and declaring his infatuation to yet another woman, Sofia Bettini, whom he had met on Staten Island some eight years earlier. That same year, he also had a child with his housekeeper (a girl whom he named Anita, after his first wife). 'All this sexual activity', as Riall puts it, reached crisis point in January 1860, when he married Raimondi and rejected her on the same day, on discovering she was four months pregnant with the child of another man.[21] Betrayed, as he saw it, in his love of both woman (or women) and country, Garibaldi was ready for revolution in Sicily.

To everyone's surprise, and Cavour's great alarm, his expedition turned out to be a lightning success. Garibaldi and his 'red-shirt' volunteers disembarked in Marsala, on the western coast of Sicily, in May; conquered Palermo in June; crossed the Straits of Messina in August; and entered victorious into Naples in September. They were lucky at the start (the Bourbon garrison stationed in Marsala had temporarily left the city when his ships sailed in) and the number of volunteers grew exponentially as he advanced: the peasants hoped for relief from exploitation, the middle classes wanted greater freedom and powers for themselves. That the south was so supportive of Garibaldi must, to a degree at least, be attributed to the work of men like Settembrini and other southern 'schoolteachers'—though this is a point that has often been elided in subsequent histories of the Italian nation.

From Naples, Garibaldi planned to march up the peninsula towards Rome. Cavour, meanwhile, fearing precisely that move, had already dispatched King Victor Emmanuel to invade the Papal State, explaining to the French, meanwhile, that they needed to let this happen in order to

---

[20] Riall 2007: 184.
[21] Riall 2007: 180. For a broader study of 'the sex lives of Italian patriots', see Riall 2015: it is a great shame she does not consider the case of Settembrini, as it would complicate the picture she depicts.

prevent a growing crowd of red-shirt revolutionaries and assorted southern riff-raff from sweeping up the peninsula. Garibaldi and Victor Emmanuel met in Teano, north of Naples, on 25 October 1860: Garibaldi famously shook hands with the king and handed the south over to him. And so it was that Italy was made, 'against all the odds and largely by accident',[22] in a manner that sealed the subjugation of the southern part of the country.

Settembrini stopped working on his *Memoirs* in the course of these events. We know from a letter he wrote to his wife that, on 1 December 1859, he had finished the first nine chapters and had a clear vision for the whole book, including its structure and title, which was to be *Memoirs of an Exile*: 'I have reached the point when I saw you for the first time! How I wish you could listen and tell me your opinion... I've read some parts to others and they are well liked: I do not think they are so bad myself... were I to leave, it would have to be after publishing these *Memoirs*.'[23] By Christmas Day, he had changed his mind. Acute bouts of rheumatism and jaundice convinced him that the *Memoirs* could not be his priority: 'I am so ill I need to leave England immediately... you would not believe what kind of fog there is here... the dampness, the melancholy... if you knew how dark it is today, how dim and damp my room, and how the coal stinks as it burns in the fireplace... I kept healthy for so many years [in prison], because I followed a clockwork routine; now I have changed lifestyle, climate, country, and I have lost my health.'[24]

After a slow journey across Europe, he reached Florence in spring. There were plans to appoint him to the chair of Latin literature at the University of Bologna, but he was worried: 'I need to take a written exam to show that I know my Latin. The difficulty is that I have made my name because of my misfortunes—and suffering is not the same as competence: I need to accept that and persevere in my old profession,

---

[22] Duggan 1994: 133. [23] Settembrini 1961: xlii.
[24] Settembrini 1971: 806–7. It is indeed the case that Settembrini had managed to stay healthy, almost without exception, during his nine years of incarceration in the Panopticon. He also explicitly observed, in his description of the prison, that although violence between inmates was frequent, 'wounds heal quickly because of the good climate and the toughness of the men', Settembrini 1971: 429.

which is that of getting into trouble. Never mind, and onwards... meanwhile, Le Monnier will print my Lucian; we have not yet agreed on how much they will pay me, perhaps a couple of hundred *scudi*, but I do not mind, because I can make do with little and because I want to publish Lucian to tell the world this much: I do not just have the virtues of the donkey, I do not just know how to withstand pain for a long time, for many days on end; I am also good at something else, I do have a skill.'[25]

Despite these anxieties, Settembrini took his exam and was appointed to the Latin chair. However, he never took up the position in Bologna, because he wanted to return to Naples. He initially could not find a job or even a place to live in his native city, but was then appointed general inspector of public education.[26] In that capacity, he focused his energies on the publication of the Herculaneum papyri, insisting that they should be properly photographed (a new technology), edited, and made accessible to international scholars. His negative assessment of the old and incomplete editions of the papyri published under the Bourbons, his mounting frustration at continued scholarly incompetence, and his condemnation of local classical scholars who embezzled public funds intended to support the publication of the papyri are well documented in an excellent study by Mario Capasso.[27] Given how hard Settembrini worked to try and have those papyri properly edited, he may have approved of Cantarella's own priorities many decades later, when he decided to devote himself to the papyri rather than announce his discovery of *The Neoplatonists*. This, however, is by no means certain: as we argue in chapter 7, Settembrini invested a great deal in that tale too.

What we do know is that Settembrini devoted the rest of his life to scholarship, education, and public service. In October 1861, he was appointed to the chair of Italian literature at the University of Naples; between 1871 and 1873 he served as rector of the university. In 1873 he

---

[25] Settembrini 1971: 809. 'A couple of hundred *scudi*' would be equivalent, today, to a couple of thousand pounds, euros, or dollars. On Settembrini as a donkey, see below, p. 90. On the resonance of this passage for contemporary debates and scholarly practices in classics, there would be a lot to say: fear of failure, in a discipline that has a proud history of exacting standards, is one of the problems we currently face in the interactions between faculty and students.

[26] Settembrini 1971: 814–18.   [27] Capasso 2014.

was appointed Senator of the Kingdom of Italy—an honour which, in the view of many, arrived much later than he deserved. Between the years of 1866 and 1872 he worked on his lively and 'popularizing' *Lectures on Italian Literature*.[28] As a student, he had learnt from Basilio Puoti that a shared language and literary tradition could help create a sense of belonging; his *Lectures* now stemmed from the desire to communicate this to the first generation of Italian students after unification. He also wanted to document how, over the centuries 'our [i.e. Italian] thinking had rebelled against the oppressions of the Roman Catholic Church'.[29] Once the *Lectures* were published, he returned to his *Memoirs*. In 1875 he wrote to his grandchild: 'I am writing my *Memoirs*, which you'll read one day; I plan to end them in 1860, the year you were born' (also, of course, the year Garibaldi united the nation and Settembrini himself returned home from exile).[30]

To conclude our first line of exploration: one reason why Settembrini never finished the *Memoirs* is that, after 1860, he devoted his considerable energies to building the nation—through education, scholarship, and service.[31] His record is impressive, by any standards, and yet lack of time cannot be the only reason why he failed to complete his *Memoirs*. Careful analysis of the relevant archival material shows that, for years, Settembrini could not bring himself to tell the story of his life beyond the years 1848–9.[32] What he did, instead, was rework the first chapters again and again, lingering on his early memories, and adjusting the political positions he had articulated then to the new realities he experienced after the unification of Italy.[33] It is clear, for example, that he replaced his convinced and uncompromising republicanism with several arguments designed to explain why it was necessary to accept and support a constitutional monarchy, not least as a means of opposing the power

---

[28] 'Popularizing' is the assessment of Themelly in Settembrini 1961: xxxvi.
[29] Settembrini 1961: xxxvi. As Themelly points out *ad loc.*, Settembrini's plain and popular language was intended as a rebellion against academic, baroque, and Jesuit refinements.
[30] Settembrini 1961: xliii.
[31] Villani 2018 gives an excellent account of his activities in this period.
[32] Themelly offers careful documentary evidence for Settembrini's inability to move past 1849, which, however, he finds hard to explain, see Settembrini 1961: xliii–xliv.
[33] A point Mario Meriggi emphasized to us in conversation and is borne out by comparing the *Memoirs* with Settembrini's earlier writings.

of the pope. What he could not bring himself to do was extend his narrative beyond the revolution, first in the Panopticon and then in exile.

As we have seen, several early accounts (written in prison and smuggled out with the help of Faucitano) greatly contributed to his fame. The *Memoirs* were meant to rework those earlier publications and supplement them with details about the escape plot, which would usefully secure a role for Garibaldi in the story, as well as the adventurous tale of near mutiny on the American ship, the melancholy months of exile in London, and the final, triumphant return home to a united Italy. This kind of tale was extremely popular not just in the 1860s but also in the 1870s, the 1880s, and beyond—not least as a way of creating a new sense of the Italian nation out of the many individual contributions to its making.[34] Five other prisoners who had been on board that American ship and taken part in the quasi mutiny published their memoirs in the decades following the event; Settembrini, who was the most famous, repeatedly tinkered with the first chapters of his *Memoirs*, but otherwise worked on his *Lectures on Italian Literature,* spent his time rereading the ancient Greek and Latin classics—and worked on *The Neoplatonists*.[35] It is noteworthy that the fake ancient tale also lingered mainly on early childhood and youth, dealing with heroic adulthood in a rather quick and perfunctory fashion.[36]

It may be tempting to link Settembrini's autobiographical impasse to his experiences in prison and, more specifically, to homosexual experiences: as we have seen, this explanation has been put forward more than once, after the publication of *The Neoplatonists*.[37] For our part, however, we find it reductive. By the standards of his age, Settembrini was hardly

---

[34] A list of various patriotic biographies can be found in Riall 2007: 460–4. Leone Carpi's *Risorgimento italiano: biografie storico-politiche d'illustri italiani contemporanei*, published in Milan in 1884, demonstrates how important it was to remember the lives of the fathers of the fatherland: as Meriggi 1997 points out, minor figures as well as famous revolutionaries were remembered in order to demonstrate that Italy was made by men from many different walks of life. That Settembrini's *Memoirs* were keenly awaited is confirmed by the fact that the posthumous publication of the *Memoirs* prepared by Francesco De Sanctis, the most important literary scholar of the period, reached its tenth edition as early as 1892.

[35] In a letter he wrote shortly before dying, Settembrini expressed his distress at the infighting, opportunism, and corruption he saw around him, then concluded: 'I live as if in a different world, in a kind of anxious loneliness where only a few ancient Greek and Latin classics relieve me of my sadness...': Settembrini (1961) xli.

[36] See below, p. 119.   [37] See p. 14.

reticent: as we have seen, his *Memoirs* give a detailed account of his childhood and life-long friendship with De Silva; his 'love' for Gennaro Placco likewise features not only in his diary and letters, but also in pages intended for public consumption.[38] A poem he entitled 'The Mask' deserves special attention when thinking about Settembrini's alleged silence about homosexual experiences. Composed in the tradition of Horace's *Sermones*, it was written in 1854 and dedicated to Gennaro Placco.[39] The wish Settembrini expresses in that poem is that he may show himself as he is, namely as 'an ass' who does not hide 'under a lion's skin'; as a 'common man' who, regrettably, is neither 'a noble hero' nor, for that matter, 'a lovely, diaphanous girl'—and yet deserves respect, precisely as a common man. He wants to show himself 'without a mask', we read at the end of this tirade. Then the poem continues in the plural, including Placco in this overall declaration of disclosure: 'we want to show ourselves naked, the way our mothers made us'; the only hope for the future, the poem concludes, is to speak eloquently and clearly to the people, which Settembrini pledges to do 'without a mask on my face, which would make me die for lack of air'. To be sure, the poem is not altogether clear about what needs to be disclosed. Ostensibly, Settembrini presents himself and Placco as commoners, rather than members of the elite—a fact he wants to acknowledge and display. It must be said, however, that the poem bears comparison with *The Neoplatonists*—not just chapter 2 of that tale, where lovers show themselves naked to one another, but also the 'translator's warning', which presents the tale as 'a work of art that...hides nothing and represents man naked as he is'.[40] Just so, in *The Mask*, there is an explicit emphasis on naked male bodies.

In short, the need to hide does not seem to us a sufficient explanation for Settembrini's failure to complete his *Memoirs*; indeed, had that been the issue, it would have surely inhibited some of the pages devoted to his friendships in adolescence. It may be more promising to consider how his work relates to the various conventions of Risorgimento literature

---

[38] See p. 74, n. 57, where Settembrini suggests that Placco use some pages Settembrini had written about him almost as a reference letter, if he ever managed to get out of prison: 'one day you may show them to somebody and say: this is how somebody—a man who valued only truth and virtue—valued and loved me'.

[39] The poem was published posthumously in 1896, as part of the many publications by and about Settembrini that appeared in the first few decades after his death, see Settembrini 1971: 468–73.

[40] See pp. 149f.

and, more specifically, autobiography. Settembrini's life, as it emerges from the materials he intended to use for his *Memoirs*, is a life of stable, intense, and egalitarian relationships with both men and women. In important ways, it does not conform to the ideals exemplified by other revolutionaries and revolutionary (auto)biographies of the period. The argument we want to make here is that both the first, much revisited chapters of the *Memoirs* and *The Neoplatonists* speak of a distant past of joyous happiness. An important theme, in both texts, is mutual affection located in the past but also, and importantly, projected onto the future. It is hard to discern, in either text, the daring and often lonesome heroism that characterizes the life narratives of other Risorgimento heroes. This raises a question about Settembrini's life and work in relation to emerging narratives about Italian national characteristics and, more specifically, masculinity.

In an important essay published in 1972 and reprinted many times since, Giulio Bollati argues that Italian intellectuals of the nineteenth century used their classical learning to make exaggerated claims about their 'cultural superiority' in a situation of 'objective inferiority'—that is to say, in the face of political and economic domination on the part of local despots (like the Bourbons) and their northern European allies.[41] Foreign views of Italy as a land of degeneration from classical ideals were, in other words, internalized; and this, according to Bollati, contributed to a 'pathological form of consciousness' which he still saw as operating in the 1970s. Bollati's Marxist and Freudian framework of analysis has more recently been integrated with approaches stemming from postcolonial and gender studies. Silvana Patriarca, for example, sees nineteenth-century Italy as a 'contact zone', arguing that Italian patriots 'felt the burden of outsiders' representations and often spoke within parameters that were not of their own making'.[42] What makes her perspective interesting for our work is that she pays attention to gendered metaphors in definitions of national character, reaching the following conclusion: 'to the historical "degeneration" of the Italians, conceived as a process of almost literal feminization, patriots opposed

---

[41] Bollati 1972, revised in 1996.   [42] Patriarca 2005: 383.

a national "regeneration" conceived as a process of almost literal re-virilization of the people'.[43]

This is an idea that deserves attention. Italians, as has often been argued, acquired a sense of themselves by seeing their image in the 'mirror of the Grand Tour'.[44] Visitors admired the ruins of the past and deplored the degradation of those who now lived in the land of Virgil and Horace. Gladstone's comments about the beautiful landscape hiding 'festering masses of human suffering' conformed to that trope.[45] When he presented Settembrini and other political prisoners as honorary Englishmen, he was quick to add that, on closer examination, they seemed surprisingly docile and cheerful in their subjugation: 'I must say I was astonished at the mildness with which they spoke of those at whose hands they were enduring these abominable persecutions, and at...their forgiving temper, for they seemed ready to undergo with cheerfulness whatever might yet be in store for them.'[46] Cheerful submissiveness was, as Patriarca points out, often presented as a female and even more specifically 'oriental' trait. She traces the discourse in Madame de Staël's influential *Corinne, or Italy* (1807), where an Englishman declares that Italian men have 'women's faults as well as their own' and the heroine Corinne concludes they are 'as indolent as orientals in their daily lives'—because of the hot climate: 'life is nothing more than a dream-filled sleep under a beautiful sky'.[47]

Italian intellectuals of the period internalized these tropes while also, as Bollati and Patriarca point out, trying to resist them. Arguments based on climate, for example, could be countered by reference to the much-admired Greeks and Romans, who had once lived in the same lands and therefore, it was assumed, in the same climactic conditions. In his *Plato in Italy* (1804–6), the influential Vincenzo Cuoco sought to present the peninsula as a site of an exceptionally ancient and wise civilization admired by Plato himself—a civilization that flourished in a beautiful climate. He explicitly invited modern Italians to have some self-respect and abandon their habit of self-denigration: 'a moderate and reasonable opinion of oneself is the true principle of national

---

[43] Patriarca 2005: 383.   [44] de Seta 2014.
[45] Gladstone 1859: 14, quoted more extensively above, p. 63.
[46] Gladstone 1859: 29.   [47] De Staël 1998: 102.

energy'.[48] That energy, moreover, was explicitly presented as the opposite of the current state of feminine, supine passivity. Italians needed to 'rise again', as the very word Risorgimento implied, and live up to their glorious past—a past, incidentally, that remained rather vague, between Cuoco's pre-Roman and pre-Greek civilization, the Roman empire, the communes of the Middle Ages, the Florentine Renaissance, and other scattered moments that might inspire national pride.[49]

Given the wealth of this composite Italian past, there were reasons to be optimistic about the future of the nation, as Antonio Gallenga, an exiled revolutionary in London, argued in his two-volume *Italy: Past and Present*, published in English in 1848. He insisted that republican ideals could be found not only in the early history of Rome, but in Dante, Machiavelli, and in the many, virile members of an Italian 'republic of letters'.[50] In his grandiose vision, Italian classical scholars were paragons of masculine energy, heroes devoted to the strenuous recovery of the glorious past from recalcitrant manuscripts that needed to be wrestled into submission. This is, for example, how he introduced the scholar Antonio Muratori (1672–1750), one of the heroes of his book:

> the national history...lay in scrolls, parchments, and manuscripts; huge folios and ponderous quartos piled up—the shelves groaning under their weight, dark, dusty, and silent, like spell-bound warriors, threatening the daring man who should attempt to break the enchantment. Yet the enchantment was broken and with luminous success. A hero was found, not enervated even by the seductions of a southern climate, or of an effeminate age, willing to shut himself up in those haunted chambers [i.e. the Ambrosian library in Milan and the Estense library in Modena], abjuring all the ties and charms of social and domestic life, to grapple with the phantoms of the dead—to rescue from them the secrets of the past.[51]

This image of the classical scholar was of a piece with the representation of other virile Risorgimento heroes, who had abjured quiet domesticity

---

[48] Patriarca 2005: 388, translating Cuoco 1928: 259.
[49] On Cuoco, see further the excellent discussion in De Francesco 2013, ch. 1. In excavating the antiquity of the Italian nation as a political myth, De Francesco points out that just as the country itself was divided so were various and competing versions of the past.
[50] Gallenga 1849 (vol. 1): xxxi.   [51] Gallenga 1849 (vol. 1): 421.

in their patriotic pursuit of national glory. We have already seen how King Victor Emmanuel cultivated his reputation as a sexual conqueror of his own nation. We also saw how Garibaldi had a series of passionate, overlapping relationships at the height of his fame—and how these fuelled, in various ways, his most daring exploits. It would be possible to explore the subject in greater depth than can be done here: Garibaldi's affairs with northern European women, in particular, could be approached as a reversal of the common trope whereby Italian men were figured as passive, feminized partners in relation to male (and more virile) northerners.[52] That Garibaldi's women 'had to know their place'[53] emerges not only from his immediate repudiation of his young and pregnant bride in 1860 but also, for example, from his decision to dismiss the German noblewoman Espérance von Schwartz as his official biographer (after she refused to marry him) and entrust the task to Alexandre Dumas instead. Riall argues that, among other things, Garibaldi did not appreciate von Schwartz's depiction of his first wife, Anita, as a veritable Amazon on the battlefield and that he had become 'tired of the independent behaviour of von Schwartz herself'.[54]

Settembrini's enduring and egalitarian relationships with men (De Silva, Placco) and women (Faucitano and, as we shall see, Guacci) differed from these conquering models of Italian masculinity. In a letter from prison, which Settembrini wrote to his wife when he was twenty-eight, he expressed, as often, anxiety about her physical wellbeing, insisting that she should look after herself: 'I need to see you again: a beautiful little old woman, with a shock of white hair, erect, full of spirit, in a temper, surrounded by at least ten children and grandchildren; I'll be an old lunatic covered in tobacco.'[55] How this autobiographical vision of future, unconventional domesticity relates to classical scholarship and, specifically, to Settembrini's works of Platonic fiction is the topic of our next three chapters.

---

[52] These affairs are briefly set out in Riall 2015, as is Mazzini's reliance on English women for many of his needs, both personal and political. These relationships would lend themselves to the kind of analysis offered in bell hooks 1981: there she focuses on contemporary interracial sexual relationships in the United States, arguing that the 'conquest' of a white woman by a Black man is socially more acceptable than a relationship between a Black woman and a white man.

[53] Riall 2015: 45.   [54] Riall 2015: 46.   [55] Settembrini 1971: 511.

PART II
PLATONIC FICTIONS

Καὶ ἐν αἷς νυνδὴ ἐλέγομεν μυθολογίαις, διὰ τὸ μὴ εἰδέναι ὅπῃ τἀληθὲς ἔχει περὶ τῶν παλαιῶν, ἀφομοιοῦντες τῷ ἀληθεῖ τὸ ψεῦδος ὅτι μάλιστα, οὕτω χρήσιμον ποιοῦμεν;

And as for the storytelling that we mentioned just now, since it is impossible to know the truth about ancient things, shall we not make the lie as close to the truth as possible, so as to make it useful?

Plato, *Republic* 382d

6
The *Dialogue on Women*

The influence of Plato on Settembrini spans his entire career. It is, however, in two works of Platonic fiction that the connections between ancient Greece and modern Italy, love of beauty and concern for the body politic, are most clearly articulated. The circumstances in which Settembrini wrote his early *Dialogue on Women* have already been established and are relevant, we argue, to the interpretation of this text—including its weaknesses and inconsistencies. After his first arrest on 8 May 1839, and a long incarceration in the prison of Santa Maria Apparente while awaiting trial, Settembrini was finally acquitted on 3 July 1841. Rather than being released, however, he was transferred to the even tougher Vicaria prison, where he was kept indefinitely 'at the disposal of the police'.[1] As emerged in chapter 3, his *Memoirs* express the impotence he felt at his continued incarceration—his mental state was made worse by the fact that he had no means of knowing how long his captivity might last, or how his young family would fare while he was detained. Writing, in the circumstances, became a means through which Settembrini hoped to contribute to the economic welfare of his wife and children—and that is itself a relevant detail, when it comes to assessing his focus on Plato, as we argue below.

Settembrini's *Memoirs* also reveal that it was during his first incarceration that he got to know his wife better and to 'respect her, and love her much more than before'.[2] The *Dialogue* stems from this new, curious, and admiring form of love. In a private dedication to Faucitano, he declared: 'Many of the things I wrote I learnt from you. For this reason, this dialogue is also your work.'[3] Collaboration between the two spouses,

---

[1] Settembrini 1971: 149.
[2] Settembrini 1971: 124, quoted at greater length and discussed on p. 50.
[3] Gigante 1977: 138, quoted at greater length and discussed on p. 25.

Classics, Love, Revolution: The Legacies of Luigi Settembrini. Andrea Capra and Barbara Graziosi,
Oxford University Press. © Andrea Capra and Barbara Graziosi 2024.
DOI: 10.1093/oso/9780198865445.003.0006

which Settembrini presented almost in terms of joint authorship, was coupled with the need to publish the *Dialogue* anonymously, given that a work emerging from prison could not hope to escape censorship.[4] The situation, then, was that Settembrini and Faucitano depended on each other—he for practical and moral support during his arbitrary detention; she for the little sustenance he could provide through work carried out within the confines of the prison. Meanwhile, neither could publish the *Dialogue*, except anonymously. Writing a Platonic fiction was, then, a way of circumventing severe restrictions on personal freedom of expression—as well as a means of expanding from personal experience to a more encompassing vision of the past (and the future).

It should come as no surprise, given the circumstances in which the *Dialogue* was written, that it focuses on the experiences of women as victims of men who enjoy greater freedoms than they do. There is also, and again tellingly, an emphasis on misattributed blame and lack of recourse on the part of victims. All this makes it easy to imagine, behind a number of passages, not only the voice of Faucitano and her clear understanding of female subordination, but also the attentiveness of a man who found himself in comparable circumstances, namely at the mercy of more powerful men who could keep him arbitrarily in prison, despite his acquittal, and thus treat him as guilty of faults not his own.

The *Dialogue* stages a fictional conversation between a wise old man and the libertine son of a deceased friend of his, a young dandy intent on seducing women. While the young man blames the seductiveness of women for his own behaviour, his older interlocutor offers an alternative assessment of the responsibilities involved:

> She, innocent and unaware of your tricks, trusted you, fell in love, and assumed that this beautiful body of yours hid a generous soul—a soul ready to defend her. Seduced, she abandoned herself into your arms and you did with her every single thing you pleased. Then, not content with abandoning her in a flood of tears, and with a broken heart, you boasted about your great triumph with your friends. As a result, you gained great honour and she was vilified and called the most

---

[4] For discussion, see p. 51.

unspeakable names. Do you not think that the judgement of men is not only unfair, but cruel? Is there anything worse and more unbearable than suffering an injustice and, on top of that, gain a bad name from it? Is this situation not equivalent to honouring the executioner and vilifying his victim?[5]

There are other ways in which the *Dialogue* encourages a straightforwardly biographical interpretation. Settembrini's reliance on his wife, for example, helps to explain statements like 'how true it is that the man who despises women never suffered a misfortune!' and 'if you suffer a misfortune and turn to women, you will find true support'.[6] It is, in fact, disappointing that Marcello Gigante, the first and so far only editor of the *Dialogue*, misunderstood these statements and, in the case of the first one, even offered an incorrect emendation. He adds a negative in order to have the text read as follows: 'how true it is that the man who does *not* despise women never suffered a misfortune'[7]—as if despised women were in a position to inflict harm on those who treated them ill. Settembrini's *Dialogue* makes precisely the opposite claim, namely that women have no recourse when they are mistreated by men, while adding (as in the transmitted sentence) that men can absolutely rely on women despite this. That addition clearly reflects Settembrini's experience of Faucitano's active, ingenious, and unwavering commitment to him.

Gigante rightly emphasized Settembrini's exceptionally progressive classicism.[8] Unfortunately, his emendation suggests a certain lack of progress—indeed a regression—on another front, namely on issues of gender equity: the twentieth-century editor of the *Dialogue* misrepresented the nineteenth-century author, turning a sentence that praises the

---

[5] Settembrini in Gigante 1977: 142–3. Note, also in this *Dialogue* dealing exclusively with heterosexual love, Settembrini's emphasis on the physical attractiveness of men: 'this beautiful body of yours' and his hint at the possibility of various sexual acts in the phrase *ogni voler tuo*, translated here as 'every single thing you wanted'.

[6] Settembrini in Gigante 1977: 141 and 142.

[7] Gigante 1977: 141, his italics: 'O quanto è vero che non fu mai sventurato chi *non disprezza* le donne'; a note explains *non* as Gigante's own editorial intervention.

[8] Gigante 1987a: xi and xii describes Settembrini as a *neoghibellino* (i.e. as a secular rather than Catholic thinker) and insists that, for this reason, he was ignored in the account of nineteenth-century Italian classical scholarship offered by Treves 1962. Timpanaro 1965 criticizes Treves for his 'conservative' account, but then he also marginalizes Settembrini, see p. 138, n. 4.

reliability of women, especially in times of need, into a complaint about their power to cause misery to men. The editorial intervention also points to a problem of disciplinary specialization. Gigante, a classicist and papyrologist well used to proposing textual emendations when dealing with ancient texts, published the *Dialogue* in a volume that was meant to offer a recontextualization and, arguably, a defence of Settembrini as a fellow classicist, after the sensationalist publication of *The Neoplatonists* earlier in the same year.[9] The problem with Gigante's aim and approach in *Settembrini e l'antico*, however, is that the work of Settembrini as a classical scholar cannot be separated from his life experience as a revolutionary, champion of homosexuality, and crucially, as we argue in this chapter, husband of Faucitano.

The very opening of the *Dialogue of Women* suggests a coincidence of the classical and the familiar. We are offered the image of an old man 'of modest means and few desires', enjoying his evening *passeggiata* up via Capodimonte towards the park and summer residence of the Bourbon king, on the outskirts of Naples. On his way, he runs into the young son of his deceased friend and engages him in a conversation about loving women. The opening sequence recalls Plato's *Phaedrus*, where the old Socrates runs into a beautiful young friend as he enjoys a 'stroll in the fresh air' on the hills on the outskirts of Athens—an encounter that occasions a long conversation on the nature of love.[10] While clearly Platonic, the setting of Settembrini's *Dialogue* is also rooted in the landscapes of Naples: Capodimonte was (and remains) a good place for a romantic stroll and the young man, we are told, considers it an ideal location to pick up girls. More importantly, perhaps, according to the report of a police informant, it was a location used by Settembrini and fellow revolutionaries to meet, talk, and plan the overthrow of the Bourbons without arousing suspicion.[11] As for Settembrini's own romantic memories with Faucitano, his open-air strolls, 'your weight in the crook of my arm', are a recurrent theme in his letters from prison and find obvious correspondence in the opening of the *Dialogue*.[12] What we

---

[9] Gigante 1977, answering Cantarella 1977.   [10] *Phaedrus* 227a.
[11] Informant Luciano Margherita, as per report quoted in Settembrini 1971: 284.
[12] Letter to Faucitano, dated 10 December 1856, in Settembrini 1971: 673. There are many other references to his walks with his wife, a veritable *topos* of remembered happiness in prison, e.g. Settembrini 1971: 451 and 566.

have, then, is a place of Platonic inspiration which is, simultaneously, a site of romantic love and revolutionary plotting.

All these different strands need to be recognized as simultaneously active in the *Dialogue*—for all that they do not necessarily lead to a coherent position on the alleged subject of this work, namely the condition of women. In fact, our reading suggests several tensions. The most obvious is this: whereas the text begins with an impassioned eulogy of women as morally superior to men, it carries on by making the case for their potential but not yet realized equality. The two positions can perhaps be reconciled;[13] but our contention is that Settembrini never convincingly does so within the *Dialogue* (or, in fact, anywhere else). It seems that Settembrini's lived experience, and specifically the trust and support that characterized his marriage, limits his political imagination.

An outpouring of gratitude for a specific woman, Faucitano, and no doubt for various other wives, mothers, and daughters he could see supporting fellow prisoners, can surely be detected at the beginning of the *Dialogue*:

> Women offer help in every disgrace; cry together with the afflicted; stand by those who are ill; take care of them with loving patience; and visit every prison—when fathers, brothers, and male friends withdraw in fear, busy with their own affairs, abandoning our prisoners, women withstand every threat and every fear, for they alone know how to pray and they alone are capable of true love.[14]

In passages such as this, we can trace how autobiographical experience expands into a general statement about the greater kindness and devotion of women compared to men—a statement that owes something to the *mater dolorosa* of the Catholic tradition, but where the influence of Enlightenment literature can also be detected. From about the mid-eighteenth century, increased rates of literacy among women led to the production and consumption of sentimental novels in which heroines

---

[13] Most obviously, and taking our cue from a position Settembrini articulates but never quite develops, the first step would be to question women's alleged greater capacity for love: how women are represented or appear to be reflects the education they receive and the subaltern position they hold in relation to men.

[14] Settembrini in Gigante 1977: 141.

were depicted as exceptionally kind and devoted to men—yet also in need of guidance and correction, given their excessive propensity for love.[15] Settembrini, to his credit, never slides from women's loving nature to their alleged irrationality and need for guidance (as we have seen, he was given to expressing his own complete reliance on Faucitano's 'excellent judgement').[16] Still, the writing here owes much to Enlightenment clichés and that sets up the critique of Rousseau he goes on to offer.

After illustrating female devotion and kindness, Settembrini pursues a different line of argument altogether. The old man soon concedes that women display all the faults his young interlocutor ascribes to them— they are indeed vain and mischievous flirts—but this, he adds, is because they are in a subaltern position in relation to men and therefore behave as the men themselves would have them do:

> We blame them unjustly when in fact we are the ones who turn them into something sad; were they given a different education, they would be capable of every beautiful and honourable thing.[17]

The programme of education Settembrini recommends for women follows exactly the same principles, and pursues the same aims, as those espoused by Plato in the *Republic*. In book 5 of that dialogue, Socrates challenges the view that men and women are predisposed by nature to act in separate spheres, the *polis* (city-state) in the case of men and the *oikos* (household) in that of women. While conceding that on average men are physically stronger than women, Socrates maintains that there is no functional difference between the two genders and that, therefore, women should be granted full access to the highest political offices in the ideal city, sharing power with men on an equal basis, for the good of the city. In the course of that argument, Plato deplores the huge waste of female talent caused by widespread misconceptions about the separate nature of men and women and sets out a radical reform of education.

---

[15] It should be stressed that even the most progressive thinkers of the Italian Enlightenment indulged in such prejudices, see Messbarger 2002.
[16] See p. 77.   [17] Settembrini in Gigante 1977: 142.

Insofar as they share one and the same nature, Plato argues, men and women should train their souls and their bodies in exactly the same way.[18]

The parallels between the position set out in Plato's *Republic* and what we read in the *Dialogue on Women* are straightforward. Here too we are told that current social norms are based on the wrong assumption that women and men are predisposed by nature to different activities and spheres of action.[19] After exposing the shortcomings of a system of education based on that assumption, and its negative impact on the soul, Settembrini turns his attention to the body, reaching the conclusion that 'the physical education for both sexes should be one and the same'.[20] As in Plato's *Republic*, his argument stems from societal concern: an education system that fully develops the physical and intellectual capabilities of women 'would make it possible to improve humanity', the old man claims towards the end of the *Dialogue*.[21]

In order to support these statements of principle, the old man offers several examples to prove the intellectual excellence of women, as well as their physical strength. Here Settembrini draws from a long tradition, which can be traced to Boccaccio's *De mulieribus claris* and typically mixes ancient and modern *exempla*. Within this tradition, Settembrini's own arrangement and selection suggest a distinctly patriotic and revolutionary stance. In a long *praeteritio*, he claims he will not mention the Amazons, or the women of Sparta, or the modern Greek heroines who died at Suli (1803), or those who died in Chios (1822), in their determination not to submit to Ottoman rule.[22] No, he will not linger on Madonna Cia degli Ordelaffi either, although she bravely led an army in defence of her native Cesena in 1357, or on Emilia Plater, the Polish revolutionary who rose against the Russian Empire in 1830. His list of examples ends, rather, in the fields near Naples 'with our strong

---

[18] *Republic* 451d–457c.
[19] Settembrini in Gigante 1977: 160 where, as so often, he expresses a Platonic idea not by reference to the soul, but in very material and indeed peasant language: 'we are all made with the same flour', *siam tutti di una farina*.
[20] Settembrini in Gigante 1977: 153; compare Settembrini's almost obsessive focus, in his letters from prison, on the physical wellbeing of his wife, pp. 69f.
[21] Settembrini in Gigante 1977: 162.
[22] On these episodes from the Greek War of Independence and their significance for the emerging nation of Italy, see Zanou 2018.

countrywomen, who show me the muscles in their arms...and divide with their men all the hard work of agriculture', and with the Albanian women who live in Calabria, who work much harder than their unspeakably lazy husbands, 'and who are nevertheless so beautiful—indeed, they possess a beauty that is truly Greek'.[23] So here we have a popular, ethnically mixed patriotism of the Italian south, where ancient Greek beauty and modern Italian aspirations can be recognized in the example of Albanian women working in the fields—the most oppressed members of an oppressed ethnic minority, belonging to the peasantry of Calabria, the most oppressed social class in the Kingdom of the Two Sicilies.

It is not difficult to recognize, in all this, not only an awareness derived from observation, but the influence of Vincenzo Cuoco's influential *Plato in Italy* (published in three volumes between 1804 and 1806).[24] Reprinted five times in the course Settembrini's lifetime alone (1820, 1842, 1843, 1852, and 1861), the novel presented itself as a collection of letters written by Plato and associates during their travels in southern Italy—travels which, in Cuoco's fictional conceit, inspired Plato's later philosophy, including the *Republic*. Cuoco's novel enjoyed tremendous success in the nineteenth century: although it addressed itself primarily to Italian patriots, it found considerable favour also abroad, not least because of its sophisticated, philological constructions.[25] It was quickly endorsed by the international elites in Rome. Alexander von Humboldt ensured its immediate translation into German; others belonging to his same circles, including Madame de Staël and the Schlegel brothers, were likewise effective in promoting it.[26] Settembrini, as he struggled to think of ways to support his family from prison, is likely to have turned his mind to Cuoco for his commercial as well as intellectual success.

Later in life, Settembrini described Cuoco as 'able to present the glorious lives of their ancestors' to his Italian readers, 'thus awakening them from their slumbers and inspiring them to some generous work of their own'.[27] This statement must be taken as a prophecy after the fact: in his old age, Settembrini was thinking of himself in his youth, while also

---

[23] Settembrini in Gigante 1977: 152f. [24] See also pp. 92f.
[25] See Andreoni in Cuoco 2006: cxxxi–cxxxvii. [26] See Andreoni in Cuoco 2006: cxix.
[27] Settembrini 1964: 1042.

hoping that the next generation of Italian students—the first in a united country—would continue to be inspired by Cuoco. *Plato in Italy* offered a pan-Mediterranean vision of the ancient past that minimized the differences between Greeks, Italians, and other ethnicities: ultimately all those living in the south of Italy were the inheritors of an ancient, vaguely 'Etruscan' or 'Italic' civilization, which even Plato admired and which was eventually subjugated by the imperialist Romans descending from the north.[28] Settembrini did not explicitly endorse Cuoco's fiction concerning the pre-Roman past, but that fiction informed his treatment of Italians, Greeks, and other ethnic groups living in the Kingdom of the Two Sicilies in his own time, including those Albanian peasants whose husbands made them work like mules, but who nevertheless displayed 'a beauty truly Greek'.[29]

Settembrini must also have appreciated Cuoco's position on the education of women. In the novel we read that, when Plato and his young disciple Cleobulus arrived in Italy, they were amazed to find 'as many women philosophers as men'. It was this discovery, we read, that led Plato to argue for 'equality between the sexes' in the fifth book of the *Republic*.[30] As often in Cuoco, fiction was deeply informed by classical learning: the prominence of Pythagorean women, well attested in ancient sources which Cuoco knew, inspired the description of an ancient, epichoric, south Italian culture which valued the education of women and gave Plato himself a few good ideas on the subject.[31] The conceit of

---

[28] On the political import of this construct, see Ceserani 2010 and De Francesco 2013.

[29] See also his *Lectures on Italian Literature*, which emphasize the connections between Italy, and especially southern Italy, with ancient Greece and Rome, e.g. Settembrini 1964: 32 and 34, when discussing the Italian language and its various dialects: 'in Calabria and Sicily, you will find Greek words and manners'; 'we [southern Italians] are closer to Latin...than the Piedmontese and Lombards'.

[30] Cuoco 2006: 18. The theme is prominent from the very beginning of the novel: after the first letter on the beauty of the south Italian climate and landscape, the next already emphasizes the high education of women. Then, in the sixth letter (which owes a lot to *Republic* 5), Plato embarks on an extended critique of Athenian customs, which, he says, prevent women from accessing a proper education and therefore from making a full contribution to the state. This problem, he says, can only be remedied through reaching 'equality between the sexes' (Cuoco 2006: 26–9).

[31] For an introduction to Pythagorean women, see Pomeroy 2013; that Cuoco knew the relevant ancient sources is confirmed by the notes he took for the planned 'first appendix' to *Plato in Italy*: Cuoco 2006: 626–8.

the novel was clearly explained in the introduction, where Cuoco pretended to have published, after the death of an older relative, a translation of a sheaf of ancient letters that this older man had discovered when digging into the ground 'where Heraclea had once been', in order to build the foundations for a modest country home for himself. This same old man had then painstakingly translated the letters for his private consumption, given there was no point, in his view, in reminding the Italians that they were once 'excellent, powerful, and happy'.[32] Cuoco claimed in the introduction that he had, for his part, decided to publish the old man's translations, because in his view modern Italians had a right to know all about their glorious past: a discussion of the authenticity and authorship of the letters, an assessment of alleged 'lacunae', a commentary indicating where the letters matched information already known from ancient sources (including on Pythagorean women), and four appendices on the pre-Roman and pre-Greek history and philosophy of southern Italy completed Cuoco's scholarly pastiche.

It is hard to judge the tone of *Plato in Italy*: some of the writing was clearly parodic, such as the hilarious non-discussion of the 'authenticity' of the letters, but there was also earnest engagement with actual ancient Greek and Roman texts, as well as British, French, and German scholarship which, Cuoco implied, sometimes also amounted to self-serving fiction.[33] Settembrini, who belonged to a more fully professionalized generation of scholars than Cuoco, never quite mixed fiction, philology, history, and Risorgimento politics in the same way, though he also used the conceit of the 'translation from the Greek' when he came to write *The Neoplatonists*. More importantly, like Cuoco, Settembrini turned to Plato for inspiration when writing about gender, love, and the body politic. In fact, his engagement with Plato was philosophically more serious and

---

[32] Cuoco 2006: 6. The discovery of the Herculaneum papyri and the antiquities at Paestum clearly influenced the fiction. In fact, in decrying the shortcomings of the Italians Cuoco clearly endorsed the perspectives of foreigners interested in visiting the ancient sites: 'Paestum, where today you cannot find even a hotel to accommodate those whose laudable curiosity takes them there from the remotest parts of Europe'.

[33] De Francesco's extensive introduction to Cuoco 2006 is a good starting point here, as are Ceserani 2010 and De Francesco 2013, though the topic would repay further attention on the part of classicists, given the philological ingenuity of the whole construction and the detailed engagement with classical scholarship, as well as ancient sources.

textually more detailed than Cuoco's—even if it remained implicit. Whereas Cuoco flaunted his classical learning by adding a whole scholarly apparatus to his novel, Settembrini kept his *Dialogue on Women* accessible to readers unwilling or unable to engage with scholarly paratexts. We suspect this is, in fact, one reason why Settembrini's own engagement with classical literature has been misrecognized. We have already seen how the setting of his *Dialogue on Women* recalls the opening of Plato's *Phaedrus*. On closer inspection, it turns out that Plato's dialogue on love underpins the entire structure of Settembrini's *Dialogue*—though this is something readers either manage to work out on the basis of their own classical learning or never realize.[34] Plato, for Settembrini, is not the source of dazzling erudite displays, as he was for Cuoco, but a matter of inner structure.

In the *Phaedrus*, Socrates and his young interlocutor Lysias align their views with those of two competing intellectuals, namely Isocrates, on Socrates' side, and Lysias, on Phaedrus'.[35] In the *Dialogue on Women*, during their stroll in via Capodimonte, the old man and his young acquaintance present their arguments not just as reflecting their own views, but as aligned with those of two specific authorities, who remain pointedly unnamed. The young man quotes a 'modern philosopher' early on in the *Dialogue*:

YOUNG MAN: Woman is called a *mischievous animal*. In fact, a great modern philosopher says that it is women who shape men. And for this reason it seems it is they who corrupt us.

OLD MAN: This is the philosophy of the strong—and those who are strong, even when they are wise, are almost always unjust. And now go, and tell this philosopher of yours that if it is true that the weak must always be governed by the strong, then women have their vices from us, just as they have our opinions and our laws.[36]

---

[34] Cuoco too draws heavily on the *Phaedrus* at the beginning of his third volume of *Plato in Italy*, when he discusses love—but he then develops his argument through a general pastiche of Platonic tropes: Cuoco 2006: 369–77.
[35] See *Phaedrus* 278b–279b, a climactic conclusion to the whole dialogue.
[36] Settembrini in Gigante 1977: 140.

The expression 'mischievous animal' as a definition of woman occurs in Cuoco, where it is put in the mouth of a charlatan who pretends to espouse proper Pythagorean doctrines.[37] The modern philosopher quoted immediately afterwards, however, must surely be Jean-Jacques Rousseau, whose approach to antiquity Settembrini is implicitly criticizing.[38]

Running like a red thread through Rousseau's popular novels *La Nouvelle Héloïse* (1761) and *Emile* (1762), as well as his *Discourses* (1750–5) and *Social Contract* (1762), is an argument that starts by asserting the physical weakness and moral inferiority of women and continues by insisting on their formidable corrupting power over men, as a result of their sex appeal and (self-)destructive libido. The power of women, so goes Rousseau's argument, should be repurposed for the good of society, according to a form of homeopathic logic whereby a poison can be used as its own antidote: 'the very causes that have corrupted people can safeguard them'.[39] In practice, this means that women should be strictly confined to the home and, within that private setting, become agents working towards the establishment of democratic relationships, among men, in the public sphere. Egalitarian sociability is not in itself natural, according to Rousseau, but can be established among men, through early education and by co-opting women for that purpose. Indeed, it should be imbibed quite literally from a woman's breast: 'Let mothers deign to nurse their children,' he writes in *Emile*, 'morals will reform themselves, sentiment will be reawakened in every heart, the state will be repeopled.'[40] Desire will be confined within the home and not create conflict between men.

Emile makes clear that republicanism and democracy need to be inculcated into men when they are still children, first through sentiment, so that they will one day desire to marry just one woman and rule within their own family, and then through the egalitarian educational

---

[37] Cuoco 2006: 106.
[38] Rousseau's position on women was well known in Settembrini's Naples. In particular, Ferdinando Galiani had endorsed it and popularized it in a work whose title was none other than *Dialogue on Women* (1789), see Cases 1979. Settembrini used the same title in order to argue the opposite case. On Rousseau and the *Querelle des Anciens et des Modernes*, see below, pp. 111f.
[39] Translated and discussed in Fermon 1994: 433.   [40] Rousseau 1969: 258.

institutions of the State.[41] Even though, according to Rousseau, women are not *naturally* inferior to men, women cannot take part in this democratic polity as equals. Indeed, for Rousseau, democracy is predicated on the sacrifice of women—just as he explicitly predicates it on the subjugation of slaves.[42] In *La Nouvelle Héloïse*, the heroine is sexually incontinent and ends up dead but, through her sacrifice, transforms her aristocratic husband into a proper democratic commoner.[43] The conclusion of the novel is not in contradiction with Rousseau's political philosophy, as some have argued, but rather, Fermon points out, 'underscores its practical intent: in a utopia Julie would not have to die'.[44] It would be sufficient for her to stay at home and obey her husband.

Settembrini, through the figure of the old man, makes his argument, point by point, in opposition to Rousseau's claims (and the young man who parrots them).[45] Democratic society, according to the *Dialogue on Women*, is to be achieved not through the enforced domestication of women but through the sexual re-education of men. As for women, the aim is to ensure they receive exactly the same intellectual and physical education as men, since they are, by nature, equal to them; this also means they are capable of political self-determination.[46] Indeed, the old man (following Plato) argues that women are able to make outstanding contributions in all areas of public life: 'If a woman is capable of occupying a throne, why should she not occupy a chair in the sciences or the humanities?'[47] Rousseau argued that a perfect democratic order could be achieved only 'if women were to abandon the government of

---

[41] Rousseau 1969. [42] *First Discourse*, in Rousseau 1964b.

[43] Rousseau 1964a. Fermon 1994: 438 suggests a parallel with de Sade: 'The powerful image of the helpless Julie, struggling with herself, seeking help from natural and supernatural forces and finding that they are not only indifferent to her cries but indeed that they succour her enemy, is repeated later by De Sade with more tragic consequences. The virtuous Sadeian heroine, having been raped, jailed, despoiled, tortured, and generally betrayed by all in spite of frequent appeals to both God and nature, dies struck by lightning which tears through her womb and obliterates her features. Julie, in the throw of despair, implores heaven, but wisely realizes that "heaven is deaf to the cries of the weak."'

[44] Fermon 1994: 436

[45] This makes it especially galling that De Leo, who seems never to have read the *Dialogue on Women*, quite erroneously aligns Settembrini with Rousseau in her preface to *The Neoplatonists* (in Conoscenti 2019: 41).

[46] Settembrini in Gigante 1977: 157: 'Why is it that when legislating about them, their vote is not solicited?'

[47] Settembrini in Gigante 1977: 158.

literature and business to take up that of the household'.[48] By the end of the *Dialogue on Women*, the young man declares himself convinced by the old man's arguments and asks him how he thinks humankind might make progress. The old man initially refuses to answer this large question, stating that he lacks the relevant philosophical and political expertise. At the young man's insistence, however, he eventually agrees to outline a way forward—with one qualification: he will not offer his own views, but rather those of a friend, 'a man of vigorous intellect and fervid heart', who again remains pointedly unnamed.[49]

There can be no doubt that the friend in question is none other than Plato: the very terms in which the young man sets up his question, 'how to improve humankind', verbally match the articulation of the central problem addressed in the *Republic*.[50] As for the answer the old man offers, it expresses Plato's thought not just in content but also in the language used: phrases such as 'the class of peasants' or 'the authentic doctor' are all of Platonic coinage—and Settembrini, with his fine ear for language, remembers and works them seamlessly into the old man's speech.[51] In the last pages of the *Dialogue on Women*, we learn that it should be compulsory for every male or female citizen to get married (as argued in the *Laws*) and that every citizen should exercise an art or a science according to individual ability (as in the *Republic*): those suited to agriculture should devote themselves to it; those with a head for science should use it.[52] Moreover, we read that there should no longer be any idle aristocrats doing nothing at all—just as there should be no oppressed peasants living in squalor.[53] As for 'libertines, who harass women', there should be none of those either in future.[54] And here the manuscript of the *Dialogue* breaks off: the bottom half of the last page got torn off

---

[48] Rousseau 1964a: 299 n. 6.   [49] Settembrini in Gigante 1977: 162.
[50] Book 5 of Plato's *Republic* culminates with the famous claim that only the fusion of politics and philosophy can deliver 'humankind' (ἀνθρώπινον γένος) from evil (473d).
[51] See *Timaeus* 17c and 24b for the 'class' (γένος) of peasants. The familiar Platonic notion of the 'authentic' (ἀληθινός) expert is found e.g. at *Republic* 488d. The opposition between authentic and fraudulent medicine takes centre stage in Plato's *Gorgias* 464d.
[52] The principle that citizens should do what they are best suited to do (τὰ αὑτοῦ πράττειν) is fundamental to Plato's *Republic* (see 433a and *passim*) as well as to Settembrini's dialogue (see Gigante 1977: 157–8). Book 6 of Plato's *Laws* contains detailed provisions on marriage, including fines for unmarried citizens (774a–b).
[53] Settembrini in Gigante 1977: 163.   [54] Settembrini in Gigante 1977: 164.

and went missing before Gigante began work on the first (and so far only) edition.[55]

Whatever the final sentences contained, Settembrini recasts the *Querelle des Anciens et des Modernes* in distinctly political terms, pinpointing Plato and Rousseau as eminent representatives of each camp.[56] And, for all his criticism, Settembrini takes from Rousseau the idea that what happens in the bedroom shapes democratic relationships between citizens: in so doing, he offers an important insight into Rousseau's political thought. As Fermon points out, 'although sociologists from Durkheim to Marx acknowledge their debt to Rousseau for his delineation of the social, distinct from the political and the economic, as well as for his discussion of childhood and political socialization to maturity, none address the specifically erotic/sexual dimensions of the political education which Rousseau proposes'.[57] Settembrini clearly does so, even while rejecting Rousseau's misogyny and, more fundamentally, what he calls his 'philosophy of the strong'.[58] It would be possible to explore here a more specific contrast between Rousseau's sadistic eroticism and Settembrini's egalitarian approach to sex, based on what he called *reciprocanza*, a drawing pleasure from giving pleasure (between men and women, as well as between men)—but this would be to stray into the subject of *The Neoplatonists*, which we treat in our next chapter. For now, and in line with the *Dialogue on Women*, our conclusion focuses on the public rather than the private sphere. For Settembrini, the question of who may be corrupting whom in the sexual politics of his day has a straightforward answer: men damage women—and not the other way round. His rejection of a 'philosophy of the strong', combined with this insight, profoundly informs his engagement with Plato.

In the *Dialogue*, rather than defining the democratic future of the nation by limiting the power of women, as happens in Rousseau, Settembrini insists that men listen to women and allow them to legislate

---

[55] Gigante 1977 gives no indication of how much of the *Dialogue of Women* may be missing, but our own examination of the manuscript suggests no more than a paragraph or two.

[56] Rousseau himself, of course, was closely associated with representatives of the 'ancient' camp, such as Perrault. In terms of his political philosophy, however, he has been recast as an eminent voice among the 'moderns' not just by Settembrini but, over a century later, by Leo Strauss 1959.

[57] Fermon 1994: 431.   [58] See above, p. 107.

on all matters bearing on their lives. His argument in favour of granting legislative powers (and the vote) to women is remarkably progressive, when we consider it was articulated as early as the 1830s and in the south of Italy—where, to this day, women vote in fewer numbers than men and also in lower proportion than northern Italian women.[59] Settembrini's political argument was accompanied by a life-long commitment to female education—first expressed in theory, in the *Dialogue on Women*, and then acted on in practice, as general inspector of education, in a newly united Italy. We may add that, throughout his life, Settembrini remained a vocal champion not only of women in general, but also of specific women who impressed him. His attitude towards Maria Giuseppa Guacci (1807–48), a poet and patriot who had studied with him in the school of Puoti, is a case in point. The grudging praise of other contemporaries did much to consign her to oblivion.[60] Settembrini, for his part, expressed his admiration unstintingly not only in his *Dialogue on Women* and in his later *Lectures on Italian Literature*,[61] but also when presenting her as a role model to a younger generation of girls who were just beginning their studies in a school for girls he had worked hard to establish.[62]

Against the backdrop of the Risorgimento discourse on women, Settembrini's 'Platonic' views are extraordinary and deserve much broader attention than they have received.[63] We must, however, add that there were limits to his political imagination: in the *Dialogue* he insisted on what men needed to grant to women, rather than consider what women might take for themselves, potentially even against the resistance of men. There is a difference, in short, between Settembrini's revolutionary commitments and his gender politics: whereas he incited the oppressed to take up arms against the oppressors in the revolution, he never imagined women confronting the patriarchy through an independent and organized movement of their own. It may be argued that such a vision did not fit the late 1830s and the south of Italy—but this

---

[59] Sarlo and Zajczyk 2012.   [60] See De Sanctis 1953: vol. 2, 60.
[61] Settembrini in Gigante 1977: 158; Settembrini 1966: 1042–5.
[62] Settembrini 1876: 3–5.
[63] Patriarca 2011 provides a very useful discussion of the limited roles women were expected to play, without discussing Settembrini's heterodox position.

would be to deny Settembrini the power of a utopian imagination, which he possessed in relation to other issues.

Our argument is different. We believe that there was an autobiographical component to Settembrini's position on women: locked up in the Vicaria and totally dependent on Faucitano even for the paper and ink he needed to write the *Dialogue*, he was in no psychological condition to imagine how women might assert their interests at the expense of men. His description of women's devotion reflected his need and—fortunately for him—also his experience. Besides these biographical considerations, we also believe there was an ideological component to his position. Rather than tell women what they needed to do (whether at home or in the public sphere) he focused on the responsibilities that men had in relation to them. Even in the early *Dialogue on Women*, his principal concern was not the intellectual education of women, after all, but the sexual education of men. As for *The Neoplatonists*, by the time he came to write that second Platonic fiction, the issue had become the entire focus of his attention.

7
The Neoplatonists

From the moment *The Neoplatonists* was discovered until now, Settembrini's erotic fiction has been kept as far away as possible from the rest of his oeuvre. This, as we argued in chapter 1, is the result of two contrasting impulses: initially, the manoeuvre was meant to protect Settembrini's reputation as a revolutionary hero; from the late 1970s onwards, however, a growing disengagement with the foundations of the Italian nation meant that *The Neoplatonists* became his only work to have sustained currency both in Italy and abroad—if only as a curious chapter in the history of homosexuality.[1] The one exception to this schizophrenic approach to the legacies of Settembrini was Marcello Gigante's *Settembrini e l'antico* (1977) which, not coincidentally, was published precisely at the moment when Settembrini was pivoting, in the public imagination, from father of the Italian nation to champion of Greek love.[2] Gigante included the first, and so far only, edition of the *Dialogue on Women* in his book and, although we have offered a different interpretation of that text in chapter 6, we agree with him that Settembrini's work as a classical scholar provides the clearest point of contact between his political and sexual legacies. The *Dialogue on Women*, in particular, helps to bring under a single purview the erotic fantasist, classical scholar, and revolutionary hero.

---

[1] French translation Patrick Dubuis 2010; German translation Gerd Gauglitz 2017; Portuguese translation La Regina and Chiarini 2016; Spanish translation Carlos Sanrune 2019. Further editions in Italian include Benvenuto 2001, Zanotti 2006, Palladino 2010, and Conoscenti 2019, as well as several reprints of Cantarella 1977. On the shortcomings of these various editions, see Capra 2018. Conoscenti 2019 stands out for its precision and overall quality.

[2] Gigante 1987b elaborates on Gigante 1977: 11–122. D'Antuono 2012: 103–12 builds on Gigante's work. Conoscenti 2019 provides an excellent contextualization as regards problems of chronology, Settembrini's position in the history of homosexuality, and the tale's debt to Italian literary models.

We have seen how the *Dialogue* makes the case for the intellectual advancement of women and the sexual education of men. *The Neoplatonists* moves beyond political and social considerations to practical suggestions for what to do in the bedroom. These range from leisurely foreplay involving all the senses, to the thrills afforded by voyeurism and group sex, to precise instructions on how to proceed between men ('I'll hold this beautiful flower, which now stands erect on its stem, so very boldly... and seems to want to open its mouth and talk to me... and now my hand will caress behind and with a finger sweetly try the door'), to the delights of giving oral pleasure to women ('I greeted the sacred door of life and pleasure... it looks like a cave sacred to some mysterious God, covered in lush, soft vegetation... I saw it, I greeted it, I kissed it again, and we celebrated the third mystery')—all the way to the general insight that the more pleasure a man gives to his partner, whether male or female, the more intense his own. As for women, one remarkable aspect of *The Neoplatonists* is that it contains no instructions at all about how they may please men—the only implicit suggestion is that, like Hymnis, they should talk to men about what they like and pursue what gives them pleasure. It is no coincidence that Dorus' attempt to instruct Hymnis and persuade her to accommodate his anal fantasies is wholly unsuccessful. She easily wins the argument she has with him on the subject and retains her role as teacher.[3] Again, far from this being an anomalous detail in Settembrini's oeuvre, this fits not only Settembrini's reliance on his wife's 'excellent judgement' (see p. 77 ch. 4), but the position of principle adopted in the *Dialogue on Women*: as we have seen, there too Settembrini focuses on how men should behave towards women, without seeking to legislate on the behaviour of women at all—whether sexually, socially, or even politically (beyond expressing the view that they should have a say in all laws concerning them).[4]

The erotic curriculum set out in *The Neoplatonists* is impressive in its range—and especially detailed when it comes to anal sex. The explicit claim, when it comes to it, is that the practice can be painful at the

---

[3] Hymnis is clearly modelled on Longus' Lycaenion in *Daphnis and Chloe* 3.15–20, where she teaches the male protagonist how have intercourse face to face.

[4] See pp. 109f.

receiving end and that it is therefore important to adopt some precautions in order to minimize discomfort: Callicles and Dorus are delighted when they discover the advantages of olive oil and, after making full use of the revelation, run to the temple of Athena to thank her for the gift of the olive tree. There are many such comical touches in the tale, suggesting that it is meant to entertain and delight, as well as offer instruction. We discuss Settembrini's gentle humour below—foolish as it is to try and explain jokes, let alone translate them. For now, we linger a little longer on the educational aspects of *The Neoplatonists* because, for all his titillating lightness of touch, Settembrini does have an agenda.

Anal sex inspires social and political commentary, as well as being the focus of practical advice and jokes. Because pain and pleasure are, in Settembrini's account, distributed unequally in this kind of intercourse, he insists on the importance of 'reciprocity', which in practice means swapping roles between men. Moreover, because taking turns in anal penetration does not feature in heterosexual relationships, he suggests that men should not ask women for what (in the words of Hymnis) 'brings no advantage to them'. Despite this difference, symmetry is possible in heterosexual relationships as well. This is explained along lines that recall Aristophanes' speech in Plato's *Symposium*: 'each body part meets and mates, thigh with thigh, belly with belly, breast with breast. The arms embrace; the hands run up and down everywhere on the back and apples: no part of the body is excluded from this pleasure.'[5] The result, we read, is 'something much stronger than the usual sweetness' which Callicles and Dorus experience among themselves. We further read that love between man and woman, in which each body part finds its 'mate', is something that defines humanity: 'animals experience pleasure in the body, and not even the whole body; human beings experience pleasure in the whole body—and, if that pleasure is coupled with love, they experience it in the whole of their soul too'.

Consideration of the soul leads Settembrini to acknowledge upfront something that remains implicit in the *Dialogue on Women*, namely his objections to the views on heterosexual love found in Plato's best known works. In the *Symposium*, Aristophanes presents male homosexuality as

---

[5] Cf. Plato, *Symposium* 189c–193d.

superior to heterosexual love, something Settembrini explicitly denies. The *Republic* advocates sexual communism between men and women,[6] not least as a means of ensuring cohesion among the ruling class of guardians.[7] Settembrini, by contrast, sees this arrangement as incompatible with love. *The Neoplatonists* concludes with this scenario:

> Each man lived in his own home, had children, enjoyed family life and was held in high esteem by his fellow citizens. The two friends no longer followed Plato's teaching, according to whom women should be held in common, but rather followed the laws of their fatherland and those of love. Each of them loved and honoured his own wife. And yet, they always continued to love each other too and, even in old age, if they happened to share a bed for any reason, they would entangle their feet and embrace as they did long ago, in the first years of their youth.

In contemporary terms, what we have here is a bisexual and quasi-bigamous arrangement: loving, heterosexual marriages are seen as compatible with a loving, homosexual, lifelong relationship between two men. Indeed, both *The Neoplatonists* and the *Dialogue on Women* present relationships between men as analogous to marriage and explicitly involve the task of bringing up children: in the *Dialogue* 'the old man' tries to educate the son of a deceased male friend of his; in *The Neoplatonists*, when Callicles becomes an orphan, his father's best friend adopts him and raises him together with his own son Dorus.[8] Although *The Neoplatonists* has often been read against an imagined background of homosexual promiscuity in prison, what we have is, rather, an attempt to fit both homosexual and heterosexual sex within a framework of stable, lifelong commitments that are, moreover, fully invested in the next generation. How this fantasy may relate to Settembrini's lived experience is something we tackle in greater detail in our next chapter. For now, it seems important to point out that, as a critic of Plato,

---

[6] Plato, *Republic* 5, 457b–458d and 461e–462e. For further discussion of Settembrini's engagement with Plato and Neoplatonism, see pp. 121f.
[7] Saïd 1986.
[8] Settembrini himself, of course, largely entrusted the education of his own son to Antonio Panizzi, see pp. 67f.

Settembrini isolates a well-recognized problem in Platonic philosophy, which we might summarize in the words of Luc Brisson: 'because he considers that human beings are defined more by their soul than by their body, Plato is led, quite logically, to place women on the same level as men, from every viewpoint. This position, which was shocking or laughable in Antiquity, has become the rule in our societies. On the other hand, our societies cannot accept sharing women and children, which reduces sexual union to its reproductive function, and therefore has nothing to do with pleasure or desire.'[9]

A focus on pleasure and reciprocity is crucial not just when it comes to heterosexual relationships, but also in Settembrini's treatment of love between men—where, impressively, he foreshadows a fluidity of roles which is not usually associated with nineteenth-century homosexuality.[10] In *The Neoplatonists*, this emerges early on in the tale, when Codrus, the old teacher of philosophy, tries to reveal to the boys the true nature of Platonic love—and ends up being taught a lesson instead. The scene displays a typical mixture of the alluring, the learned, and the comical:[11]

> 'Please let me kiss your shoulders, back, and apples,' Codrus added. 'What beautiful apples of the Hesperides; here comes Hercules to pick this precious fruit.' At this, good old Codrus anoints his Hercules with perfumed oil, embraces Dorus and, after two or three sweet attempts, enters the divine orchard of the Hesperides. They lie, embracing tightly on the rug, conjoined, and Callicles, at that sight, can no longer keep himself in check and, after anointing his own nail, directs it between Codrus' fleshy apples—and sinks in at once. Startled, Codrus lets go of Dorus but immediately takes him again, saying, 'Well done, boys, stick

---

[9] Brisson 2012: 134. One could object that Plato acknowledges the importance of sexual desire in the *Republic*, but the important point here is that Brisson expresses a common assumption in Settembrini's time and our own, namely the presumed incompatibility between sexual communism and desire.

[10] As Duncan 2006: 18–19 points out, one of the most widely read books on homosexuality in Italy (Barbagli and Colombo 2001) claims that equality and reciprocity are recent developments in homosexual relationships which, in the nineteenth century, were allegedly 'structured round inequalities of social and sexual authority'. He rightly points out that the authors should revise their claims in light of Settembrini's *Neoplatonists*. See also Zanotti 2005: chapter 15 contains a sensible, if brief, discussion of *The Neoplatonists*; chapter 23 correctly presents Settembrini as anticipating later attitudes.

[11] See pp. 160f. for notes on details of language and references to ancient texts.

to it! You, Dorus, ahead of me and you, Callicles, behind: we need to hold on tight and keep on track.' After they had run the course of one station, Codrus said, 'I wanted to teach you the art—but you, divine boys, are teaching me something quite new, how to take the two pleasures of love at one and the same time. I thank the Gods for having learnt this more refined art.' 'Enough,' said Dorus, 'time for reciprocity.' And with this all three turned around, Codrus held the expert Callicles, while Dorus, with equal impetus and skill, entered Codrus' garden, who sighed loudly. After they completed that second stadion, and after washing their limbs in a basin, Codrus insisted that they pour a libation of wine in memory of Plato, naked as they were, and then drink from the same cup.

It is through the surprisingly contemporary insistence on reversing roles that we move from the bedroom to the nation, in *The Neoplatonists*. The starting point for that transition is the idea that you must be able to do to your lover what he does to you, otherwise the result 'is not love at all, but rather some kind of fury that overwhelms and damages somebody else'. The emphasis on equality is such that, in Settembrini's view, the best form of love is between partners 'of the same age'. He does, however, countenance the possibility of true sentiment between partners of different ages and/or social status: the young dancer Hymnis, for example, cares for her older benefactor and lover, even while he cares more for her. Just so, Codrus loves a young man from Larissa who answers that feeling—even if only up to a point. The implication here is inescapable: the most powerful form of love is between equals. It is for this reason that Callicles and Dorus are presented as the paradigmatic couple in the story, for all that Settembrini acknowledges and honours other forms of love as well.

In the second half of *The Neoplatonists*, the two lovers put an end to their promiscuous experiments: after making their discoveries about pleasure and reciprocity, they remain faithful to each other—and their respective wives. The arrangement is presented as good for their bodies, their souls, and also, importantly, for their fatherland. We are told that they fight bravely in war (albeit in the rather late and perfunctory chapter 7, whose only aim is to make that point). Moreover, they come to reject the sexual communism advocated in Plato's *Republic* out of respect for the laws of their country and, we are told, out of love for their wives.[12] The movement from sexual promiscuity to stable, long-lasting relationships is probably the main reason why Settembrini calls *The Neoplatonists* 'an obscene narrative up to midpoint'. It is true that the first half of the tale is also more insistently homosexual than the second but, as we have seen, Callicles and Dorus continue to go to bed together right until the last sentence. What we never see, in *The Neoplatonists*, is a transformation of love all the way from the physical to the purely spiritual. Indeed, the tale is nothing less than a manifesto against that very notion of Platonic love—which is underscored by many jokes. The verb *platoneggiare*, for example, is used as a synonym for having anal sex and, more elaborately, a professor of 'Platonic' philosophy insists that practice is more important than theory—a position that runs entirely counter to the hierarchies between theory and empirical knowledge, not to mention soul and body, which underpin Plato's thought. And then there is the title of Settembrini's alleged 'translation from the Greek', which is at once hilarious and polemical.

Settembrini drew a sharp distinction between Plato's philosophy and the way it was interpreted in Late Antiquity and the Renaissance. In his *Lectures on Italian Literature*, for example, he criticized Marsilio Ficino (1433–99) by insisting on the difference between the 'strange mysticism' of Neoplatonist thought and proper Platonic philosophy: had Ficino 'had access only to Plato's works, which he translated with admirable clarity and fidelity, he would have understood them and commented on them in a broad and serious manner; his misfortune was that he also had to hand the works of Plotinus and other Neoplatonists of the Alexandrian school'.[13] Settembrini's understanding of the reception of Plato tallies, in this as in other respects, with current scholarship: Reeser, for example, has recently shown how Marsilio and other Renaissance men reinterpreted Plato so as to create the concept of Platonic love.[14] But Settembrini's polemic was not directed only against Hellenistic, Late

---

[12] Settembrini seems to echo Plato's own recantation in his last work, the *Laws*, which famously abandons the sexual communism advocated in the *Republic*. Note that Callicles and Dorus opt for marriage out of respect for the 'laws' of their country.
[13] Settembrini 1964: 294.   [14] Reeser 2015.

Antique, and Renaissance Platonism. He was also aware that influential contemporaries were committed to Neoplatonism in both their religious and their political positions. The clergyman and philosopher Vincenzo Gioberti (1801-52), in particular, made one of the most effective arguments for Italian unification by proposing the establishment of an Italian federation overseen by the pope. Settembrini recognized the importance of Gioberti in the cause of Italian unification, though he categorically rejected his proposed system of government. A convinced republican throughout his life, he came to accept the monarchy—but only as a measure needed in order to counterbalance the secular power of the pope.[15]

Now, it was none other than Gioberti who had first imported the modern term 'Neoplatonism' (first coined by Friedrich Schleiermacher, 1768-1834) into Italian.[16] Thus, by choosing a conspicuous neologism for his title, Settembrini was not only undercutting his own fiction of a faithful 'translation from the Greek', but also signalling his polemical engagement with Gioberti's Neoplatonist views. It must be said that, in terms of metaphysics, Settembrini had no great quarrel with ancient Neoplatonism. Indeed, it seems that his own religious views were largely inspired by it: the priority of 'the Good' or 'God' or 'the One'— and the origin of everything from the One can easily be paralleled in Settembrini's own thoughts on God.[17] His idea of the universe as a manifestation of divine beauty is again very close to what might be called 'pagan' Neoplatonism.[18] It is in the spheres of ethics and politics that his objections to Neoplatonist doctrine, whether ancient or modern, became trenchant. Lovemaking, for Settembrini, was itself a form of celebration and even worship of beauty: the boys in his tale are repeatedly compared

---

[15] Gioberti's most influential work, *Primato morale e civile degli Italiani* (*On the Moral and Civic Primacy of the Italian People*), was first published in 1843. In his *Memoirs*, Settembrini vividly describes the effect it had: suddenly Italian patriots could speak openly about unification, without immediately putting themselves in danger. This meant that 'the concept became clearer, started to spread, became action, and finally turned into fact', Settembrini 1971: 169. In the *Lectures*, Settembrini 1964: 1176-7, he added that Gioberti's attempts to reconcile the Italian nation with the Roman Curia had been, in themselves, an utter failure.

[16] Cortellazzo and Zolli 1983: 799.

[17] Settembrini's religious thought, however, changed over time: his late writings arguably contain professions of atheism, Themelly 1977: 56-9.

[18] Francesco De Sanctis (1817-83), whose *History of Italian Literature* is a revered model in the genre, famously defined Settembrini as 'a pagan born and bred' (*un pagano purosangue*, De Sanctis 1965: 310).

to the Dioscuri, in that typical blending of fun-making, classicizing parody, and sincere celebration of lovable men that we see so often in his work. If there is any missionary zeal to *The Neoplatonists* at all, it resides in its rejection of asceticism in favour of a joyous, uninhibited celebration of sex.

This can be seen in the criticism of hypocrisy fronting the entire tale. The 'translator's warning' suggests that ascetic Neoplatonism is nothing but a ruse invented by some 'clever types', some *furbi*, to disguise their love affairs with men: 'this tale... reveals the antiquity of the view, held by men of discretion, that Platonic love is not absolutely pure and free of all sensuality—for all that some clever types have spread the notion in order to hide their own love affairs with other men'.[19] In short, (Catholic, Neoplatonic) hypocrisy is seen as the opposite of ancient, sensual, and properly Platonic celebrations of beauty: 'one of the principal traits of Greek Art is that it is not hypocritical... moralists may well condemn this tale; artists will certainly take pleasure in it and say that art makes everything beautiful'.

It is possible, and even likely, that Settembrini's celebration of beauty and homosexuality, combined with deep hostility towards hypocritical Catholicism, had its roots in his early experiences. As we outlined in chapter 1, he entered a Catholic boarding school at the age of ten and soon became close with another boy, Luigi De Silva: their friendship was so intense that it attracted the attention of other children, who started calling them *i dottorelli* ('the little doctors', on account of their intense classical studies), and later *i monaci* ('the monks', when they began to undergo extreme devotional practices together). Linguistically, *i neoplatonici* follows the same pattern—except that, in the story, the boys share physical pleasures rather than penitence and prayers. Moreover, in the story, the boys continue to love each other and have sex together all the way into old age, without experiencing any hostility on account of their homosexual relationship. In real life, by contrast, Settembrini and De Silva were first placed in separate bedrooms and then Settembrini's father took him out of the school altogether. For all that, in his *Memoirs* Settembrini described De Silva as a lifelong friend.[20] When we consider

---

[19] See p. 150. [20] See p. 42.

that Settembrini was copying out *The Neoplatonists* and his *Memoirs* at the same time and on the same paper, towards the very end of his life, the parallels in the stories and the names used to describe the fictional and the real-life boys become all the more significant.

And yet the story cannot be reduced to autobiographical account or idiosyncratic sexual fantasy—just as it would be reductive to see it simply as a stylistic exercise in imitation of the Greeks.[21] We argue that Settembrini's critical engagement with Plato provides the key to access the broader aspirations of his tale. The first point to make here—and this is a point that, to our knowledge, has never entered discussions of *The Neoplatonists*—is that Settembrini drew inspiration from a genuinely ancient tradition of pseudepigrapha. The very first author in Greek literature to appeal to an (invented) ancient document in order to express what ought to happen in the ideal city was, after all, none other than Plato himself. In the *Timaeus*, which is conceived as a sequel to the *Republic*, the myth of Atlantis is offered as a 'true' account of the distant past, recorded in an Egyptian archive allegedly consulted by Solon during his travels and translated into Greek.[22] This invented document 'proves', in the *Timaeus*, that early Athens was exactly like the ideal city Plato had already described in the *Republic*. On this same model, *The Neoplatonists* 'proves' that, in the ancient past, men and women related to each other in the loving and mutually respectful ways already advocated, at the level of political discussion, in the *Dialogue on Women*. In short, for Plato, as well as Settembrini, political utopia found confirmation in the pseudepigraphic past.

The *Timaeus* inaugurated a long tradition of pseudepigraphic experiments—a tradition that proved especially influential in Greek prose fiction and the later literature it inspired.[23] We note, for example, that an ancient novel by Antonius Diogenes, *The Wonders beyond Thule* (dated to the end of the first or the beginning of the second century CE),

---

[21] Conoscenti 2019 discusses this kind of reading in his first chapter.
[22] For a first orientation, see Gill 2017. Gill has persuasively shown that Plato's Atlantis story can be taken as marking the 'birth of fiction' (Gill 1979).
[23] It is a tradition that includes Cuoco's *Plato in Italy* (1804–6), itself an important influence on Settembrini, as we argued on pp. 104–7. In fact, one of the main characters in Cuoco's pseudepigraphic novel is called Timaeus.

began with the trope of a newly discovered ancient manuscript as the source for the story the reader was about to enjoy. Though the novel itself is now lost, Photius (working in the ninth century) summarized its plot and drew attention to its influence on Apuleius and Lucian—the author whom Settembrini spent years translating in prison. Lucian himself, in his *True History*, not only included a pseudepigraphic inscription, but offered a whole series of references to genuine ancient literature in order to support the 'veracity' of his grandiose and self-confessed 'lie'.[24] And this is what Settembrini had to say about Lucian's pseudepigraphic games in *True History*: 'It is an imaginary tale that offers much enjoyment because of its novelties, pleasant subject and style, bizarre inventions and, above all, for the fact that all these inventions are spicy allusions to tales and wonders told by ancient poets, historians, and philosophers—who are never mentioned by name, because the allusions are clear enough in themselves.'[25]

We have already seen, in our last chapter, that Settembrini set up a contrast between Plato and Rousseau as authorities on women's role in society—without ever mentioning their names because, he must have thought, the allusions were surely 'clear enough in themselves'. In fact, in part because of unhelpful disciplinary specializations, it seems we managed to point them out, for the first time, in this book. We now uncover a similarly tacit but precise operation of silent allusion in *The Neoplatonists*. Settembrini works with two ancient traditions engaged with Plato, one fictional, the other more strictly philosophical. Between the two, he privileges 'the popular and sensual Platonism found in the works of Aristaenetus and Achilles Tatius' (and more generally the ancient novel), rather than the ascetic, philosophical positions articulated in doctrinal Neoplatonism.[26]

It is remarkable how Settembrini's understanding of the ancient reception of Plato aligns with the most up-to-date scholarship on the subject. As Richard Hunter has recently shown, it is possible to trace a

---

[24] The prologue of *The True History* confirms that Lucian expected his readers to enjoy a text that tested their paideia by alluding to the ancient classics they had studied in school; it also used this testing to blur the boundaries between truth and lies, in much the same way as Antonius Diogenes' novel did.
[25] Settembrini 1988: 1135.   [26] Capra 2018: 45.

line of influence from the speech of Aristophanes in Plato's *Symposium* all the way to the symmetrical conception of heterosexual love found in the ancient Greek novel.[27] Settembrini's description of intercourse, with each body part finding its 'mate', clearly draws inspiration from Aristophanes' mythical explanation of love as the reunion of two divided, semi-spherical halves in the *Symposium*. What has become a cliché in current parlance (as in 'my better half') was, in Plato's time, a revolutionary and recognizably comical conception of eros, involving symmetry in heterosexual as well as homosexual relationships, both male and female. While dominant ideas of love in the ancient Greek world were characterized by a hierarchical distinction between active lover and passive beloved, whether in heterosexual or homosexual relationships, Aristophanes' speech shaped the conception of love later found in the Greek novel. As several recent scholars have argued, that conception distinguishes the ancient novel, as a genre, 'from all other amatory literature in the classical world, as well as from those prose fictions, also called novels or romances, composed in ancient Rome'.[28]

Scholars tend to assume that Lucian's *Amores* is the dominant influence on Settembrini's *The Neoplatonists*—and it is of course true that he drew from that work.[29] The conception of love underpinning *The Neoplatonists*, however, is quite different. Settembrini himself seems to have been aware of that, since this is what he had to say about Lucian: 'his poetic and fantastic spirit was destined either to dry up or to survive with some addition of feeling—and, because noble feelings had themselves been extinguished, it latched on to sensual love, the only kind of love that existed, and powerfully so, in that corrupt age. And so it was that many erotic tales started to be written in this century and continued to be common in the centuries that followed.'[30]

Settembrini's own novella is introduced as a 'Milesian tale', i.e. an erotic narrative—but we are also told that it remains obscene only 'up to midpoint'. After that, it moves beyond erotic experimentation towards an understanding of love (whether homosexual or heterosexual) as satisfying to both body and soul, symmetrical, based on reciprocal,

---

[27] Hunter 2012.   [28] Konstan 1994: 7.
[29] Conoscenti 2019: 164–5.   [30] Settembrini 1861, paragraph LI.

lifelong commitments, and therefore supportive of the fatherland. As David Konstan points out, 'it is peculiar to the Greek novel, among ancient forms of love literature, that the protagonists are invariably a young boy and a young girl, both of free status and eligible for marriage, and each equally enamoured of the other. This pattern of symmetrical or reciprocal love, in which the attraction is both mutual and between social equals, has a profound effect on the entire structure of the novel and gives it its raison d'être.'[31] Settembrini transformed this ancient pattern by allowing some sexual experimentation before the protagonists settle into their bisexual and quasi-bigamous arrangement.[32] He also makes homosexuality more prominent, though it is attested also in the ancient novel, as Hippothous and Hyperanthes (in Xenophon's *Ephesiaca* 3.3–3, 5.15) and Cleinias and Charicles (in Achilles Tatius 1.7–14) demonstrate. Beyond this tradition of symmetrical love, extending from Plato's *Symposium* to the ancient novel, there are many other aspects of *The Neoplatonists* testifying to Settembrini's close engagement with the Greek romances: ring composition;[33] the comparison of the two protagonists to the deities they worship;[34] the capacity of their beauty to subdue even barbarians;[35] the late and somewhat perfunctory show of martial valour on the part of male protagonists;[36] and the general atmosphere of escapism and romantic reverie.[37]

---

[31] Konstan 1994: 7; see also Fusillo 1989: 186–96.
[32] Fusillo 1989: 207–18 underlines the 'monomania' characterizing love in the Greek novel.
[33] Ring composition is especially clear in the novels by Xenophon of Ephesus and Chariton. In Settembrini the protagonists begin and end in bed together: as children they fall asleep 'intertwining their legs and feet like the two snakes round Mercury's wand' (p. 152) and as old men they would still 'entangle their feet' (p. 183). The image of the snakes is also found on a bracelet worn by Hymnis, which acts as a *mise en abîme* within the novella (p. 167). A similar narrative device can be found in Heliodorus' *Aethiopian* 3.4.3–7, where the heroine's breastplate is adorned with sinuous snakes, again a significant image in that story.
[34] The protagonists of the Greek novel are often presented as the living embodiment of the god they worship: e.g. Anthia resembles and worships Artemis, Callirhoe worships and resembles Aphrodite, and both girls are often mistaken for the goddesses themselves (Cioffi 2014); just so various characters call Callicles and Dorus 'the Dioscuri' and they themselves worship the twin gods.
[35] Ancient examples include Chariton 5.3.9; Xenophon of Ephesus 2.4, Heliodorus 8.9.4; Callicles and Dorus impress the Syrians with their beauty.
[36] Chariton's Chaereas and Heliodorus' Charicles are rather querulous and helpless, in particular compared to the female heroines, until shortly before the end they prove their valour, almost as an afterthought; cf. Callicles and Dorus in the rather brief chapter 7.
[37] On *The Neoplatonists* and the ancient novel, see further Capra 2018.

It is that very atmosphere, we argue, that suggests some political as well as aesthetic parallels. The Neoplatonists can easily be dismissed as an erotic fantasy with no political significance at all. Just so, the ancient novel has, until very recently, been seen as escapist entertainment—entirely detached from broader ethical, let alone political, concerns. Recent scholarship has entirely transformed our understanding of the ancient novel, however. Today we read this genre of ancient literature not only as promoting an unusually egalitarian conception of love, but also as a deeply, if implicitly, political genre.[38] The total lack of reference to the Roman domination of Greece and the rise of Christianity has been argued to be, in itself, a form of resistance to both these developments.[39] Just so, Settembrini's escapist fantasy amounts to an act of resistance to the subjugation of Italy to northern, foreign powers and a rejection of hypocritical forms of Christianity extolling ascetic, i.e. 'Platonic', love. The image of *Graecia felix*, which finds its most attractive expression in the ancient novel, is foundational for Settembrini's own utopian, anti-clerical, and deeply egalitarian vision of a future Italy.

In short, then, Settembrini's reading of the ancient novel suggests a form of political resistance which derives its strength from enjoyment—and this, as we argue in our next chapter, finds remarkable parallels in contemporary discourse, also beyond the field of classics. That said, it is also important to recognize that Settembrini could assume his contemporaries to recognize the divided history of Platonism, between fiction and philosophy, underpinning his tale. We have already seen how Cuoco's *Plato in Italy*, an epistolary fiction pretending to be a translation of actual ancient Greek letters, included a whole apparatus of scholarly disquisitions and notes, pointing out where the fictional translation matched genuine ancient sources, and particularly Plato.[40] This kind of game trained readers in specific forms of exegesis which Settembrini not

---

[38] New Comedy and Menander, which constitute a major influence on the novel, have recently undergone a similar reassessment, while private in subject and distant from Aristophanes' political satire, New Comedy tacitly advocates major societal changes. What we argue here is that this holds true of Settembrini's *Neoplatonists* as well.

[39] This is of course a thorny question, which can be viewed from very different angles, see Whitmarsh 2011: 8.

[40] See pp. 105f.

only absorbed himself but could assume in some of his readers. Fake translations with a strong scholarly apparatus were prominent in his time, also beyond Cuoco—and some of them focused specifically on the ancient Greek novel. Settembrini's own teacher, Basilio Puoti (1782–1847), wrote a love romance which he presented as a translation from a Greek original. Melchiorre Cesarotti (1730–1808) composed a tale entitled *Calliste and Philaretes: Fragment of a Greek Novel* (first published in 1777), which explicitly engaged with Platonic and Neoplatonic conceptions of love.[41] In one edition of this tale, the frontispiece even described its subject as *Ravings of Platonic Love*.[42]

Cesarotti's *Fragment* deserves special attention here, not least because of its dialogue form. The young female protagonist, Calliste ('Most Beautiful'), discusses with Love himself which potion to offer to her sweetheart, Philaretes ('Lover of Virtue'), and drink herself. The choices are: a murky liquid, which is responsible for 'attraction between animals'; a pure, transparent, celestial love; and an attractive amber drink which turns out to be a mixture of the other two. Initially, Calliste chooses the pure vial. The effects, it turns out, are exhausting. After a long conversation in which the young protagonists 'inveigh against the imperfection of matter, despise their own bodies, and speak about the contemplation of the soul', they fall asleep, some distance apart. On waking up, Philaretes quickly reverts to his previous sentiment and attraction for Calliste, while she engages in a second conversation with Love, when he explains how the potions work. We are left wondering whether Calliste will choose the amber drink after all, since the fragment breaks off, we are told, 'exactly at the point of greatest interest: we do not know whether Calliste drank from that vial, nor whether she fully loved Philaretes in the end—though it seems he deserved to be so loved'.[43]

---

[41] Cesarotti's novella first appeared in the *Giornale enciclopedico di Vicenza*, vol. 4, published 26 April 1777, and was subsequently published as *Callista e Filetore: Frammento d'una novella greca tradotto dall'abate Melchior Cesarotti* (Piacenza 1794), cf. Papani 1871: vol. 1, 98–9.

[42] This is the frontispiece of a copy of the tale Gigante consulted in the National Library in Naples and therefore something Settembrini may possibly have seen: *I delirij dell'amor platonico: Frammento d'una novella greca tradotta dal signor abate Melchior Cesarotti, Pubblico professore di lingue orientali nell'Università di Padova*: Gigante 1977: 32.

[43] Cesarotti 1863: 131.

As in Rousseau, the focus is on how women should love men—and more specifically on how they might try to maintain their purity while somehow satisfying male sexual needs. In *Settembrini e l'antico*, Gigante recognizes the potential relevance of Cesarotti's *Fragment* to *The Neoplatonists*—though he concludes that it is 'impossible to say whether Settembrini knew of it'.[44] In fact, this can be established—not by looking for references to *Calliste and Philaretes* in Settembrini's *Lectures on Italian Literature* (which is where Gigante sought confirmation) but by consulting the Pessina archive in the National Library in Naples: unpublished materials kept there include a list of Settembrini's books at his death, among which we find an anthology of romances, *Mescolanze d'amore*, which includes Cesarotti's tale.[45] This archival find proves interesting also because the specific anthology within which Settembrini read Cesarotti's 'fragment' prints, as its preface, nothing other than Plotinus' own discussions of love in the third *Ennead*.[46] Settembrini's engagement with Neoplatonism mocks the mystifying apparatus surrounding Cesarotti's fiction, which is itself, as we have seen, quite coy—breaking off precisely at the point where the heroine may just decide to have sex with her sweetheart.

Leaving aside Cesarotti's fake translation, genuine ancient Greek novels were popular in late eighteenth- and nineteenth-century Italy. Authors were keen to write new novels in emulation of ancient ones— also in order to avoid the impression they were simply imitating foreign French and English fiction. Pietro Chiari's *La filosofessa italiana* (1753), generally regarded as the first novel in Italian literature, grapples with precisely that anxiety, as Warholm Haugen has shown.[47] Alessandro Verri's *The Adventures of Sappho, Poetess of Mytilene* (1793) gives us a love story based, allegedly, on a classical, Attic Greek original, itself based on 'ancient inscriptions, volumes that were written in the ancient Aeolic dialect, and oral songs transmitted from earlier times'.[48] Actual ancient Greek novels became available in Italian translation in 1815–16, under

---

[44] Gigante 1977: 34. [45] Pessina Archive B6.4.
[46] Cesarotti 1863: 3–7, translated by Anton Maria Salvini. [47] Haugen 2015.
[48] Verri 1793: 'dichiarazione del traduttore' and chapter 1, pp. 6–7.

the title *Erotici greci*, and then in an expanded edition of that collection in 1833: together with the five main ancient Greek romances, that edition provided access also to Aristaenetus, Alciphron, and Eumathius Macrembolites' Byzantine novel *Ismene and Ismenias*.[49]

Given this general background, it is perhaps unsurprising that the most influential Italian novel of all time, Alessandro Manzoni's *The Betrothed* (published in different versions in 1827 and 1940-2 and, still today, a tool used to educate Italians on the unity of their nation), displays some of the same patterns as the ancient Greek romances and, once again, pretends to be prompted by the discovery of a forgotten document (in this case a seventeenth-century eyewitness account of the plague in Milan).[50] The ruse allows Manzoni to offer his own commentary on the love story he is telling, as well as his criticism of Spanish rule in seventeenth-century Lombardy (and, of course, implicitly, Austrian rule in his own day). Without going into detail here, we note that Manzoni's heroine, Lucia, is quite as pure and clueless as Cesarotti's Calliste. Settembrini, by contrast, suggests that women too, just like men, enjoy having sex and sees in this no cause for reproach. On the subject of female sexual pleasure, *The Neoplatonists* is in line with actual ancient Greek novels—a fact that distances Settembrini from the Enlightenment concerns of Cesarotti or the Catholic commitments of Manzoni (not to mention the heteronormativity of both).[51]

The analysis we have offered so far does not come close to accounting for the density of Settembrini's allusions to ancient and modern literary models. Our notes on *The Neoplatonists* offer some more guidance but, for now, we focus on the cumulative effect of Settembrini's engagement

---

[49] The full title was *Collezione degli erotici greci tradotti in volgare*, first published in Pisa by Capurro in 1814–16 and then in Florence by Passigli in 1833. The five main romances were translated by different writers. Settembrini criticized Annibal Caro's version of Longus in this volume when he came to write the introduction to his translation of Lucian (Settembrini 1861, paragraph LI, n. 17).

[50] Like Settembrini, Manzoni was familiar with, and inspired by, Longus' *Daphnis and Chloe*. See Brambilla Ageno 1965: 555–6.

[51] Dario Del Corno 2008 (incidentally a student of Cantarella, who succeeded him as Professor of Greek in Milan) rightly argues that *The Neoplatonists* expresses Settembrini's exasperation with the classicizing Italian novels written in the eighteenth and nineteenth centuries.

with classical sources.[52] This line of analysis reveals him as more radical and, we argue, even more fun-loving than has been recognized to date. Our main contention is that *The Neoplatonists* attempts to rewrite the history of Platonism by foregrounding a popular, sensual, fictional line of ancient reception at the expense of the 'subtleties and obscurities' of doctrinal Neoplatonism and, to quote Settembrini again, the 'hypocritical' reception it inspired in his day.[53] Recognizing allusions not only helps to understand this broader intellectual framework but also increases readerly pleasure: what Settembrini says of Lucian can be applied to his own fiction, since it too offers 'much enjoyment because of its novelties, pleasant subject and style, bizarre inventions and, above all, for the fact that all these inventions are spicy allusions to tales and wonders told by ancient poets, historians, and philosophers—who are never mentioned by name'.[54]

Beyond giving learned readers the pleasure of discovering allusions by themselves, there is a second—and arguably more important—reason why Settembrini avoids labelling his references to ancient literature: it would compromise the accessibility and popular appeal of his tale. His work, in general, can be seen as poised between eighteenth-century classicism and nineteenth-century romantic commitments to the people. What we see in *The Neoplatonists*, as a result of this confluence, is a deep and detailed knowledge of the classical past combined with an inclusive attitude towards potential readers: the only explicit assumption Settembrini makes of his readership is that we all appreciate the pleasures of sex. When the two boys get too heated in their theoretical comparisons between heterosexual and homosexual pleasures and end up making love, he winks at his imagined readers, concluding: 'What do you expect? They were eighteen.'[55]

His style, popular as it is, should not be seen as a departure from classical models but rather as a specific way of engaging with them. As he put it himself, 'the very wise Greeks wrote up the highest doctrines in

---

[52] For more ample guidance on allusions and intertexts, see Conoscenti 2019. Our notes focus mostly on ancient literature; allusions to Italian literary sources are mostly established through Settembrini's lexical choices—and those choices are largely lost in translation so it seems a little pointless to linger on those in this short book.
[53] Settembrini 1964: 297.   [54] Settembrini 1861, paragraph LI.   [55] See p. 166.

humble and colloquial form'.[56] He accordingly privileged the two Greek prose genres that stood out for their stylistic simplicity and accessibility, namely the dialogue and the novel. The fact that Settembrini read out his translation of Lucian to his cellmates in the Panopticon, who were often illiterate and had difficulties understanding standard Italian (let alone speak it), is relevant here: their reactions guided the development of his style at least as much as the ancient prose works he admired and knew so intimately.[57] That he avoided explicit quotations from ancient authors and (unlike Cuoco) refrained from appending a scholarly apparatus to his Platonic fictions should, then, be seen as a stylistic choice in its own right. It was a choice made, to be sure, in imitation of Lucian and other ancient authors but was also, and importantly, an expression of his commitment to the people of Italy—undereducated, linguistically divided, and politically subjugated as they were.

And here we need to deal with a passage in *The Neoplatonists* that seemingly contradicts everything we have argued so far. Gone is Settembrini the learned classicist and accessible writer, for what we have here is a heavy-handed, explicit reference to Plato—a reference, moreover, that is spectacularly wrong. When Codrus tries to instruct the boys about the true nature of Platonic love, he engages in a little textual exegesis:

> Plato, our divine teacher, means to talk about this kind of love in his works, and not some other kind of love, as people believe. Remember the last words in the *Phaedo*, which are these: "Grant me, ye gods, always to be liked by the beautiful."

The trouble is that the *Phaedo* does not end like that at all—though it does end memorably in its own way. In Plato's actual dialogue, Socrates is in prison, surrounded by his friends, awaiting execution; he has

---

[56] The quotation is taken from an unpublished treatise on Italian literature (Pessina Archive B.C.1-C9 folio 53), discussed in Themelly 1994: 517.

[57] We note here the regrettable fact that the latest editions of Settembrini's translation of Lucian have been tacitly modernized—without marking editorial interventions which are also, in themselves, unnecessary: see further Condello 2014. This lack of respect for Settembrini's prose is, in some ways, a result of his own lack of self-importance.

rejected the very real option of evading and going into exile, as well as the opportunity to have sex (which, in classical Athens, was offered to all inmates on death row), and decided instead to drink his hemlock in the company of friends. Shortly before dying, he uncovers his face one last time, reminding one of them, Crito, 'we owe a cock to Asclepius; pay it and do not forget'.[58] Given that Asclepius was the god of health, and that the sacrifice of a cock was a normal offering after recovery from illness, this final remark—in what is easily Plato's most ascetic dialogue overall—seems to present death itself as a cure from the disease of life.[59]

In his notes on *The Neoplatonists*, Cantarella (followed by Gigante) points out that the words Codrus attributes to Plato do not feature at the end of the *Phaedo*, nor anywhere else in Plato. On that basis, he concludes that the alleged quotation must either be 'a failure of memory' or 'an invention'.[60] Here, however, Cantarella's otherwise precise notes contain an error. First of all, Settembrini is actually quoting from Plato—not from the *Phaedo*, that is true, but from Socrates' conclusion to his so-called 'Palinode' in the *Phaedrus* (257a-b), when Socrates recants all he has said about love and declares himself ready to make amends:

ὦ φίλε Ἔρως ... δίδου τ' ἔτι μᾶλλον ἢ νῦν παρὰ τοῖς καλοῖς τίμιον εἶναι.

Dear Eros ... grant me to be honoured, even more than now, by the beautiful.

It seems, then, that Settembrini is replacing one famous Platonic ending with another, offering not a celebration of death as a release from life (as at the end of the *Phaedo*), but rather an insistence that love requires celebration (as at the end of Socrates' 'Palinode', i.e. his recantation about love, in the *Phaedrus*).[61] What we have, as a result, is not a simple 'invention' but rather something resembling the 'inventions [that] are spicy allusions to ancient poets, historians, and philosophers—who are

---

[58] *Phaedo* 118a.
[59] While in recent years scholars have advanced a number of clever alternatives, this explanation of Socrates' last words remains the most obvious and widely accepted solution.
[60] Cantarella 1977: 113 n. 32. Cf. Gigante 1977: 13.
[61] Cf. Capra 2018: 55–6 and Conoscenti 2019: 128.

never mentioned by name', which Settembrini so enjoyed in Lucian. Still, our initial problem remains, because here the allusion is *not* anonymous and, moreover, involves a blatant *mis*quotation.

Now, before we proceed further in our argument, it may be useful to consider the possibility that Settembrini made a mistake—after all, writing *Phaedo* for *Phaedrus* is easily done. However, the quotation is not found at the end of either dialogue, so we cannot dismiss the whole business as a mistake prompted by a simple switch of titles. More importantly, given that Settembrini copied *The Neoplatonists* more than once, he had the opportunity to notice his mistake, and in general the copy of *The Neoplatonists* in the Biblioteca Nazionale is very carefully produced. Had the tale been an extemporaneous composition written in prison (as Canteralla assumed), the switch from *Phaedrus* to *Phaedo* would seem even easier to make. As it is, we think it possible to explain the misquotation along quite different lines.

We begin, as ever, with Settembrini's training as a classicist and, more specifically, his work on Lucian. In his remarks on *Philosophers for Sale*, he points out a possible error in Lucian's text, when Dion of Syracuse is said to buy Socrates rather than Plato: this, Settembrini insists, is not actually an error 'but fine satire, meant to indicate that Socrates was the true founder of the so-called Platonic school'.[62] Just so, instead of quoting the actual end of the *Phaedo*, and Socrates' famous last words on death, Settembrini quotes the conclusion of Socrates' celebration of love in the *Phaedrus*: this fits the context of the quotation, to be sure, since Codrus and the boys are about to embark on an exploration of lovemaking—but also fits Settembrini's own take on Platonism and, simultaneously, his life experiences.

As we have seen in chapter 5, Settembrini himself became famous because, like Socrates, he was condemned to death for crimes against the state and, after his sentence, had to wait in prison because, again as in the *Phaedo*, a religious holiday delayed the execution. All these similarities must have been obvious to Settembrini, given how well he knew Plato's work. The differences, however, are equally important. Unlike Socrates, who according to the *Phaedo* refused to escape from prison and chose

[62] Settembrini 1988: 1153-4.

death as a cure for the ills of life, Settembrini entrusted himself to joyous and life-affirming recollections, even while the gallows were being erected outside his cell: 'Whenever fortune inflicted on me the worst suffering and sank me into the deepest abyss of pain, the rare moments of happiness in my life came right back to me.'[63] Meanwhile his wife was relentlessly pursuing every available avenue to ensure that his death sentence would be commuted to life imprisonment. And later she coordinated first some daring plans of escape from prison and then petitions in favour of exile.[64] It was because of these efforts, and this joyful devotion to love, rather than ascetic acceptance of death, that Settembrini could see through the work set in motion by the revolution of 1848.

We do not know when Settembrini wrote *The Neoplatonists*, though the version we have is likely to date to around 1872.[65] What we do know for sure is that he copied out the tale shortly before his death in 1876, when he was also working on his *Memoirs*. His deliberate and mistaken quotation—or, we might now say, using his own words on Lucian, his 'fine satire'—replaced Socrates' last words on death with Socrates' wish to remain ever pleasing to the beautiful—a wish devoted to life, pleasure, and the next generation. It is tempting, then, to see in the figure of Codrus at least an element of autobiography: the old professor gets things wrong, to be sure, but he wants to live and love, and is therefore prepared to learn from the young.

Despite the richness of these parallels between fiction, scholarship, and lived experience, Settembrini's deliberate misquotation should not be reduced to autobiography. We expand on its significance for his (and our) views on love, classical literature, and political activism in the next chapter: for now, we note that it expresses, once again and most concisely, his rejection of ascetic Neoplatonism and his celebration of a sensual, popular, and even comical Platonism of the living body. We like to imagine that he introduced his little 'error'—or rather, his moment of autobiographical reminiscing and classicizing allusion—with a smile.

---

[63] This passage, quoted more extensively and discussed on p. 27, refers to Settembrini's first ever night in prison, but also fits with his account of 'three days in the chapel', awaiting execution, discussed on pp. 62–3.
[64] See pp. 55f.   [65] See pp. 26f.

8
How to Live and How to Read

And in the way that, dealing with the dead, you always want to tell them to just come off it—resume being
                                                    Eve Kosofsky Sedgwick[1]

Luigi Settembrini never completed his autobiography, choosing instead to devote his energies to scholarship, public service, and family life—after surviving the revolution. His choices raise the question of what we ourselves may be doing, as classicists,[2] writing about him instead of prioritizing more direct approaches to the study of antiquity, let alone other personal and professional duties. Cantarella, as we saw in chapter 1, sidelined *The Neoplatonists* in order to devote himself to the 'more urgent' task of editing the Herculaneum papyri. His decision may well have been in line with Settembrini's own priorities, given how much he too cared about the papyri and how reluctant he was to present himself as a revolutionary hero in a celebratory autobiography. Still, there is one moment, in *The Neoplatonists*, when he allows himself a reference to one of the most dramatic events in his life—the time when he was almost executed for the role he had played in the revolution of 1848. The passage is, as we have shown, simultaneously a personal memory and a critical reading of Plato and his legacies. And so it is that we start from Settembrini's misquotation—his packaging of his life and revolutionary

---

[1] Kosofsky Sedgwick 1999: 121.
[2] We do not address here the history, practice, and problems of referring to the study of ancient Greece and Rome as 'classics': a good place to start investigating that issue is provided by Hall and Stead 2020. We are not especially attached to this nomenclature and can see good reasons why it might be changed in future, though we also think that a change of name—on its own—is unlikely to signify much. For now, we call ourselves classicists on the basis that we both work in classics departments and feel we belong to the same field as all our departmental colleagues, whatever their specific approaches and areas of interest.

Classics, Love, Revolution: The Legacies of Luigi Settembrini. Andrea Capra and Barbara Graziosi, Oxford University Press. © Andrea Capra and Barbara Graziosi 2024.
DOI: 10.1093/oso/9780198865445.003.0008

convictions inside a philological error, or 'fine satire'—in order to conclude our own intervention.

Settembrini and Socrates are on death row, their execution delayed by a religious feast. Socrates rejects the final opportunity for sex, together with the possibility of escaping, launching instead on a recollection of the metaphysical world beyond sensory perception. Settembrini, by contrast, escapes by returning to the most pleasurable memories of his actual life—while his wife Faucitano works relentlessly, first to have his sentence commuted to life imprisonment and then to have him actually escape from the Panopticon. At the level of Settembrini's biography, then, life and love win over an ascetic acceptance of death. At the level of Settembrini's reading of Plato, the palinode in the *Phaedrus* comes to replace the conclusion of the *Phaedo*.

The reason why Settembrini's palimpsest, his deliberate overlaying of one text with another, has eluded recognition is not that the game he plays is particularly recondite. He engages with two of the most famous passages in the most popular works of one of the most widely read philosophers of all time. The reason, rather, rests in disciplinary specialization. To put it bluntly, scholars interested in the history of sexuality, historians of the Risorgimento, classicists, and philosophers do not talk to each other as frequently or effectively as they might.

The current challenges in the field of classics can themselves be seen, at least in part, as the result of increased disciplinary specialization. Historians rightly insist on the fact that Greece and Rome were slave societies—that is to say, societies whose structure was rooted in the practice of enslavement.[3] This makes it difficult to present the cultural products of those societies, whether literary, artistic, architectural, or philosophical, as models worthy of emulation—without, that is, resorting to wilful selectivity or downright fiction. Settembrini himself was prepared to invent a story that served his purpose and present it as a

---

[3] E.g. Padilla Peralta 2017 and Forsdyke 2021. This historical fact has wide-reaching implications, also at the level of psychology, cf. Carl Jung 1928: 187: 'Every Roman...liv[ed] constantly in the atmosphere of slaves...The explosive spread of Christianity which, so to speak, sprang out of the sewers of Rome—Nietzsche called it a moral slave rebellion—was a sudden reaction that set the soul of the lowest slave side by side with that of the divine Caesar.'

'translation from the Greek', though he also signalled his ruse by choosing a title that had no Greek equivalent.

We are not prepared to write fiction ourselves—though we have certainly been selective. We retrieved from the historical archive the life and work of Settembrini because we were inspired by his rejection of ancient hierarchies placing mind over body, male homosexuality over heterosexual love, and, within male homosexual relationships, an older, active lover above a younger, passive beloved. We also thought it enabling, for our own normative thinking, that Settembrini resisted placing philosophy above literature—and that he approached ancient literature itself in a manner that eschewed hierarchical distinctions between the classical canon and ancient works which, in his time, were excluded from it on the basis of their belatedness, popular appeal, and perceived lack of quality. As we showed in chapter 7, classicists have only recently re-evaluated the erotic and political import of Lucian and the ancient novel, together with their significance as chapters in the reception of Plato.

That Settembrini recognized all this already in the nineteenth century has everything to do with his egalitarian stance in matters both political and sexual. It is a pity that his perceptive reading of imperial Greek literature has attracted so little attention—not only abroad, but also in Italy, and despite the ongoing popular appeal of his translation of Lucian. The reason for this is not that classicists necessarily fail to share Settembrini's political commitments, but rather that the connections between those commitments and his engagement with Lucian and the Greek novels have not been understood.[4] We emphasize the links between Settembrini's various legacies in the hope that this book may be read as a token of our own commitment to an 'expanded classical tradition', a phrase we borrow from Emily Greenwood's current work on Black classicisms. At this moment in the history of classics as a discipline, we believe it useful to foreground the contributions of scholars and

---

[4] The history of nineteenth-century Italian classical scholarship offered by Timpanaro 1965 is a case in point: Timpanaro's own Marxist commitments did not result in an expansion of the classical canon, not even to include later Greek literature; this is in part because he did not share Settembrini's interest in the body and in modelling political equality on the erotic paradigms of the novel. On the relationship between politics and classical scholarship in Timpanaro's own work and its reception, see now Anderson 2021 and ongoing work by Tom Geue.

fiction writers (and Settembrini was both, after all) who, in various ways, testify to the vitality of classical scholarship beyond northern European and North American traditions. We take Settembrini seriously as a representative of the Italian south: his approach to classics was rooted in the *meridione*, a fact that helped him establish fugitive commonalities with Albanian prisoners, disaffected policemen, Black sailors, Sicilian students, and Calabrian peasants.[5] Those encounters, in turn, suggested to him new ways of reading Plato, translating Lucian, and articulating his ancient/future vision of equality and reciprocity in the face of the extreme injustice he denounced in the *Protest of the People of the Two Sicilies* and experienced in his life. Settembrini, we argue in this book, knew how to read ancient Greek texts in relation to the revolutionary potential of the motley crew.[6]

When it comes to his political legacies, there are specific reasons why those too, just as his contributions to classical scholarship, have been sidelined. We have shown how he failed to capitalize on his status as a revolutionary hero: completing and publishing his autobiography in 1860 or in the following decades would have been an advantage to him but, as a contemporary put it, he did not seem too concerned with self-promotion: 'had Luigi been ambitious, he would have held the top positions in government: he, the author of the *Protest*, and extremely popular as he was'.[7] We have offered various explanations, in chapter 5, as to why he never completed his *Memoirs*. The most general can perhaps be stated as follows: he could not fit himself to the pattern of heroic, virile, revolutionary (auto)biography that was becoming canonical during his lifetime—and which set the terms for how the Risorgimento was to be remembered in subsequent histories of the Italian nation.[8] More specifically, Settembrini's conception of equality

---

[5] The Italian *meridione* has been influential in suggesting useful positions for the global south: most famously, Ranajit Guha 1983 and other pioneers of the Subaltern Study Group adopted and expanded the semantic range of the term 'subaltern', coined by Antonio Gramsci, making it one of the most useful concepts in postcolonial criticism. On fugitive commonalities and the vitality of intellectual life beyond—and in opposition to—academic structures, Harney and Moten 2013 is essential reading.

[6] On the motley crew in the eighteenth and nineteenth centuries, and its revolutionary potential, see Harris 2012.

[7] De Sanctis, in his introduction to Settembrini 1892: xii.

[8] Nay 2014 emphasizes the anti-heroic features of Settembrini's autobiographical writings.

and reciprocity in love between men and women, as well as among men, did not conform to emerging notions of Italian masculinity. And so it was that he was soon dismissed as a 'kind rather than a great man'[9]—an assessment that, we believe, confirms the accuracy of our analysis.

And here it may be useful to broaden our discussion to consider, however briefly, an aspect of revolution that has long been identified as a problem: 'women have consistently been let down by revolutionary promises for equality. They have made progress only where they have undertaken their own mass campaigns for the right to vote and women's rights.'[10] This is true in general and also specifically of the French Revolution and the 1848 uprisings inspired by it.[11] In taking down Rousseau, Settembrini was targeting that failure, as we argued in chapter 6. Beyond this, though, he never considered that women may organize as a political force in their own right, or acknowledged the possibility that they may compete rather than collaborate with men. This is in line with Settembrini's general silence on female homosexuality, beyond some telling remarks on Lucian's *Dialogues of the Courtesans*.[12] There were, then, limitations to his vision. Our point stands nonetheless: both his homoerotic imagination *and* his attitude to women clashed with emerging, revolutionary Italian masculinities. Settembrini differed from other revolutionaries also when it came to ethnic diversity—and here too it is worth pointing out that, across different periods and places, post-revolutionary regimes tend to be 'particularly harsh on minorities, who often are scapegoated for social problems and singled out as traitors or

---

[9] This is the verdict of Benedetto Croce (1866–1952), arguably the most influential intellectual in Italy from the late nineteenth century until the Second World War: Croce 1921: 351. For criticism of this position, Conoscenti 2019: 31–2. Tellingly, Settembrini receives almost no attention in recent standard works on Risorgimento Italy such as Banti and Ginsborg 2007 and Banti, Chiavistelli, Mannori, and Meriggi 2011. The same is true of popular anthologies of Risorgimento authors such as Pedullà 2021.

[10] Goldstone 2014: 39–40.

[11] Mastroberti 2012 makes this point and explores it in relation to the making of Italy. As one historian puts it, Italian women were 'citizens without citizenship', who began to compete with men only when they found out that their efforts to support the Italian cause had left them wholly disempowered (Fruci 2006).

[12] What he writes about Lucian's *Dialogues of the Courtesans*, which includes a scene of group sex between three women, suggests his general appreciation and support—at a time when such an attitude was exceedingly rare. He calls the *Dialogues* 'exceedingly useful' as well as beautiful and morally sound. As in *The Neoplatonists*, he uses the thematic verb *compiacersi* (cf. p. 150, n. 7) to describe not only the relationships described in the *Dialogues* but also its effect on readers, Settembrini 1988: 1190.

enemies'.[13] We have already seen how Settembrini emphasized the multiethnic character of ancient and modern Italy—and particularly the south. In this too he was unusual.

A statement he made early on in life, in his *Dialogue on Women*, reveals how in tune he was with current ways of describing the failures of allegedly 'successful' revolutions: as we have seen, he worried that 'those who are strong, even when they are wise, are almost always unjust'.[14] The only answer he had to that problem was an insistence on love as rooted in equality, reciprocity, and justice. Indeed, he saw justice as a *condition* of love in a manner quite as strict as bell hooks's dictum that 'without justice there can be no love'.[15] Settembrini's position on the revolutionary potential of love—indeed on love as a necessary precondition for the revolutionary project—may seem naïve and was often so described in the years after his death. Still, he recognized a problem that is now generally identified as a failure of revolution, namely the unjust treatment of women and minorities. As he pointed out, 'those who are strong'—including those who win revolutions—'are almost always unjust'.[16]

It is for all these different aspects of his life and work that we thought it worthwhile to devote our time to writing this book. It is possible, of course, that we have idealized Settembrini, despite our commitment to factual accuracy. This is all the more likely because we have ourselves been trained in an intellectual tradition that, to use Settembrini's words, places value on 'revealing what is beautiful' rather than 'pinpointing faults'.[17] As an antidote to this risk, we provide our readers with the critical tools needed to judge our own work as well as Settembrini's—including the first English translation of *The Neoplatonists*. This will, we hope, provide more direct access to this text, even when expressed in our English words.[18] We have also included extensive quotations from Settembrini's other works, in order to show on what evidence we have

---

[13] Goldstone 2014: 38–9.   [14] Settembrini in Gigante 1977: 140.
[15] hooks 2001: 30.   [16] Settembrini in Gigante 1977: 140.
[17] Settembrini 1964: 619. On the mechanisms whereby positive evaluation creates literary value, rather than simply reflecting it, Herrnstein Smith 1983 remains a useful point of reference.
[18] We have struggled to match Settembrini's deceptive simplicity; indeed, as one contemporary put it, 'you read him and by some, easy illusion, you believe you can write like that; you try and you fail; you try again and the difficulties just multiply' (Fiorentino in his preface to Settembrini 1879: i).

based our claims. Still, the problem endures: even if we are not prepared to replace literary and historical research with fiction, our selection of quotes, our choices as translators, and our overall selection of Settembrini as a figure on which to focus our efforts, cannot be reduced to a quest for accuracy.

Our approach can, in fact, be compared to that adopted by Constanze Güthenke in her recent study *Feeling and Classical Philology: Knowing Antiquity in German Scholarship, 1770–1920* (Oxford, 2020). In the course of her monograph, she repeatedly draws attention to the language of love used by classical German scholars in describing their relationship to one another and to the ancient subjects of their studies. She rightly points out that although German scholarship is often characterized, especially in the Anglo-Saxon world, as objective and aloof, the language of feeling pervades it. This is also true of Settembrini, as we have seen, even if his conception of love is more explicitly invested in physical pleasure—and in humour—than that of the roughly contemporary scholars on whom Güthenke trains her attention. There is also another and more important difference between her study and ours: Güthenke explicitly withholds love from the subjects of her own enquiry, recommending critical distance, whereas we are happy to treat Settembrini with all the love of which we are capable as scholars and critics.[19] There are two main justifications for our affective investment.

First of all, we have chosen to focus our attention on a marginalized figure: quite apart from the extremes of hardship and injustice he suffered during his lifetime, Settembrini represents a strand of classicism—popular, anticlerical, invested in the pleasures of the body, supportive of homosexuality, affirmative of women's emancipation, and prepared to celebrate ethnic minorities—which current debates about classics are in danger of claiming never existed before current efforts. Secondly, and perhaps more importantly, our mode of reading may help to bring about a transformation: to echo Bruno Latour, it seems important to us to care for 'matters of fact' so that they may become 'matters of

---

[19] Contrast our position with that of Manganelli, who names and shames Settembrini in his preface to the first edition of *The Neoplatonists*: 'we all know who he is... and we do not love him', discussed in chapter 1, pp. 13f. See also our comments on exposure and shame at the end of this chapter.

concern'.[20] The purpose of criticism, then, is not so much to 'debunk but to protect and to care, as Donna Haraway would put it'.[21]

In the past few years, classical scholarship has been rightly exposed as complicit with white supremacy: the Greeks and Romans have routinely been invoked in order to support claims to cultural and, often, racial superiority on the part of European, North American, and specifically white subjectivities. Settembrini's commitment to symmetrical relationships and what he called *reciprocanza* stems from a different reading of the ancient record—a reading informed by the injustices he experienced, witnessed, and denounced in the *Protest of the People of the Two Sicilies*, but also by his critical engagement with Plato's work and its reception history. For all his lightness of touch, Settembrini was not lacking in critical acumen—in fact, his attitude towards the future and the ancient past was, in our view, postcritical: he was interested in what to do *after* pinpointing a fault. He was also interested in postclassical Greek literature: as we have seen, his engagement with Lucian and the Greek novels is in line with current re-evaluations.

We have, then, offered a reading of his work which, we hope, adds care to matters of fact. In an important essay, Eve Kosofsky Sedgwick argues that, confronted with systemic injustice, we may choose various strategies of response: exposing and shaming represents just one possibility among several.[22] The specific example she chooses, in order to launch her argument, is that of the AIDS epidemic: whether or not the virus was deliberately engineered and spread by white, heteronormative forces of oppression (a popular conspiracy theory when she was writing), the lives of Africans, African-Americans, gay men, and drug users were held cheap when the disease broke out—and continue to be of little account also today. That, then, is the fact that deserves affective investment so as to become a matter of concern. This thought has considerable impact on many different domains, including classics as an academic discipline. Exposing the study of ancient Greece and Rome 'as the product and accomplice of white supremacy', to quote a recent article in the *Chronicle of Higher Education*, is one possible move.[23] Sedgwick's point is that it is

---

[20] Latour 2004.   [21] Latour 2004: 232.
[22] Kosofsky Sedgwick 2003: 123–51.   [23] Hanink 2021.

not the only and perhaps not even always the most effective move in confronting the fact of systemic injustice. For one thing, it encourages combative criticism rather than collaboration towards a shared goal—and the splintering into individual antagonisms hardly bodes well for political action. Sedgwick observes that to apply a hermeneutics of suspicion in order to expose sinister mechanisms of power or compulsion is 'widely understood as a mandatory injunction rather than a possibility among other possibilities' in critical theory today. She points out that exposure does not necessarily bring change and proposes, as an alternative, a 'move toward a sustained *seeking of pleasure* (through the reparative strategies of the depressive position)'.[24]

Whatever exactly a reparative reading may turn out to be, and it is a matter of regret that she died before fully exploring the concept, her intuition seems important—and timely.[25] It may even be that practices of reading developed in the field of classics can help to articulate some possibilities for reparation and, as Settembrini would have it, pleasure. The term 'hermeneutics of suspicion' was coined to describe approaches pioneered by Marx, Nietzsche, and Freud in a context that also included alternative practices such as philological and theological attempts to recover meaning. Classics, as a discipline, is still closer to philological concerns than most other humanities, which is why suspicious readings have hit late and, it seems, especially hard. Current debates about the discipline have inspired polarized reactions, whether of self-destruction or denial, which may in fact amount to the same affective stance, namely a fundamental suspicion about the motives and capabilities of our discipline. And here what Sedgwick had to say about the AIDS epidemic seems pertinent: exposing a sinister plot is never the only possible move, whether or not such exposure would correctly represent the facts. The point is never just accuracy, then, the point is care. And the fact that needs an investment of care is the fact of oppression. The question becomes what to do about that, also as classicists.

Reading Plato in the company of Settembrini suggests a few possibilities. The first has to do with exercising the historical imagination:

---

[24] Kosofsky Sedgwick 2003: 137.
[25] Bettini 2023 offers one interesting way to explore the space opened up by suspicious criticism, specifically in relation to the study of Greco-Roman antiquity.

focusing on the distant past helped Settembrini consider models and possibilities for a more equitable future. Secondly, and crucially, the exercise gave him intense pleasure. He survived in the Panopticon also because he was able to escape the harsh realities of the present by travelling in his mind, back and forth, between an idealized past (inspired by the popular, sensual Platonism of Lucian and the novels) and a utopian future. The pleasure he experienced was, moreover, something he was ready to share with his inmates, which may in itself have helped him preserve his life, as well as his sanity, among men who killed one another easily. Beyond prison walls, he also shared his pleasure with more distant readers, including the two of us. We found in his work many sources of inspiration and joy. It so happens that we carried out the bulk of our research and writing in lockdown, during the Covid-19 pandemic: surrounded by every comfort, but separated from our dying mothers, and unable to meet one another in person, we learnt from Settembrini some techniques for better living, grounded in the study of the classical past. One measure involved reading in company, for shared beauty. A second amounted to regular habits of study.[26] A third meant learning from his example: having a laugh, willing the past into the present, and telling Settembrini to 'come off it'—come off the business of being distant and dead, that is—and spend some time with us.

Turning to the past with longing and love can be empowering: we highlighted the nostalgic bend of the new nationalisms in chapter 1; Settembrini, for his part, harnessed his pleasure and nostalgia towards a non-nationalistic and inclusive form of patriotism. We are not alone in suggesting that emotional stances other than critical suspicion may be important in the fight for social justice.[27] In her autobiographical account of Black feminism, Brittney Cooper ends with a postscript on joy which, she insists, 'is different from happiness, because happiness is predicated on "happenings," on what's occurring, on whether your life is going right', whereas 'joy arises from an internal clarity about our

---

[26] On confinement and the psychosomatic habits of intellectual labour, see Gramsci 2001: 498–501 and esp. 500: he explicitly linked his ability to work in prison to the classical training he had received in high school and university.

[27] The point was, of course, already influentially made by Hannah Arendt: she argued for love in response to Nazism, and more specifically for an Augustinian *amor mundi* which bears comparison with the opening sentences in Settembrini's *Memoirs*, quoted on p. 37. For Arendt, love, and totalitarianism, see now Herberlein 2021.

purpose'.[28] That purpose can be tinged with nostalgia, itself a largely pleasurable affect, according to experimental psychologists.[29] We have seen, in chapter 1, how longing for a fictional past can be used in the service of political ends that we find alarming. In response, we have argued that historical accuracy, pleasure, and a commitment to social justice can align—at least occasionally. In order to show this, we have tried to bring out of the historical archive one true story.

This focus on one example from the past as a way of outlining joyful possibilities for the future raises three problems, which we may as well acknowledge by way of conclusion. The first is authorial: we may not have managed to give joy to our readers, for all that we tried. It is not easy to be as pleasure-giving, and seeking, as Settembrini. The second is infrastructural and educational: the historical archive needs to remain open, accessible, and well organized, in order for scholars to go fishing in it for both truth and pleasure.[30] The radical disinvestment not only in classics but in the humanities gives cause for alarm and may jeopardize future scholarly projects of the kind we have attempted here. The third difficulty is affective: seeking pleasure brings with it the risk of shame.[31] To quote Sedgewick one last time, 'the innate activator of shame is the incomplete reduction of interest or joy'; in other words, we may end up feeling ashamed of our own curiosity and pleasure as classical scholars.[32] Settembrini understood this risk and realized that it was best met by trusting in the possibility of being both exposed and loved.[33] As a revolutionary, he had to operate in secret. As an author, he never completed his *Memoirs*. As a classical scholar, he only pretended to translate *The Neoplatonists* from the Greek. And yet he did reveal himself—to our delight—even if only in the form of a playful misquotation.

---

[28] Cooper 2018: 274. [29] Sedikides, Wildschut, Arndt, and Routledge 2008: 52.
[30] Settembrini was a forerunner in both historic preservation and heritage conservation: D'Antuono 2018.
[31] There can be many sources of shame: admitting love for the Greek and Roman classics has, in some contexts, become one of them. There are different ways to deal with the issue: reception studies is, as we argued in chapter 2, one of them.
[32] From the essay 'Shame in the Cybernetic Fold', Kosofsky Sedgwick 2003: 97.
[33] On the importance of shared pleasure and Settembrini's programmatic use of the verb *compiacersi*, lit. 'taking pleasure together', see p. 140, n. 12; p. 150, n. 7; p. 181, n. 6.

PART III
THE NEOPLATONISTS
English Translation and Notes

9
The Neoplatonists by Aristaeus of Megara

Translation from the Greek

Translator's Warning

The Neoplatonists,[1] by Aristaeus of Megara,[2] is one of those Milesian tales[3] which so delighted the supremely delicate Hellenes.[4] It is an obscene narrative up to midpoint,[5] but it is a work of art—and it is translated into Italian because it is a beautiful work of art. We modern men have all the vices and perhaps even more and worse vices than the ancient Greeks. However, we hide them—I do not know whether out of

---

[1] On the title, see pp. 29–31 and 120.
[2] The Italian *Aristeo* is probably meant to translate the Greek Ἀρισταῖος (*Aristaios*), Latinized as Aristaeus in this English translation. The less common Ἀριστεύς (*Aristeus*) is another possibility. Settembrini quotes a fourth-century *Aristeo* in his *Lectures on Italian Literature* (see Conoscenti 2010: 168, for the significance of this) and surely he also had in mind Aristides (late second/early first century BCE), who wrote erotic fictions entitled *Milesian Tales*, now lost but famous in antiquity. Settembrini will have remembered the beginning of Pseudo-Lucian's *Amores*, which he translated in prison: 'This morning I have taken great pleasure in the sweet and wily seductiveness of your immodest stories, so that I almost thought I had turned into Aristides, full of delight at those Milesian tales.' We do not know Aristides' place of origin. Settembrini's choice of Megara seems inspired by Plato's *Phaedrus* 227d (cf. pp. 100 and 107 for the importance of this dialogue) and perhaps also *Theaetetus* 142c: these passages in Plato emphasize proximity to Athens, a detail that is also important in *The Neoplatonists*.
[3] Aristides (see n. 2) wrote tales that were, in all likelihood, set in Miletus; afterwards, however, the term 'Milesian tales' came to describe short obscene fiction as a genre, irrespective of setting.
[4] The phrase *delicatissimi Elleni* recalls Settembrini's description of Lucian in his memoirs (1961: 367): *leggiadrissimo Luciano*.
[5] The midpoint (chapter 5) marks the moment where Hymnis makes the case for heterosexual love; the last three chapters of the tale are not obscene at all, though the story does end with the male protagonists in bed together, as in their youth.

Classics, Love, Revolution: The Legacies of Luigi Settembrini. Andrea Capra and Barbara Graziosi,
Oxford University Press. © Andrea Capra and Barbara Graziosi 2024.
DOI: 10.1093/oso/9780198865445.003.0009

decency or hypocrisy.[6] The ancients hid nothing and, through their art, beautified even their vices. One of the principal traits of Greek Art is that it is not hypocritical: it hides nothing and represents man naked as he is, even in his shameful parts. Moralists may well condemn this tale; artists will certainly take pleasure in it and say that art makes everything beautiful.[7]

This tale, in addition, reveals the antiquity of the view, held by men of discretion, that Platonic love is not absolutely pure and free of all sensuality—for all that some clever types[8] have spread the notion in order to hide their own love affairs with other men. Of this I wanted to warn those who will read the tale.[9]

---

[6] Hypocrisy is one of Settembrini's key criticisms of Catholicism, see e.g. his comments on the effects of the Council of Trent (1964, vol. 1: 372). At the same time, Settembrini also takes direct inspiration from Lucian, especially the end of the *Amores*, where Theomnestus claims that Platonic love is but a hypocritical ruse. For further discussion, see p. 125.

[7] 'Take pleasure in it' translates the Italian verb *compiacersi*, which Settembrini uses, programmatically, in its etymological sense of 'taking pleasure together with somebody else/ others'. The idea is that artists will share in the pleasures experienced by the protagonists and, indeed, the writer. See also the authorial comment below, with n. 9.

[8] 'Clever types' translates *furbi*, a key word in the Italian collective imagination, usually opposed to *fessi*, 'fools'. The term expresses both intellectual admiration and moral distaste. In his influential *Codice della vita italiana* (1921), Giuseppe Prezzolini observed: '*fessi* have principles, *furbi* only have aims'. Hooper (2015: 33) argues that 'an entire history of modern Italy might be written in terms of the never-ending struggle between its *fessi* and its *furbi*'. Settembrini chose this word with precision, then: it underlines the moral corruption of hypocritical *furbi* who invented purely spiritual Neoplatonism, but also expresses admiration for their ability to protect their homosexual love affairs.

[9] This 'translator's warning' can be usefully compared to a handwritten note, kept in the National Library in Naples, in which Settembrini issues another 'warning', *avvertenza*, concerning his translation of Lucian: he insists that the 'five obscene works' by the ancient author should be published separately from the rest of his work: see Conoscenti 2019: 75. The same plan also features in a letter to his wife, discussed on p. 72.

THE NEOPLATONISTS BY ARISTAEUS OF MEGARA   151

Chapter 1

In the city of Athens, district of Collytus,[1] there lived a wealthy citizen called Euphranius.[2] His wife, a woman from Andros named Tecmessa,[3] was very beautiful and gave him a baby boy, whom he named Callicles.[4] The child was very pretty and looked just like his mother.[5] A friend and neighbour, called Phemius,[6] also became the father of a boy, by a woman from Megara called Doris:[7] the child, who was beautiful and had sweet eyes, was named Dorus.[8] The two boys grew up together and loved each other wonderfully: if one cried, his mother knew no other way to calm him down than to call the other child; as soon as the second boy arrived, the first would dry his tears, break into a smile, and walk towards his friend; they would then amuse themselves together for many hours a day. When Callicles was given some fruit, or some honey cakes, he wanted to share his food with Dorus; when Dorus had a new little dress, he begged Tecmessa to make a similar tunic for Callicles. Every day the two boys, fresh, clean, and bright, would walk together to school, accompanied by their servants. They soon learnt to read and write, showing great intelligence, and, after school, they attended the gymnasium for the young, where they trained naked—running, wrestling, and throwing the discus.

---

[1] One of the districts or 'demes' of Attica, located within the city walls of Athens: ancient biographies of Plato claim that it was his neighbourhood (see Nails 2002: 243–4 and 353).

[2] The opening echoes the beginning of various ancient Greek novels, especially those by Chariton and Xenophon of Ephesus. The difference is that we start with a 'citizen' rather than a prince or a king. The name 'Euphranius' means 'of cheerful mind'.

[3] Tecmessa is a rare name in Greek: Settembrini must have taken it from Sophocles' *Ajax*.

[4] 'Callicles', i.e. 'famous for his beauty', is the name of a young philosopher in Plato's *Gorgias*: there are some common traits between the two characters, particularly their youth, beauty, and appreciation of pleasure; but also important differences (Plato's Callicles is antidemocratic). Settembrini seems to have been primarily influenced by the etymology of the name, its generally Platonic flavour, and the names of the two main adversaries in the *Amores*, Callicratides and Caricles (the latter features in the manuscript of *The Neoplatonists* and is corrected to Callicles, in Settembrini's hand).

[5] This is one instance where Settembrini gently corrects ancient notions according to which the mother is merely a receptacle for the male seed, without otherwise contributing to the makeup of the child. Here and elsewhere in Settembrini, male and female beauty are undifferentiated, cf. 1971: 776–7.

[6] This is the name of the singer working at the palace of Odysseus in Ithaca: he is prominent in the *Odyssey* and is also mentioned in Lucian, *On the Hall* 18.

[7] A common Greek name, meaning 'Dorian woman', it also features in Lucian, *Marine Dialogues* 1.1. On Megara, a Doric city, see p. 149, n. 2, and p. 152, n. 10.

[8] The boy is named after his mother, see above, n. 7.

152 CLASSICS, LOVE, REVOLUTION

In short, they were beautiful, clever, and strong. And they were always together, never leaving each other for a moment, and holding hands in the street: those who saw them took great pleasure in them and called them 'the Dioscuri'.[9] They assumed they were brothers and said, 'How blessed the mother who gave birth to them!'

Now it came to pass that Tecmessa fell ill and soon died. Euphranius, who loved her very much, suffered such acute grief that he died himself shortly afterwards, leaving his only son in the care of Phemius, with the recommendation that he bring him up as his own son, together with Dorus. Poor Callicles cried bitterly at the loss of his mother and father. He moved into Phemius' house, where his dear Dorus was always near him, tried to console him, and often cried with him. Phemius and Doris brought up Callicles lovingly, as if he were their own child, faithfully managing his inheritance and increasing it in value.

The two boys, who were of the same age, were now about twelve: they went to school together and then to the gymnasium; they learnt the poems of Homer, Hesiod, and Theognis;[10] and they read Herodotus' *Muses*.[11] Callicles was the fastest runner among their peers and Dorus the strongest wrestler. They lived in this manner for some more years, acquiring useful knowledge and strengthening their beautiful, alert bodies. They lived in the same house, ate at the same table, slept in the same room, and shared the same bed: often, intertwining their legs and feet like the two snakes round Mercury's wand,[12] they would caress each other, embrace, and sweetly fall asleep. They grew their first soft beards at the same time and each took pleasure in the other: together they went into the city, together to the countryside, and together I saw them in Megara, on a farm that belonged to Doris.[13] At the festivals in honour of

---

[9] The twin demigods Castor and Pollux, whose mother, Leda, also gave birth to Helen of Troy.

[10] It may be relevant that Theognis was from Megara and that many of his elegies dealt with love between men and boys.

[11] Ancient grammarians named the nine books of Herodotus' *Histories* after the Muses, cf. Lucian, *Herodotus* 1 and *On How to Write History* 42.

[12] The caduceus, a short staff entwined with two snakes and sometimes surmounted by wings, was the symbol of the Greek god Hermes (Roman Mercury). In Italy, it represents the order of pharmacists: Settembrini wrote for readers who could easily picture it.

[13] On the basis of Pseudo-Lucian *Amores* 1 (quoted at p. 149, n. 2), it is tempting to conjecture that the original *Milesian Tales* by Aristeides also contained a first-person claim of this kind by

the gods, they stood out in the chorus of boys: all the girls in the other chorus had their eyes on them.[14] Everyone said that the sons of Phemius were the most beautiful boys in town.

One day, after a procession, Callicles said, 'Did you notice, Dorus, with what loving eyes those virgins looked at us—those right at the front, walking closest to the statue of the Goddess?'[15] 'You are right, they are beautiful,' Dorus answered, 'they have beautiful eyes and lovely, golden hair.' And Callicles replied, 'Yes, but your eyes are more beautiful!' then kissed his eyes. Callicles kissed him back, saying, 'This hair that tumbles down like apium[16] is more beautiful than their tresses! How beautiful you are, Callicles, my friend.' 'And how beautiful you are, Dorus, my Dorus.'[17] Speaking these words, they embraced, held tight, pressed their mouths together, and gave each other a long kiss, then sighed.

They had already become ephebes[18]—and already felt that inner stirring, that anguish, which is the first sign and whisper of love. Dorus spoke, 'I feel, Callicles, that I love you with a new intensity, greater than what I felt so far. I think it is the kind of love that, according to the divine Plato, the Gods place only in the heart of the wise, the kind of love that nourishes wisdom and makes it pure, that unites young warriors and

---

the author. Settembrini seems to have drawn this conclusion, which is shared by scholars today. The fact that the alleged author of *The Neoplatonists* comes from Megara, a city not too distant from Athens, makes the conceit of eyewitness testimony sound more plausible.

[14] This is a standard scene in the Greek novel, see esp. Chariton 1.4–6, Xenophon of Ephesus 1.2, and Heliodorus 3.3–4.

[15] The goddess in question is Athena, patron deity of the city: later in the text, Settembrini specifically mentions the ancient Panathenaic festival dedicated to her. The description here may be influenced by Thucydides 6.56, where a girl is asked to carry a basket in a procession, but is then not allowed to do so because her virginity is doubted: the incident contributes to the assassination of the tyrant Hipparchus, p. 157, n. 6. Settembrini's description of this scene also recalls Catholic processions. In *Lectures on Italian Literature* (ed. Settembrini 1964: 372), he explicitly suggests a parallel: 'Catholicism, with its rituals, processions, symbols, its cult of saints and images, absorbed a great part of pagan religion: this suits the Italian character, since it is imaginative, cheerful, and alive amidst beautiful, smiling nature—nature both adorable and pagan.'

[16] The likeness is taken from *Amores* 26; several different species of plant belong to this genus, among them celery.

[17] See above, n. 5, on the lack of differentiation between male and female beauty, as well as pp. 170 and 181.

[18] In Athens in the fourth century BCE, the term 'ephebe' specifically described eighteen-year-old boys who entered a two-year period of military service, but Settembrini seems to use it in the more general ancient meaning of 'boys who have reached sexual maturity'.

makes them brave.' 'Yes, Dorus,' said Callicles, 'I love only you, and more powerfully than before: I think this Platonic love has taken root in us. Let us enjoy it now, because now is the right time.'

When the two boys lay in each other's arms they looked like two *medimnus* measurements of purest flour.[19] Their bodies were of the whitest white, with touches of pink. They shone bright and had the fresh smell of youth, and were constantly clean from bathing. They kept looking at each other, caressing and touching each part of their bodies. They kissed each other's eyes, faces, chests, stomachs, thighs, and feet—feet that seemed made of silver. They held each other tight, intertwining, one tongue in the other's mouth, drawing from it the nectar of the Gods. They would spend a long time sucking that nectar, interrupting only once in a while to smile at each other, call each other by name, and then drawing each other close to their chests, drinking that sweetness again.

Not content with embracing each other chest to chest, one youth would hold the other from behind, and attempt to enter between his two beautiful apples,[20] but the other would feel pain, so the first would withdraw, not wanting to cause agony to his beloved. Repeatedly each tried this game in turn, but neither managed to succeed—until Dorus got up and said, 'A Deity suggests a solution to me.' He took a flask of the purest oil, which shone like golden amber, and added, 'Let us anoint both key and lock with this oil and try again whether we can manage to open up.' They thoroughly anointed key and lock and, in this manner, Dorus entered victorious, without much trouble for himself or discomfort for Callicles. In the same manner, Callicles also entered and enjoyed the same victory. That way they both felt happy and both enjoyed the first fruit of their love. On that same day they climbed up the acropolis, entered the temple of the virgin Pallas Athena, patron of the olive tree, and thanked her for the solution she had suggested, namely to use oil, as

---

[19] The *medimnus* was a unit of measurement standardly used for cereals.
[20] The buttocks are never described as 'apples' in ancient Greek sources, where the term is reserved for breasts (e.g. Aristophanes, *Lysistr.* 155; *Thesm.* 903; Theocritus, *Id.* 27.30). In Italian, 'apples' for 'buttocks' is well attested; Settembrini uses the term not only here but also in his translation of Lucian, *Amores* 14, see Settembrini 1988: 493, with Casi 1991: 61.

students and lovers do.[21] From that day onwards, love caused them no more craving or anguish and in fact made them calm.[22] The boys attended to their studies and to their duties, in the home and on their land; they talked sensibly to people; and, after their various daytime occupations, entered their faithful little room, enjoying every sweetness, sip by sip. They would take time to look at and admire each other's bodies; touch and caress each other; exchange the sweetest kisses in the mouth; and finally anoint each other, using that divine flask, and enter into the final enjoyment. Afterwards, they would feel tired and fall asleep. Often, on waking up in the morning, they would find they were still holding each other in an embrace.

Thus they lived, enjoying themselves with temperance. Each would have an equal share, taking turns in everything and always, as love and justice demand. The two boys swore on this—and they kept to their promise for the rest of their lives.[23] I think that, if the Gods take an interest in what men do,[24] they must have taken great pleasure[25] in this most beautiful thing. Perhaps they even felt some envy[26] for two blooming boys who were in love and delighted in each other, in accordance with justice and love.

---

[21] Lovers need oil for the purposes just illustrated, cf. Aristophanes, *Clouds* 977, extolling a past of greater chastity, when 'no boy oiled himself below the navel' (a play and passage that was on Settembrini's mind, cf. p. 168 n. 8 where he is thinking of the lines immediately following). Students need oil lamps to read

[22] In Plato's *Symposium* 191a–c, Aristophanes presents sex as a device ($\mu\eta\chi\alpha\nu\dot\eta$) for reaching a state of calm productivity.

[23] The one and only anticipation in the whole narrative.

[24] The idea that the gods rejoice at the sight of human lovers is prominent in ancient literature, including Plato's *Symposium* 179b–180b. Settembrini may also have been influenced by Lucretius.

[25] Again, the thematic verb *compiacersi*, see p. 15, n. 7.

[26] In Greek myth, the gods are often said to feel envy for mortals, especially when the latter are in their prime.

Chapter 2

The boys attended the school of Codrus,[1] a Platonic philosopher who enjoyed great repute in Athens. The school faced onto the main road leading to Piraeus, not far from the little temple of Apollo.[2] Athenian and foreign youths gathered there to listen to Codrus, who was a good speaker and had a pleasant appearance, lacking the scowl of the philosopher: he was about forty, dressed neatly, and had an easy smile. People said that he was the only teacher who really understood Plato and could explain his doctrine. The two boys listened to him with great attention, writing down on their tablets the beautiful things they heard, in order to remember them more easily: after school, they would often go to the sacred grove of Apollo and, taking leisurely walks by themselves, would discuss what the teacher had said. One day, they saw Codrus himself taking a leisurely walk in the grove all alone, so they went to him and extended a greeting. He answered with a smile, 'What are you doing here, you two beautiful boys?' 'We were having a discussion.' 'About what?' 'About what we heard you say in school today.' 'And will you let me intervene between the two of you?[3] Let us sit on this marble bench here, where laurel[4] branches offer the thickest protection against the rays of the sun.'

After seating himself between the two boys and taking each by the hand, he said, 'A poet would declare that you two boys resemble the steeds of the sun: you are so beautiful and bright, and you always travel together.[5] But I, for my part—and I have observed you for a while—I declare that you are in love. Please do not blush because being in love is nothing shameful; in fact, it is a precious gift that the Gods grant only to the few and the best.' Callicles answered, 'Yes, we love each other and we

---

[1] Codrus was the name of the last, mythical kings of Attica; Settembrini probably had in mind a passage in Lucian where somebody is described, ironically, as 'nobler than Codrus, more beautiful than Nireus, wiser than Odysseus' (*Dialogues of the Dead* 9).

[2] Settembrini may be referring to the small temple of Apollo Patroos, on the west side of the agora, near the road to Piraeus (cf. Pausanias 1.3.4).

[3] This prefigures more concrete interventions later in the chapter.

[4] Laurel is sacred to Apollo.

[5] Codrus speaks in a pastiche of Platonic allusions, starting with the allegory of the chariot pulled by two horses (*Phaedrus* 246a–254) and ending with the deliberate misquotation allegedly from the *Phaedo*, but in fact *Phaedrus* 257a.

have no reason to blush or feel shame because we do not harm anyone else—nor, indeed, do we harm ourselves.' Codrus added, 'You, boys, behave like Harmodius and Aristogeiton, who freed Athens and also loved each other.[6] The Athenians set up statues commemorating those two lovers and made sacrifices in their honour, as they do in honour of the Gods. Achilles and Patroclus, those two great heroes who gave their lives in Troy, were likewise lovers: when Patroclus died, Achilles cried bitterly and, remembering all the sweet things they had enjoyed together, missed with greater passion

"that sweet habit
of lingering between your thighs, in all devotion".[7]

Among the various armies of Greece, which is the bravest? The one made up of lovers who fight in couples, helping each other. Love turns them into heroes and they accomplish the greatest feats, which are then remembered in our stories. In short, boys, let me tell you that all the best Hellenes, those who have the greatest wisdom, and most cultured mind, and most gentle habit, are lovers in their youth, just in the same way as you are—and some remain lovers also later, in their maturity and old age.'

At this point, Dorus asked, 'You too, Codrus, are in love?';[8] 'Yes, young man,' answered Codrus, 'and when I was a boy, my teacher Cleobulus[9] loved me, and I remember him fondly. Now I love a young man who is as old as you are: he went to Larissa a few days ago in order to claim his father's inheritance.' Dorus asked, 'And does this Thessalian boy love you?' 'Yes, he does, because I love him: he wants to come back

---

[6] Harmodius and Aristogeiton, who were lovers, killed the tyrant Hipparchus in 414/13 BCE and were celebrated in Athens as paving the way for democracy: Thucydides 6.57.2. They feature in Plato's *Symposium* 182c and Pseudo-Lucian's *Amores*.

[7] A fragment of Aeschylus' lost tragedy the *Myrmidons* (fr. 136 TrGF), which Settembrini knew from a quotation in Pseudo-Lucian's *Amores* 56 (without knowing its provenance). He translates the original μηρῶν τε τῶν σῶν εὐσεβὴς ὁμιλία (lit. 'the pious company of your thighs'), turning the second line into an hendecasyllable, the main metre of Italian poetry.

[8] A nice touch: the young are startled by the possibility that Codrus, old as he is, may also be in love.

[9] A common name in Greek, which means 'famous for his good counsel'.

soon and live with me; just as I wish to see him again.[10] Without him I am unhappy, as you see me. Let us therefore discuss this kind of love. Plato, our divine teacher, means to talk about this kind of love in his works, and not some other kind of love, as people believe.

'Remember the last words in the *Phaedo*, which are these: "Grant me, ye Gods, always to be liked by those who are beautiful."[11] This is the pure and sacred love which he discussed so often and in such depth. Now, this kind of love is perfect when found in two young people such as you are, graceful of body, quick of intellect, and nourished with good Literature: this is because they take pleasure in their love with temperance (since the characteristic feature of this love is, very precisely, temperance). They do not exhaust and ruin their bodies by loving women, whose desire is insatiable;[12] nor do they deplete their own households by offering mad and lavish gifts to courtesans, who the more they receive the more they demand; nor are they tormented by jealousy: they never get involved in abductions, fights, wounds, or murders;[13] but, rather, after sharing some delight, they study together—and go to war together, and act as shields for each other. This kind of love is based on the law of reciprocity and, for this reason, is best practised by young people of the same age and, second best, by those who are not too distant in age from each other.'

Callicles asked, 'So was there any reciprocity between you and your teacher Cleobulus—and between you and the boy from Larissa?' 'Let me tell you this, Callicles,' answered Codrus, 'love without reciprocity is barbaric rather than Greek; it is not love at all, but rather some kind of

---

[10] There is a suggestion here that Codrus is a little more in love with the young man from Larissa than the reverse, just as the old man Cleonymus loves young Hymnis more ardently than she loves him (see pp. 168f.). This fits with Settembrini's view that lovers should ideally be of the same or similar age and his insistence on symmetry and reciprocity.

[11] As we discuss in chapter 7, this quotation does not conclude the *Phaedo*, but rather Socrates' speech on love in the *Phaedrus*, 257a–b.

[12] The insatiability of female desire was a commonplace in ancient Greek thought. Hesiod complains about women being most demanding at the end of summer, when men are most exhausted from the harvest: *Works and Days* 586. The Hesiodic *Melampodia*, fr. 275 MW (= Apollod. 3.6.7) is the earliest attestation of the myth according to which Teiresias, having been both man and woman, said women experienced far greater pleasure than men. Settembrini himself does not seem to have shared Codrus' view, cf. p. 172, n. 4.

[13] Settembrini reports several stories of abductions, fights, wounds, and murders he heard in the Panopticon. The most significant, from the point of view of this passage and *The Neoplatonists*, are those concerning Gennarino, for which see Settembrini 1971: 459 and our discussion of this important person in Settembrini's life on pp. 73f.

fury that overwhelms and damages somebody else, who is in no position to do to you what you did to him.' 'And yet,' Dorus observed, 'many criticize this kind of love; and even more people find fault with the law of reciprocity.'[14] 'And who are these people?' Codrus replied. 'They are people who have no knowledge of this kind of love and criticize what they do not know. Those who have felt this amorous delight thank the Gods for it. And I'll tell the others: try, see, learn first, and then we'll talk about it again. And to those who argue against the law of reciprocity I will say that they deny that two is a greater number than one, meaning that two pleasures amount to more than just one. Love is something sacred; taking pleasure in love without offending anyone or shaming oneself, taking pleasure equally—well this is how love grows to fulfilment. Boys, you must not listen to those who do not know what they are talking about. Moreover, in this case, knowledge does not originate in the mind, but rather stems from experience and action. Those who never tried should not talk. And you, dear boys, should know that this kind of love, like everything else, needs art in order to reach perfection—and this art is a subject that can be learnt.' 'What kind of art is it?' asked Callicles. 'You, who know so many things and have entered so deeply into the doctrine of the great philosopher, do you perhaps master also this art?' 'I do master it, and I could teach it to you, if you so wished.' Dorus answered, 'Please do, we would like to make you our teacher also in this kind of art. Please tell us and we'll listen to you'. 'Every art is learnt by practising rather than talking. If you want to come home with me, I'll show you the art in question and I will explain it to you to the best of my powers.' The two boys looked up and, after exchanging a few meaningful looks, Callicles answered, 'We'll come with you and see how you practise this art!'

They thus set off for Codrus' house. When they arrived, he gave orders to a servant to prepare a table with a few sesame cakes,[15] some beef with

---

[14] An important sentence in *The Neoplatonists*, linking sexual fantasy to political programme.
[15] Lucian mentions sesame cakes at *Piscator* 41. For sesame cakes as food traditionally served at weddings, see Aristophanes, *Peace* 868-70: 'The girl is coming out of the bath, with her beautiful backside, the flapjack is baked and they are kneading the sesame cakes too. Nothing's lacking except for the bridegroom's tool.'

gravy, a bowl of fruit picked just then from the garden, and a bottle of Chian wine. Then he sent out the servant on some errand and, turning to the two boys, said, 'You are my guests, please accept this gift of hospitality.' After they had eaten and drunk that excellent wine, and had a chance to relax, Codrus led them to a small room. A deep, soft rug from Tarentum lay on the floor, scattered with cushions on which the three men sat, after taking off their sandals. Codrus then said, 'First, we need to reveal our bodies, because there is beauty in all body parts, and it is for the eyes to take the first pleasure.' So all three lay naked: the two boys were bright and trim; Codrus displayed his white, clean flesh, an appetizing sight. He had very beautiful hands. The two young men touched his sizable apples and chest, while he squeezed and kissed each boy in turn.

'Herein lies the art,' he said, 'except that it can be practised only with one person at a time. Let us start with you, Dorus. First, it is necessary to kiss these eyes, my beautiful Dorus, for your eyes are so sweet. Then comes a long, long, long kiss in the mouth, my tongue darting inside yours and yours in mine.' 'We already knew this,' said Callicles, 'love taught us as much.' Codrus continued, 'I'll kiss your nipples, just so, and suck a little. I'll stroke your belly with my hand, lightly, and all the way down to the hair covering your lap, and I'll hold this beautiful flower here, which now stands erect on its stem, so very boldly. What a beautiful flower! It has the colour and perfume of a rose; it seems to want to open its mouth and talk to me! And now my hand will caress further and with a finger sweetly try the door.' 'This is no new art for us either,' said Callicles. 'Please let me kiss your shoulders, back, and apples,' Codrus added. 'What beautiful apples of the Hesperides; here comes Hercules to pick this precious fruit.' At this, good old Codrus anoints his Hercules with perfumed oil, embraces Dorus and, after two or three sweet attempts, enters the divine orchard of the Hesperides.[16] They lie, embracing tightly on the rug, conjoined, and Callicles, at that sight, can no longer keep himself in check and, after anointing his own nail,[17] directs it

---

[16] On the switch from the past to the present tense, see below, p. 172, n. 5.
[17] 'Nail' for penis is used also in antiquity: Aristophanes, *Ecclesiazousae* 1020 and *Palatine Anthology* 5.129.

between Codrus' fleshy apples—and sinks in at once.[18] Startled, Codrus lets go of Dorus but immediately takes him again, saying, 'Well done, boys, stick to it! You, Dorus, ahead of me and you, Callicles, behind: we need to hold on tight and keep on track.'[19] After they had run the course of one station, Codrus said, 'I wanted to teach you the art—but you, divine boys, are teaching me something quite new, how to take the two pleasures of love at one and the same time. I thank the Gods for having learnt this more refined art.' 'Enough,' said Dorus, 'time for reciprocity.' And with this all three turned around, Codrus held the expert Callicles, while Dorus, with equal impetus and skill, entered Codrus' garden, who sighed loudly.

After they completed that second stadion, and after washing their limbs in a basin, Codrus insisted that they pour a libation of wine in memory of Plato, naked as they were, and then drink from the same cup. After making their libations, and drinking, and kissing one another, Codrus embraced both boys and said, 'Two pleasures at the same time! Still, if I had to choose between them, what you gave me seemed to me the sweeter pleasure.' 'We too, teacher, experienced a new pleasure as we entered the deepest recesses of your Platonic wisdom.' 'May the Gods bless you, boys. Do not forget that you acquired this new knowledge of pleasure in the company of a Platonic philosopher.' The two boys got dressed and left. They Platonized a few more times with their teacher in that manner, until the young man from Larissa returned to Athens.

---

[18] The same arrangement features in an epigram by Strato, *Palatine Anthology* 12.210.
[19] The metaphor comes from ancient athletics and, more specifically, running the length of a stadion in one direction and then, after turning round the post, in the other.

Chapter 3

It was the time of the Panathenaic festival and a multitude of people, local citizens and foreigners alike, thronged the streets of Athens.[1] Callicles and Dorus held hands in the crowd in order not to get separated, but there was a sudden surge of people, a commotion, and some jostling, so the two friends were torn apart and did not see each other for a few hours. Eventually, Dorus recognized Callicles in the distance, near the temple of the Dioscuri,[2] and called out to him. When they got together, he said, 'What is going on, Callicles? You seem happier than usual.' 'Yes, my Dorus, I'm happy because the Gods granted me some good fortune and I have conceived a new idea. Come here, let us sit at the foot of this column, far away from the crowd, so you can listen to me.' 'Oh, what could this be, my brother?' Callicles began as follows:

'When the crowd tore me away from you and I could no longer see you, I looked for you everywhere and kept asking any acquaintances I met whether they had seen you. Then I saw a band of young women and, among them, Hymnis, the beautiful dancer—do you remember her?[3] The one who always giggles as soon as she sees us, and winks, and calls us the philosophizing Dioscuri?' 'That lass with black hair and lively looks? Yes, I know her!'

'So I ask her, "Have you seen Dorus?" "Yes," she says. "And where is he?" "Here," she says, and she opens up her dress and shows me her nipples, adding in a whisper, "If you follow me, we'll find him." Easily she gets rid of her friends and goes into a narrow alley. I follow her and, after a short walk, we enter her house. "O Hymnis," I say, "please let me see exactly where you are hiding my friend." And she answers, "Sure, you little philosopher!" And so it was that I saw and kissed two little titties: they were of the whitest white—and quite hard. "He's not here," she said. "But we'll find him somewhere else." So I answered, "Hymnis, I don't

---

[1] The Panathenaic festival was the most important festival in ancient Athens: it celebrated the patron goddess of the city. As Settembrini states, it attracted foreign visitors as well as local crowds.
[2] See p. 152, n. 9: the boys resemble the deities to whom the temple is dedicated. For discussion see also p. 126.
[3] The atmosphere is that of New Comedy: a play by Caecilius Statius was entitled *Hymnis*.

know the place you mention and have never been there, nor has my friend, so you'll have to guide me." And she, bursting with delight, exclaimed, "Is that so?", stroking my face and kissing me. "In that case, I'll be the one who picks this flower!" Then, taking my flower into her hands, she admired it at length, kissed it all over, smelled it, and said, "It looks like a rosebud that is about to bloom." Then she throws herself belly up on the bed and pulls me over, while, with her hand, she places my bud inside her little vase. She tightens her arms around my neck, crosses her legs over my back, and starts to meow. Her eyes turn inside her head, and she starts to waggle, and she bites my lip, and, after quite some waggling, we come to a halt together. "Don't get out," she says, and tightens her legs around my back: after a while, we give it another working, reaching the same sweetness.[4]

'Afterwards, she dried and cleaned my flower, held it, and touched it; and I drew into my mouth first one breast, then the other, and delighted myself caressing her thighs and apples. And what beautiful apples are those! White and shiny like Parian marble! And round and large and utterly fresh! Suddenly a thought crossed my mind and I exclaimed, "Say, Hymnis, you feasted your eyes on my flower. Now please let me do the same with the little basket where we placed it—since I've never seen such a basket. It is my first!" She gets up, refreshes herself with water, dries herself with a perfumed little towel, and returns to me, saying, "You should have seen this basket when it was new! But even now it is not spoilt at all; it's small and smells lovely." I saw it, O Dorus, and I greeted the sacred door of life and pleasure, the door through which man comes out into the light of the sun: it looks like a cave sacred to some mysterious God, the cave of Pan covered in lush, soft vegetation. I saw it, I greeted it, I kissed it again, and we celebrated the third mystery: we took our third pleasure, which was longer, if less intense. Finally, I gave Hymnis one more kiss and went to look for you, to tell you about this adventure of mine!'

---

[4] This entire description uses several expressions found in Boccaccio, Masuccio and other early Italian authors, see Conoscenti 2010, who draws attention to the implications of this for dating *The Neoplatonists,* and our own discussion at pp. 26f.

Poor Dorus, during this report, had gone bright red in the face and felt that his blood was boiling. After Callicles was done, he observed, 'Now you know something that I do not know.' 'Would you also want to acquire this new knowledge?' 'For sure, my Callicles!' he answered. 'Your words have inspired in me the most ardent desire!' 'Then come with me,' said Callicles. They went on their way and, after a while, they knocked on Hymnis' door. As soon as she saw the two young men, she declared that she was expecting them, gave them an enthusiastic welcome, and thanked Callicles with a kiss. He told her, 'Look what second lovely gift I bring for you. You'll pick this other flower and, while the two of you enjoy each other, I will take pleasure looking at you hugging and holding onto each other.' 'Please don't!' said the woman. 'All right,' answered Callicles, 'Would you like me to leave or entertain myself with your maid?' 'Actually,' she added, 'you are welcome to watch, if that is what you want.' Meanwhile, Dorus planted on her lips a long and tasty kiss and, after a few caresses, she exclaimed, 'Holy Venus of the Gardens,[5] I thank you for the good fortune you bestow upon me, since you let me pick, on the same day, that lovely rosebud and this carnation, the most beautiful flowers in the entire garden of Athens' virility!' They mingled and Callicles took pleasure in looking at Hymnis' naked feet as they tightened around Dorus' strong back. The latter, meanwhile, applied himself to the task with great vigour. Whenever Callicles caressed those lovely feet, which seemed made of crystal,[6] she twitched and he said with a smile, 'Enjoy yourselves!' Our Callicles was a true philosopher: he wanted to see, and observe, and touch everything.[7] After the work was done, the woman placed herself between the two boys and, giving many kisses to each of them, she let her head rest on the chest now of one, now of the other, saying, 'You beautiful Dioscuri, you are not men but immortal Gods! That is how beautiful you are and how powerfully

---

[5] Venus, i.e. Aphrodite 'of the Gardens', had a cult in Athens: this is something Settembrini knew from Lucian, *Dialogues of the Courtesans* 7.1.

[6] 'Made of crystal' is a detail taken from early Italian literature. Settembrini discusses the expression in chapter 9 of his *History of Italian Literature*, when illustrating Spanish and Arabic influences (1964: 68). For the relevance of this for dating *The Neoplatonists*, see p. 26.

[7] The scene mirrors the earlier encounter with Codrus—except that, in this case, Callicles limits himself to observation and does not join in the action.

your beauty affects me. Do not forget poor Hymnis, you beautiful Dioscuri, with whom you celebrated your first Panathenaic feast.' After exchanging some more caresses, the boys left.

When they got home, after enjoying a pleasant family meal, they retired to their bedroom, climbed into their bed, and intertwined their legs, as they always did. Thus entwined, Callicles asked, 'What do you think, my Dorus, of the pleasure we experienced with Hymnis today?' 'It seems to me,' Dorus answered, 'that it is a great pleasure indeed, and quite different from what we have together: it is something else entirely.' 'And what seems to you the greater pleasure?' Dorus answered, 'I cannot compare them because our pleasure is accompanied by love whereas the other happened without love.' 'Yes, but let us just compare pleasure with pleasure,' Callicles insisted. 'If you want my opinion, I'll give it to you. With Hymnis I felt a new intoxication, something much stronger than the usual sweetness.' 'You describe what I also experienced,' answered Callicles, 'and I truly do not understand why the philosopher does not praise that inebriating pleasure and goes as far as discouraging wise men from pursuing it.' 'I think,' Dorus answered, 'that this is precisely because it intoxicates and upsets reason and because, after that drunkenness, many irritations ensue: we did not experience those because we only indulged once, but jealousy, great expenditure, children, domestic worries: those irritations never accompany our other pleasure, which is always serene and unchanged, involves no waste of wealth, and for that very reason suits the wise.' 'But do you think that, should these irritations not ensue, the philosopher would still criticize the pleasure that can be had with a woman?' 'No, I don't think so,' said Dorus. 'But, in any case, whatever the philosopher might opine, I believe we should not abandon two pleasures for the sake of one, and that we should enjoy both, as best we can. This seems to me the wisest council: never refuse any of the gifts and pleasures the Gods bestow upon us, but make the most of them all, with measure, so as to make them last as long as possible.'

Callicles then asked, 'And if you had to choose? In our kind of pleasure there are two sides, whereas in the inebriating pleasure there is only one. After I embraced Hymnis and we enjoyed each other, she in her way and I in mine, we did not swap roles as we do. After I embrace my Dorus I experience a second sweetness: I feel how my dearest Dorus embraces me. Hymnis does not do to me what I do to her, whereas Dorus does.' On hearing this, Dorus without further ado embraces his Callicles from behind, holding onto him with great sweetness, and then Callicles embraces and holds the beautiful Dorus in exactly the same way. Well, what do you expect? They were eighteen! Then they fell asleep.

Chapter 4

Two days later, at the agreed time in the evening, Callicles and Dorus went to Hymnis' house and she welcomed them joyously, kissing each on the mouth. This Hymnis was a charming young woman of about twenty: she had expressive eyes, a rosy smile, delicate little hands, small feet, and such a fair complexion that she seemed to have descended directly from the Erechtheans (that is to say, the ancient Athenians of noble stock).[1] She had just now come out of her bath, all fresh and bright, and was wearing a fine robe finished with a purple band. In a lovely, childish gesture, she sat on Dorus' lap, then arranged his hair on his forehead, and looked at him with a smile full of pleasure, throwing her arms around his neck and kissing his eyes. Callicles sat next to them: she put first one little foot on his knee and then the other. He took those feet into his hands and kissed them: they looked like two pieces of crystal.[2] Then Hymnis held him by the chin and kissed him in the mouth: she did not know how to divide herself between the two boys, but she leaned towards Dorus.[3] Meanwhile Dorus put a golden ring on her finger, which was made in Rhodes,[4] while Callicles thread her arm through a golden band, artfully made of two intertwining snakes.[5]

Looking at what the two young men offered, she said, 'Actually, no ring, no armband, no necklaces or earrings could ever be as beautiful and precious to me as Callicles and Dorus: they are the most beautiful and graceful boys in Athens—and they are mine. I took them for the first time, I was the one who picked the beautiful flower of their virginity.[6] No

---

[1] Erechtheus was the mythical first king of Athens; King Codrus was a descendant. Here Settembrini abandons the pretence of translating an ancient text and offers an explanation clearly aimed at the modern reader.
[2] See p. 164, n. 6.
[3] One of several moments in which the narrative moves towards the conclusion that, *pace* Plato, women are not to be held in common, cf. p. 183, n. 8.
[4] It is unclear why Settembrini picked Rhodes as the place of provenance for this ring. Perhaps there is no more to it than a general association with impressive ancient craftsmanship.
[5] The two gifts symbolize the relationship each man establishes with Hymnis: she is more attached to Dorus, who gives her a ring, while Callicles remains close to her via his association with Dorus: the armband with two intertwined snakes recalls the description of the two young men in chapter 1 (see n. 12) and our comments on p. 126, n. 33.
[6] Settembrini uses language traditionally applied to the deflowering of girls and reverses gender roles. See Conoscenti 2019: 121–2.

woman, not even the daughter of the Archon,[7] will ever have such good fortune in her life. You offered yourselves as gifts and you are more precious to me than the treasure of Delphi. Besides, I already own four rings: did you know that? I also have an armband and two pairs of earrings: one pair in a three-almond design, the other featuring a half-moon dangling from a circle; I also have two cicadas made of gold and two bees that hold up my hair between them.[8] And all of these jewels are made in Syria. Come on, I want to show them to you!' She went into a nearby room, brought back a casket, and placed it in front of the two young men. Then she took out her jewels and, trying them on, first one, then another, she kept asking, 'What do you think? Do they suit me? I'll wear your ring and your armband at the next party: what a great impression I'll make!'

Callicles asked, 'Who gave you these other jewels? Your mother?' A cloud passed over Hymnis' face as she answered, 'Ah, my mother was a poor woman married to a sailor: he died when I was five so she supported me and brought me up through her own hard work. When I was old enough, I became a dancer and had some lovers. Then I lost my beloved mother and cried so much: when I remember this, I still cannot hold back my tears.' 'Poor Hymnis,' said Dorus, while Callicles asked, 'So your lovers made you rich?' 'I am not rich! But I live without worry and I have one maid. I want to tell you everything: Master Cleonymus,[9] the wealthy old man who owns many ships in the Piraeus and who used to sail with my father and held him dear, was the one who gave me these little gifts and who supports me in life.' 'Who do you mean? That man with a great shock of white hair on his head?' Dorus asked. 'The very one! Just like garlic, he has a white head but a green tail![10] He has a wife and children, but he also loves me!' 'And do you love him?' asked Callicles. 'How could I not!' said Hymnis. 'The same way I would love the dear

---

[7] The chief officer, which rotated every year.

[8] Settembrini probably has in mind a passage from Thucydides, 1.6.3, according to which, in an earlier age, Athenian men used to wear cicada-shaped pins in their hair. See also Aristophanes, *Clouds* 984, where the term 'cicadas' is shorthand for old-fashioned refinement.

[9] Cleonymous means 'of famous name'. Settembrini knew it from Pseudo-Lucian, *Charidemus* 4.

[10] Settembrini takes this expression from the programmatic introduction to the fourth day in Boccaccio's *Decameron*: 'As for those who express doubt because of my age, they only reveal they do not know that the leek, though sporting a white head, has a green tail! Jesting aside...' See Conoscenti 2010 and 2019: 119.

soul of my father. He is good to me. I would be a scoundrel if I did not love him.' And Callicles, 'You love him and you love the two of us.' 'I feel a different kind of love for you—and have long felt it, although you did not notice. I love him as I would love a father and I love you as lovers. I admire his kindness just as I love your beauty. Still, let him not notice anything, by the immortal Gods, otherwise I am ruined.' 'Is he jealous?' asked Callicles. 'Of course he is jealous: he is old. Are you jealous of each other? If I love Dorus better, are you jealous of him, Callicles?' 'Not at all,' said Callicles, 'nor would he be jealous of me, because we are friends and we share everything.' 'Ah, you are philosophers and quite unlike other men!' said Hymnis. 'What I mean is this: you do not love me, because love is jealous. You think that poor Hymnis is just a dancer like any other, while I am a woman in love with your beauty, and have been in love with it for a long time. Your beauty made me lose my mind.' With these words, that lovely woman let herself fall into Dorus' arms and cried.

Dorus lifted her into his arms and placed her on the bed, saying, 'Now is the time for pleasure, so let us take our pleasure.' The two young men lied next to her, kissed her, and caressed her. First one and then the other did what they wanted and what she wanted in turn—and what I would also want, as would you![11] I say no more. And thus, for some time, with discretion, in order not to make old Master Cleonymus suspect, now Callicles, now Dorus, now both at the same time philosophized with Hymnis.[12] For her part, she never tired of admiring the two beautiful boys and talking with them about love.

---

[11] On the complicity of the reader, see also the translator's preface, with n. 7.
[12] Lucian uses 'philosophize' in ways that suggests this meaning, see for example *Amores* 36 οὐκ ἐρῶσι λέοντες, οὐδὲ γὰρ φιλοσοφοῦσιν, '(male) lions do not have sex with one another nor do they philosophize'. Earlier in the tale, Settembrini goes further and coins 'to Platonize' (p. 161).

Chapter 5

A few months went by and Dorus fell violently ill with a fever: he took to his bed for over twenty days while his mother and his friend looked after him with every care. Eventually, as he got himself up, felt better, and could leave the house again, he went to see Hymnis by himself. She welcomed him with the sweetest caresses. 'How are you, my beautiful Dorus? It seems a year since I last saw you, my boy! Your pasty little face makes you even more beautiful, don't you know? Callicles told me about the high fever you ran.' 'What a fever, Hymnis! I would dream of you when it ran really high and it seemed to me you were curing me.' 'Really? And how?' 'You seemed to me to be sitting on my lap: you took my carnation in your little hand and placed it in your other vase—and I felt I was getting cured. Oh, please, Hymnis, by Venus Callipyge,[1] do cure me in that manner: you are the only one who can make me bloom.' 'I hear you, my little philosopher, I hear you. You would like to behave with me the way you men behave among yourselves—and so you come here telling me about your dreams. Listen to me, Dorus: I know a few words that have the power to cure such illnesses. No, don't laugh: let me utter them and you'll see. If they have no effect, I'll do what you want me to do.' 'Is this a magic spell?' 'Oh, yes, that it is.' 'And if the magic fails?' 'Then I promise.' 'Well, then, cast your spell.'

Hymnis loosens her hair with expert ease and lets it fall onto her shoulders, then opens her robe a little, so that her breasts peak out, and says, 'Come here, Dorus, sit opposite me, your knees touching mine, hold my hands, and look at me in the eye. Now tell me, wherein resides our beauty, the beauty of both men and women? In the face. The gaze, the smile, the kiss, the word, the whole soul is there, in the face. Hide the body in clothing, and the beauty will appear in the face; hide the face and display the body: beauty disappears. Now, taking pleasure in the body without looking at the face means having pleasure without beauty; this is not the pleasure of human beings but that of animals, who know no

---

[1] The Venus Callipyge, literally 'of the beautiful buttocks', is an ancient Roman marble statue dated to the first century BCE, probably based on a lost Greek Hellenistic sculpture of the third century BCE. It is kept in the National Archaeological Museum in Naples, once Museo degli Studi, where Settembrini will have seen it.

beauty. All animals, when they mate, go about it the same way: the male jumps onto the female from behind and, as they work on, the female looks down, the male looks up; few body parts touch each other and, when they are done, they detach and go their separate ways. Only man and woman, when they join, face each other. They look each other in the eye. They smile. They kiss and tell each other sweet little words, and they experience beauty in their pleasure. Savoured that way, this is the greatest pleasure—and it becomes divine when coupled with love: in that case, the smiles and kisses and words are, truly, most divine. When taking pleasure face to face, each body part meets and mates, thigh with thigh, belly with belly, breast with breast. The arms embrace; the hands run up and down everywhere on the back and apples: no part of the body is excluded from this pleasure, at the point when man and woman unite.[2] When animal mates with animal, the male takes hold of the female's neck with his mouth, or else, if he does not grasp her, he leaves his mouth open with the tongue spilling out. We, by contrast, unite face to face, mouth to mouth; the tongue of one partner is inside the mouth of the other. In short, animals experience pleasure in the body, and not even the whole body; human beings experience pleasure in the whole body—and, if that pleasure is coupled with love, they experience it in the whole of their soul too.'

Dorus asked, 'What sorceress taught you these words, Hymnis?' 'I am an Athenian, my Dorus, and we Athenian women all know a little magic.' She said this with such grace and looked at him with such lively eyes that Dorus fell under her spell and, kissing first her breasts and then her tumbling hair, said, 'Then let us enjoy this divine pleasure.' Naked they embraced and with sweet looks and delightful smiles, saying 'My Dorus!', 'My Hymnis!', 'O beautiful boy!', 'O delightful sorceress!', they wriggled for quite a while, until, with a sigh, they came to rest.

Resting, they remained attached and Hymnis, holding the boy's cheeks between her rosy fingers, kissed him in the mouth and said, 'There's some hair above your lip and yet, when I first saw you, you had none. My kisses made it sprout and my kisses will make it grow too. And once

---

[2] This account is clearly influenced by Aristophanes' speech in Plato's *Symposium* 189c2–193d5.

that's happened, you'll have a nice little moustache and you'll stroke it with your hand, telling yourself: "Hymnis made it sprout and grow with her kisses." Thus you'll remember your Hymnis and this pleasure. Look at me with those beautiful eyes of yours! You are so beautiful, my Dorus, my delightful flower! What lovely smell rises from your limbs! Your chest seems made of polished ivory!' 'Your eyes are beautiful, Hymnis, and beautiful is this mouth from which issue words that bind my heart. My Hymnis, my dear, sweetest, most beloved Hymnis!' ' Now, these eyes, this mouth, these words, these kisses, and this pleasure which you now enjoy, could you actually enjoy it, had you taken me in the back? You would no doubt experience a lesser pleasure yourself and you would give me pain or at least discomfort—and that to me, your Hymnis, who talks to you, and looks at you, and gives you kisses.' 'Enough, enough, you witch!' said Dorus. 'You intoxicate me with your words. Let us take our pleasure again face to face, mouth to mouth. Let our souls mingle together. This is pleasure united with intelligence; it is man's pleasure. Even the Gods wanted to experience it and mixed[3] with women: just so, I mix with the beautiful Hymnis, with the delightful sorceress Hymnis, and I feel I become a God.' And thus they took their pleasure, a second time.

'Enough!' said Hymnis. 'This amount helps you recover; any more of it would harm you.[4] Stay in bed and do what I say.' Then she leaps down, pours some wine and honey into a cup, and offers it to the boy, who drinks it with pleasure. Afterwards she sits by his bedside and starts chatting; at the same time she began stroking his forehead with her hand, and playing with his hair between her fingers to the point that the boy, overcome by all that murmuring and caressing, closed his eyes and fell asleep.[5] After an hour he opened his eyes again and Hymnis told him

---

[3] The original *mescolarsi*, to 'mix', is as unidiomatic in Italian as it sounds in English: it is probably meant to represent a literal translation from the ancient Greek μείγνυμι, 'to mix', 'to have intercourse'.

[4] Contrary to Codrus' claims that women are sexually insatiable, Hymnis imposes limits on Dorus in order to ensure his full recovery.

[5] The switch from the past to the present tense, in the previous sentence, and back to the past in this one is as harsh in Italian as in English. It seems an attempt to imitate, in a fake literal translation, the historic present typical of ancient Greek prose.

with a smile, 'Oh, you are cured! Your cheeks bloom like roses again. Didn't I tell you? Now go, get washed and dressed, then return home to your mother, who is waiting for you.' Dorus said no more, just added a few kisses, and then went home to his mother, who rejoiced at seeing him happy and in full bloom, just as he had been before his illness.

Chapter 6

Dorus told his friend what had taken place between him and Hymnis and declared he was very fond of that dear young woman. Callicles did not respond, observing only that women should not be asked to do what they do not enjoy and brings no advantage to them, adding, 'Please let us remember that this pleasure is granted only to wise men.' Dorus kept going to visit Hymnis, while Callicles went rarely and only when his friend took him there: it seemed that his thoughts were elsewhere.

One day they received a letter stating: *Please come immediately, both of you. Hymnis*. They went and, as they met the woman, she told them with a painful sigh, 'I called you in order to see you one last time. Master Cleonymus lost his wife and, since his own children are married and he is now all alone in his home, he has asked me to go and live with him.' 'And will you go?' asked Dorus. 'Yes,' she answered. 'But surely we can give you what Master Cleonymus offers you,' Dorus added. 'We have sufficient wealth; my father has entrusted me with much of the family business and Callicles is in charge of his own affairs.' 'Dearest young men, the Gods know what pain I feel at the prospect of not seeing you again, but that good old man, a benefactor of my father, somebody who generously supported my mother and who lifted me out of poverty and shame, tells me that he is now all alone in the world, and that he wants me to look after him and close his eyes when he dies. Even if he were poor, I would still have the duty to go and live with him and assist him. I would be a callous woman if I refused him. And you, would you want your Hymnis to be callous? This sailor's daughter, this dancer, may be poor, may be unhappy in her heart, but she is neither callous nor ungrateful. I had you two, the most beautiful Callicles and Dorus, and this gave me such happiness that I felt like a Goddess. Now the Gods take away this inestimable good and I return to be an ordinary woman like before.'

At these words, Dorus' face lost all colour and Callicles, who was also moved, said, 'Hymnis, how can we lose you now that we know how good you are?' 'Can't you still see us sometimes, even when you live with that old man?' asked Dorus. 'No,' answered Hymnis, 'I can't. If he found out, the discovery would kill him.' At that point the woman, who had managed to keep herself in check up till then, broke down in tears and let herself fall into Dorus' arms. 'The old man will arrive in an hour,' she said. 'Goodbye, my dearest and most beautiful Dorus; goodbye, Callicles, my first love: remember Hymnis.' The two young men did not know what to say: they had a lump in their throat, gave her many kisses and, when they left her house, had to wipe away their tears. They always remembered kind-hearted Hymnis.

Callicles was brooding over something: he kept staring into the distance, refused to talk, and would react only to Dorus, with a brief smile. At some point Dorus asked him, 'What is the matter with you, Callicles, my friend and dear brother? You must be in pain: why are you trying to hide this?' Callicles answered with great sadness, 'Alas, Dorus, I've lost my peace and feel I am about to die! When you fell ill and burned with that fever, your mother in her worry told me: "Callicles, go immediately to fetch doctor Euristheus.[1] He is at the house of Eutyches the Areopagite:[2] tell him to come here straight away." I ran to the house and found the doctor in the company of a girl who looked like a Goddess to me, as beautiful as Hebe.[3] They were reading Homer together and the doctor was explaining the beauty of the poetry. As she lifted her eyes to look at me—what eyes, Dorus, what eyes!—I felt a fire run through my whole body; I did not know what to say or do.[4] I begged Euristheus to go to our home, explaining that you were ill—and he, turning to the girl, said, "Psyche,[5] I must go and see to that young man, who is unwell: continue reading and we'll talk about it tomorrow. Tell your father that

---

[1] Euristheus means 'of broad strength'; the name appears in Lucian, *Zeus the Tragedian* 21 and *Council of the Gods* 7.
[2] The name Eutyches means 'of good fortune': in this form it is not attested in ancient Greek; an 'Areopagite' is a member of the Areopagus, a judicial council that met on the Athenian hill of that name.
[3] Hebe, daughter of Zeus and Hera, is a personification of female youth. She features in Lucian, *Dialogues of the Gods* 5.2 and *Dialogues of the Dead* 16.1.
[4] Cf. Settembrini's first visit to his future wife, at her home: 'She was working at her beautiful embroidery and even while talking to me she would not interrupt her work, though, from time to time, she would raise her eyes and look at me with a smile that made me shudder' (1971: 95).
[5] The name means 'Soul'. It is exceedingly rare as a personal name, though Apuleius tells of the famous love affair between Cupid and Psyche in *Metamorphosis* 4–6, an episode of clear Neoplatonic influence.

I have gone to Phemius' house." As I left, I turned back to look at the girl—and she was looking at me.'

'Have you ever spoken to that girl?' asked Dorus. 'Not once and I only saw her one more time by the temple of Ceres with her mother and two younger sisters.[6] Oh, I feel I am dying of love! I never knew that love could come of a single glance and burn so hot! What do you advise, Dorus?' 'What possible advice can I give you, given that I have not experienced love myself? We must beseech the Gods to let your passion reach a good end.' 'But she does not know of my passion for her and possibly despises me: she is the daughter of Eutyches, wears a cicada on her shoe,[7] and considers herself of greater nobility than Theseus.' Dorus answered with some irritation, 'So is it not enough to be an Athenian citizen, in order to be considered noble? Do we not all live as equal under our laws? Well, Callicles, do you know what comes to my mind? Perhaps my mother, Doris, knows Eutyches' wife and Psyche herself: open your heart to her; she loves you so much!' And that is what they did: Doris, in her kindness, tactfully made some arrangements: Callicles and Psyche met, talked, and loved each other.

---

[6] Ceres, Demeter in Greek, was an important deity in ancient Athens. Compare Settembrini's account of first seeing his future wife: 'One day, in the street, I saw her in the company of a nun and she seemed to me an angel: then she disappeared from my sight, though she remained in my mind and heart' (1971: 94–5).

[7] See p. 168, with n. 8.

Chapter 7

Antiochus, king of Syria,[1] irritated with the Athenians for I do not know what reason,[2] sent over several ships which infested the shore of Attica and threatened the port of Piraeus. The Athenians immediately armed their fleet and recruited a large number of warriors: Callicles and Dorus were among the first to enlist. Leaving behind their other occupations and pleasures, they devoted themselves entirely to the war effort. They armed themselves with good weapons and embarked on an exceptionally fast vessel named the *Hawk*.[3] One day, the news came that four Syrian ships were attacking an area near Cape Sunion and that they would soon capture it and imprison the local people: immediately the Commander sent off a detachment, made up of the three fastest ships, one of which was the *Hawk*; he then followed with the rest of the fleet. The Syrian ships, which had captured and sacked the land, were leaving the shore full of booty and prisoners, when the three Athenian ships attacked them with great fury.

As the *Hawk* accosted one of the enemy vessels, Callicles took one great leap and landed on it. The Syrians thought he was a God descended from heaven among them and, seized by wonder and fear, stood in a stupor. Meanwhile Callicles hit hard with his spear and brought down quite a few men: eventually, though, the Syrians came to their senses, surrounded him, and wounded him in his thigh with an arrow.[4] He fell onto his knee yet continued fighting and fending them off. 'Do not kill

---

[1] Seven different kings named Antiochus ruled over Syria between 281 and 129 BCE, though none seems to have waged war against Athens. Settembrini is probably thinking of Antiochus I 'the Saviour': Lucian mentions him several times.

[2] The war allows Settembrini to show that Platonic love is compatible with, and indeed encourages, bravery—but is otherwise dismissed: this is the shortest chapter and we are never allowed to know the causes or consequences of the war. Note the conclusion, with more than a hint at the general futility of war: 'The Athenians ... sent some ambassadors to Antiochus, patched things up with him, and the war came to an end.'

[3] *Hawk* translates *Sparvierata*, a name Settembrini takes from his own translation of Lucian: 'una nave sparvierata' for σκάφος εὐτρέπιστο at *Amores* 6 (Settembrini 1988: 490). For further discussion, see Conoscenti 2010: 160.

[4] Fighting with bow and arrow is a sign of cowardice in Homeric epic. The description of battle in this chapter is clearly influenced by Homer; see also the lion simile. It may also reflect Settembrini's youthful enthusiasm for the naval battles in the Greek War of Independence, see p. 41.

him!' shouted the Captain. 'Take him alive: we'll get a good ransom for him!' The Syrians were tightening their circle around him in order to catch him and one hit him over the head from behind: the young man fell onto his shield.

Just at that moment the *Hawk* organized a second assault, while Dorus kept shouting, 'The hooks! The hooks!'[5] As soon as they threw one hook overboard, it caught the Syrian ship, and Dorus leapt onto it. Roaring like a lion, he hit out in desperation, planting himself in front of his fallen friend: he killed, wounded, and was eventually wounded himself in the shoulder, by another arrow. Meanwhile the rest of the Athenians had arrived and, after a fierce, brief battle, the enemy ship was taken. Another Syrian vessel got rammed, broke open, and sank, amidst the screams of those inside it. The two remaining ships sailed off in bad condition, but the Commander pursued them and they too were captured. When the Commander returned, he asked to see the ship on which the fighting had taken place and gave orders to carry Callicles, who seemed dead, and Dorus, who was badly wounded, into his own ship. There they received every care and, when Callicles opened his eyes, the Commander told him, 'Rejoice, brave youth: yours is the honour of this victory and, after you, it belongs to your friend.' Callicles smiled lightly and squeezed Dorus' hand, as his friend was by his side.

The Athenian ships, after capturing the enemy vessels, returned to the port of Piraeus. The news about the two boys and their great courage soon spread. The Athenians wanted to see them and greeted them with happy cheers as soon as they disembarked. Eutyches immediately went with the doctor to the house of the two boys and, as soon as he saw them, he exclaimed with great emotion: 'Immortal Gods! Pallas, patron Goddess, preserve these two young men for our city of Athens; save this Callicles, this son of mine!' Poor Callicles was in no condition to hear those words, but Dorus did—and reported them to his friend as soon as he regained consciousness, a few days later. He was exceedingly pleased with them and, from that moment onwards, steadily got better. Dorus, for his part, recovered quickly. Callicles continued unwell for two

---

[5] An anachronism: hooks were not used in ancient Greek naval warfare.

months but eventually got up and regained his strength: both became as strong and beautiful as before and demanded to resume their naval service in order to fight in defence of their country. The Athenians, however, sent some ambassadors to Antiochus, patched things up with him, and the war came to an end.

Chapter 8

A letter addressed to Callicles arrived from the island of Andros:[1] Eurydemus,[2] a brother of his late mother, sent news that he was seriously ill and that, before dying, he wished to see Callicles and entrust him with a secret of some importance: he should visit quickly, as it would be to his advantage. The young man showed the letter to his friend and they both sailed off to Andros. As soon as they disembarked, they asked a woman who was spinning wool where Eurydemus lived and she, lifting her hand and pointing with her spindle, showed them a white house on a hill, in the middle of a meadow, 'That's the one,' she said.[3] The two young men climbed up the hill and when they arrived at a wooden gate, a dog barked his welcome: a servant arrived, tied up the dog, and let them in. They saw old Eurydemus sitting under a pergola: although he was unwell, he got himself up, embraced his nephew and asked after the other visitor. As soon as he learnt that the man was Dorus, he exclaimed, 'Oh! You are the two heroes of Cape Sunion!' Then he embraced Dorus too and the young man greeted him with the respect that is owed to the elderly—Eurydemus too had fought for the fatherland and had a generous spirit. Leaning on Callicles' arm, Eurydemus entered the house and called out to his daughter Ioessa,[4] 'Here is your brother Callicles and his comrade in arms. Tell Hecamede[5] to prepare dinner for them: they must be tired after their long journey and the rough sea.'

---

[1] Andros features at the start of the first chapter and now, in ring composition, at the start of the last, see p. 126.

[2] The name is attested in Herodotus 7.213. It fits the pattern of other names chosen by Settembrini for their etymology: many are compounds; in this case, the name is made up of *eury-* ('broad') and *-demus* ('people'), i.e. 'popular'.

[3] In his memoirs, Settembrini describes a house on top of a hill, which he could see from his prison cell during his first incarceration; he moreover describes how he grew fond of the family who lived there, simply by observing how they went about their daily lives (1961: 121). The description here may also recall his first arrival in Catanzaro, the city high on the hill, with the Ionian sea curving into a gulf below (1961: 81). Several other passages in his writings suggest a susceptibility to landscape, and especially to houses located high above the sea and associated with happiness and the comfort of family.

[4] The name derives from the Greek for 'purple'; it is attested in Lucian, *Dialogues of the Courtesans* 12.

[5] Nestor's servant in Homer, *Il.* 11.624. The whole passage recalls scenes of hospitality in Homeric epic, where guests are typically offered a bed outdoors, under the roof of a porch.

This Ioessa was one of those girls of fine beauty one sees on the Aegean islands: her eyes gave an impression of innocence and joy. She had a calm gaze and a sweet smile. After welcoming the two young men very gracefully, and spending some time with them, she went to prepare dinner with the old servant Hecamede who, bustling around the house, looked after the young guests with great pleasure.[6] Meanwhile Eurydemus was asking a million questions about Athens, about the recent battle, and about several people he knew there. After dinner, Hecamede took the two young men to their sleeping quarters under the roof of a porch, where two beds were ready for them.[7] Then Dorus grasped Callicles' hand and exclaimed, 'Ah me! This sister of yours, Ioessa! She looks so much like you that, when I saw her, I thought I was seeing you as a boy. How beautiful she is! How sweet her words! And how sweet her glances! Callicles, my friend, my heart aches!'

The next day, Eurydemus was feeling a little better: he called his nephew and, once alone with him, started speaking to him, 'Son of my good sister Tecmessa, I am so pleased to see you in your prime and enjoying such good reputation among your fellow citizens. I called you because I feel that I am about to die: the illness I have could kill me in no time and I do not know to whom to entrust my only daughter, by beloved Ioessa, who has no mother and no brothers—but only you. For you are the only relative we still have, my Callicles. I am dying. What will happen to her?' He began to cry at this point, but then resumed, 'I entrust her to you and wish you to be to her a father, a brother, and friend. What do you say to that?' 'I promise you that much and swear to it on my mother's sacred soul,' answered Callicles. The old man continued, 'Unless my fatherly love deceives me, she seems not unattractive in appearance to me and, moreover, I can certainly tell you this: she is as kind and affectionate as your mother was. She loves me dearly, keeps me company, and often sits by my bedside at night. A girl that is so good and loving will not turn out to be a terrible woman. If you liked her and wished to marry her, this house of mine is comfortable, if not luxurious;

---

[6] That Settembrini includes the pleasure of the old woman here is part of the democratic thrust of his tale, particularly since the same terms *compiacenza, compiacere* are also used of the main characters, the author, and his readers, see p. 15, n. 7.

[7] Cf. n. 5.

mine is the largest and best plot in Andros; and I have put away some savings which you could have: you would have a woman with a dowry which you would not easily find in Athens—a dowry of innocence and good habits. Moreover, she belongs to your family and finally, let me just say it, she is the most beautiful flower in Andros. I would be happy and would not feel anxious about my own death.' 'You will be satisfied, Uncle,' said Callicles. 'But you know that first there has to be love and then a promise. I only saw her once, yesterday, and only briefly: give me a few days to talk to her and learn to know her heart. But please do not doubt: I will make you happy.'

After a few days, Callicles, who had noticed how Ioessa kept looking at Dorus, and blushing, reported to his friend what his uncle had said, adding, 'You know that I love Psyche and have eyes only for her. If, as you told me, you love Ioessa and she loves you too, as I seem to have noticed, then would you like to take her as your wife? Could I tell that poor old man that Ioessa will find in you a husband and in me a brother and a friend?' Dorus hugged Callicles and said, 'Yes, my brother, I do love Ioessa and I would be delighted to take her in marriage.' Callicles went to see Eurydemus straight away, telling him, 'Here, be reassured immediately, Eurydemus. Love gives orders even to Jupiter, and nobody gives orders to Love. Dorus loves Ioessa and she loves him. He asks her hand in marriage: if you grant it, she will have two friends in life; in him she'll find a husband and in me a brother. We shall both love her and support her.' 'I like this solution too,' said Eurydemus. 'I know Phemius and Doris: this son of theirs, and friend of yours, seems a good man. If they love each other, I am satisfied.' He asked his daughter about this, then he asked Dorus, and finally agreed on the marriage; but the poor old man could not see it celebrated because his illness worsened, his heart failed, and he died in the arms of his beloved daughter. This caused great grief.

After the days of mourning had passed, and once all arrangements had been made, the two young men returned to Athens with the girl. Doris welcomed Ioessa with great kindness and began to love her like a daughter. Callicles went to live in his own ancestral home and hosted Dorus at his place until the wedding. The wedding day arrived—a double wedding that brought much joy. Callicles married Psyche; Dorus wed

Ioessa. Each man lived in his own home, had children, enjoyed family life and was held in high esteem by his fellow citizens. The two friends no longer followed Plato's teaching, according to whom women should be held in common,[8] but rather followed the laws of their fatherland and those of love. Each of them loved and honoured his own wife. And yet, they always continued to love each other too and, even in old age, if they happened to share a bed for any reason, they would entangle their feet and embrace as they did long ago, in the first years of their youth.

The End.[9]

---

[8] Plato, *Republic* 5, 457b–458d and 461e–462e. See further pp. 19f.

[9] As Plato's Socrates says in the *Phaedrus*, κοινὰ τὰ τῶν φίλων, 'amongst friends all things in common' (279c). Time and again, we have signalled the extent to which this book stems from our shared research on Luigi Settembrini—whose works, incidentally, often challenge the notion of single authorship, as we have remarked more than once. That said, Barbara is especially interested in (auto)biographies, whereas Andrea's focus is more on Platonic fictions. Therefore, for narrowly bureaucratic purposes (such as what Italian academia refers to as *determinazione analitica del contributo individuale*), Barbara should be considered the translator of the tale and the author of chapters 2, 3, 4, and 5; Andrea of chapters 1, 6, 7, and 8.

Epilogue

It is our last day of work in the National Library in Naples: we are checking references in the Pessina archive and returning documents to the cardboard boxes where they are kept. Andrea leaves briefly to consult the main catalogue and returns in some excitement, gesticulating to Barbara to come and see what is happening behind him, in the main hall of the Rare Books Department.

It is packed with young men and women in high uniform: blue buttoned jackets, white collars, double-buckled belts, grey trousers with purple stripes stretching down the sides, hats tucked neatly under each left arm. A librarian, meanwhile, is opening various manuscripts on the central table: a Renaissance herbarium, a fragment of carbonized papyrus... *questi sono i tesori della patria*, he states—'these are the national treasures you will one day be called upon to protect, not just for the benefit of Italy, but of all who want to study them: here look...'. While the young officers observe the manuscripts, we fix our gaze on them: they look really very young, hardly adults. Cadets at the Nunziatella, someone whispers. The name sounds familiar: we are sure we've come across it, in the course of our research, even though we cannot place it immediately.

Eventually, it comes to us. Francesco del Carretto, last minister of so-called justice under the Bourbons, attended the same military academy as these young women and men. He kept Settembrini in prison indefinitely, after he had been acquitted of all charges, and prevented him from teaching in school when he was finally released. These future officers, meanwhile, hear a lesson—about civic responsibility, classical scholarship, and care—which, we have argued, Settembrini lived to impart.

Classics, Love, Revolution: The Legacies of Luigi Settembrini. Andrea Capra and Barbara Graziosi, Oxford University Press. © Andrea Capra and Barbara Graziosi 2024.
DOI: 10.1093/oso/9780198865445.003.0010

Bibliography

Alatri, P., ed. 1982. *Giuseppe Mazzini e i rivoluzionari italiani*. By Benedetto Musolino. Cosenza.
Alfieri, V. E. 1986. *Maestri e testimoni di libertà*. Milazzo.
Altimari, F. 2014. 'Naples, an Important Center of the Arberesh-Albanian Renaissance in 19th Century'. *Studia Albanica* 2: 53–79.
Anderson, B. 1991. *Imagined Communities: Reflections on the Origin and Spread of Nationalism*. London.
Anderson, P. 2021. 'Timpanaro among the Anglo-Saxons'. *New Left Review* 129: 109–22.
Ashton, B., G. Griffith, and H. Tiffin. 1989. *The Empire Writes Back: Theory and Practice in Post-Colonial Literatures*. Abingdon.
Assmann, J. 2011. *Cultural Memory and Early Civilization: Writing, Remembrance, and Political Imagination*. Cambridge.
Babini, V. P., C. Beccalossi, and L. Riall, eds. 2015. *Italian Sexualities Uncovered, 1789–1914*. Basingstoke.
Banti, A. M. 2000. *La nazione del Risorgimento: Parentela, santità, e onore alle origini dell'Italia unita*. Turin.
Banti, A. M., A. Chiavistelli, L. Mannori, and M. Meriggi. 2011. *Atlante culturale del Risorgimento: Lessico del linguaggio politico dal Settecento all'Unità*. Rome and Bari.
Banti, A. M. and P. Ginsborg, eds. 2007. 'Il Risorgimento'. In *Storia d'Italia: Annali*, vol. 22. Turin.
Barbagli, M. and A. Colombo. 2001. *Omosessuali moderni: Gay e lesbiche in Italia*. Bologna.
Benvenuto, B. 2001. Foreword to *I Neoplatonici*, by L. Settembrini. Palermo.
Bettini, M. 2023. *Chi ha paura dei Greci e dei Romani? Dialogo e cancel culture*. Turin.
Bollati, G. 1972. 'L'italiano'. In *Storia d'Italia: I caratteri originali*, vol. 1 (2). Turin: 949–1022. Repr. in G. Bollati, 1996 (1983), *L'italiano: Il carattere nazionale come storia e come invenzione*, 2nd ed. Turin: 34–123.
Borgna, A. 2022. *Tutte storie di maschi bianchi morti…* Rome and Bari.
Brambilla Ageno, F. 1965. 'Riecheggiamenti e imitazioni nella tradizione letteraria italiana'. *Giornale Storico della Letteratura Italiana* 142: 550–6.
Brisson, L. 2012. 'Women in Plato's Republic'. *Études platoniciennes* 9: 129–36.
Butler, S. 2022. *The Passions of John Addington Symonds*. Oxford.
Cantarella, R., ed. 1977. *I neoplatonici: racconto inedito*. By L. Settembrini, with a foreword by G. Manganelli. Milan.

Cantarella, R. and G. Arrighetti. 1972. 'Il libro "Sul tempo" (*PHerc.* 1413) dell'opera di Epicuro "Sulla natura"'. *Cronache ercolanesi* 2: 5–46.
Capasso, G. 1908. 'I tentativi per far evadere Luigi Settembrini dall'ergastolo di Santo Stefano negli anni 1855–56'. *Il risorgimento italiano* 1, 1908: 22–65.
Capasso, M. 2014. 'Luigi Settembrini e i papiri ercolanesi'. In S. Cerasuolo, M. L. Chirico, S. Cannavale, C. Pepe, and N. Rampazzo, eds., *La tradizione classica e l'Unità d'Italia: Atti del Seminario Napoli-Santa Maria Capua Vetere 2–4 ottobre 2013*. Naples: 19–37.
Capra, A. 2018. 'A 19th-Century "Milesian Tale": Settembrini's *Neoplatonici*'. In E. Cueva, S. Harrison, H. Mason, W. Owens, and S. Schwartz, eds., *Re-Wiring the Ancient Novel*. Eelde: 45–60.
Carpi, L. 1884. *Risorgimento italiano: Biografie storico politiche d'illustri italiani contemporanei*. Milan.
Cases, C., ed. 1979. *Ferdinando Galliani: Dialogo sulle donne e altri scritti*, 2nd ed. Milan.
Casi, S. 1991. 'Un patriota per noi: Luigi Settembrini'. In *Le Parole e la storia. Ricerche su omossessualità e cultura*, special issue of Quaderni di critica omosessuale 9: 49–69.
Cassin, B. 2014. *Sophistical Practice: Toward a Consistent Relativism*. New York.
Cesarotti, M. 1863. 'Callista e Filetore: Frammento d'una novella greca tradotto da Melchior Cesarotti'. In G. Daelli, ed., *Mescolanze d'amore: ovvero Raccolta di scritti amatorii di Plotino, Leon Battista Alberti, Stefano Guazzo e Melchior Cesarotti*. Milan: 119–31.
Ceserani, G. 2010. 'Classical Culture for a Classical Country: Scholarship and the Past in Vincenzo Cuoco's Plato in Italy'. In S. A. Stephens and P. Vasunia, eds., *Classics and National Cultures*. Oxford: 59–77.
Ciampi, S., ed. 1814–16. *Collezione degli erotici greci tradotti in volgare*. Pisa.
Cioffi, R. L. 2014. 'Seeing Gods: Epiphany and Narrative in the Greek Novels'. *Ancient Narrative* 11: 1–42.
Claeys, G. 1989. *Citizens and Saints*. Cambridge.
Condello, F. 2014. 'Settembrini e Luciano: Norme e costanti di una traduzione (primi sondaggi)'. In S. Cerasuolo, M. L. Chirico, S. Cannavale, C. Pepe, and N. Rampazzo, eds., *La tradizione classica e l'Unità d'Italia: Atti del Seminario Napoli-Santa Maria Capua Vetere 2–4 ottobre 2013*, vol. 1. Naples: 39–68.
Conoscenti, D. 2010. 'Sulla datazione de "I Neoplatonici" di Luigi Settembrini'. *Critica letteraria* 146: 150–72.
Conoscenti, D. 2019. *I Neoplatonici di Luigi Settembrini: Gli amori maschili nel racconto e nella traduzione di un patriota risorgimentale*. Sesto San Giovanni.
Cooper, B. 2018. *Eloquent Rage: A Black Feminist Discovers Her Superpower*. New York.
Cortellazzo, C. and P. Zolli. 1983. *Dizionario etimologico della lingua italiana*. Bologna.
Croce, B. 1921. *La letteratura della nuova Italia*, vol. 1, 2nd ed. Bari.
Cuoco, V. 1928. *Platone in Italia*. Bari.
Cuoco, V. 2006. *Platone in Italia: Traduzione dal greco*, ed. A. De Francesco and A. Andreoni. Rome and Bari.

Daelli, G., ed. 1863. *Mescolanze d'amore: ovvero, Raccolta di scritti amatorii di Plotino, Leon Battista Alberti, Stefano Guazzo e Melchior Cesarotti*. Milan.
D'Antuono, N. 2012. *L'asino che ride: Saggi e ricerche su Luigi Settembrini*. Angri.
D'Antuono, N. 2018. 'Settembrini e l'antico'. *Critica Letteraria* 179: 293–304.
De Francesco, A. 2013. *The Antiquity of the Italian Nation: The Cultural Origins of a Political Myth in Modern Italy, 1796–1943*. Oxford.
Del Corno, D. 2008. 'Fra biblioteche e fantasia: Romanzare l'antichità greca e romana. Da Settembrini a Ransmayr, con un ritorno alle origini'. In M. Colummi Camerino, ed., *La storia nel romanzo, 1800–2000*. Rome: 29–38.
Deleuze, G. 1995. *Negotiations*. Trans. M. Joughin. New York.
Derbew, S. F. 2022. *Untangling Blackness in Greek Antiquity*. Cambridge.
De Sanctis, F. 1876. *Parole di Francesco de Sanctis in morte di Luigi Settembrini*. Naples.
De Sanctis, F. 1953. *La letteratura italiana nel secolo XIX*, ed. F. Catalano, vol. 2. Bari.
De Sanctis, F. 1965. *Saggi critici*, ed. L. Russo. Bari.
De Seta, C. 2014. *L'Italia nello specchio del Grand Tour*. Milan.
Dubuis, P., trans. 2010. *Idylles socratiques: Les néoplatoniciens*. By L. Settembrini. Cassaniouze.
Duggan, C. 1994. *A Concise History of Italy*. Cambridge.
Dunkan, D. 2006. *Reading and Writing Italian Homosexuality: A Case of Possible Difference*. London and New York.
Fabietti, E. 1936. *Luigi Settembrini: La centuria di ferro: La pattuglia dei precursori*, vol. 9. Milan.
Fagan, L., ed. 1881, *The Life and Correspondence of Sir Anthony Panizzi*, 2 vols. Boston, MA.
Felski, R. 2015. *The Limits of Critique*. Chicago.
Fermon, N. 1994. 'Domesticating Women, Civilizing Men: Rousseau's Political Program'. *The Sociological Quarterly* 35: 431–42.
Fogu, C. 2001. '"To Make History": Garibaldinism and the Formation of a Fascist Historic Imaginary'. In A. Russell Ascoli and K. von Heneberg, eds., *Making and Remaking Italy: The Cultivation of National Identity around the Risorgimento*. Oxford: 203–40.
Foot, M. R. D. 1979. 'Gladstone and Panizzi'. *British Library Journal* 5: 48–56.
Forsdyke, S. 2021. *Slaves and Slavery in Ancient Greece*. Cambridge and New York.
Foucault, M. 1995. *Discipline and Punish: The Birth of the Prison*. Trans. A. Sheridan. London.
Fruci G. L., 2006. 'Cittadine senza cittadinanza: La mobilitazione femminile nei plebisciti del Risorgimento (1848–1870)'. *Genesis. Rivista della società italiana delle storiche* 5 (2): 21–56.
Fubini, M. 1977. 'Review of Cantarella 1977'. *Giornale Storico della Letteratura Italiana* 154: 307–9.
Fusillo, M. 1989. *Il romanzo greco: Polifonia e eros*. Venice.
Gabrielli, A. 1927. *Settembrini*. Milan.
Galiani, F. 1957. *Dialogo sulle donne e altri scritti*, ed. C. Cases. Milan.
Gallenga, A. C. N. 1849. *Italy: Past and Present*. London.

Gambari, S. and M. Guerrini. 2018. '"Terrible Panizzi": Patriotism and Realism of the "Prince of Librarians"'. *Cataloging & Classification Quarterly* 56: 455–86.
Garibaldi, G. 1973–2002. *Epistolario*. Rome.
Gauglitz, G., ed. and trans. 2017. *Die Neuplatoniker: Ein erotisches Märchen*. By L. Settembrini. With foreword and afterword by W. Setz. Hamburg.
Gigante, M. 1977. *Settembrini e l'antico*. Naples.
Gigante, M. 1987a. Foreward to *La cultura classica a Napoli nell'Ottocento*, Naples.
Gigante, M. 1987b. 'Luigi Settembrini'. In *La cultura classica a Napoli nell'Ottocento*. Naples: 405–37.
Gill, C. 1979. 'Plato's Atlantis Story and the Birth of Fiction'. *Philosophy and Literature* 3 (1): 64–78.
Gill, C. 2017. *Plato's Atlantis Story: Text, Translation and Commentary*. Liverpool.
Gioberti, V. 1843. *Primato morale e civile degli Italiani*. Brussels.
Gioberti, V. 1938. *Prolegomeni del Primato morale e civile degli Italiani*, ed. E. Castelli. Milan.
Gladstone, W. E. 1859. *Two Letters to the Earl of Aberdeen on the State Prosecutions of the Neapolitan Government*, 14th ed., London.
Goldstone, J. A. 2014. *Revolutions: A Very Short Introduction*. Oxford.
Gramsci, A. 2001. *Quaderni del carcere*, ed. V. Gerretana. Turin.
Graziosi, B. 2005. 'Review of S. Settis, "Futuro del classico", Turin'. *The Journal of Hellenic Studies* 125: 206–8.
Graziosi, B. 2020. 'Uomo greco, cittadino italiano: Luigi Settembrini, lo studio del passato e la costruzione del futuro'. In A. Camerotto and F. Pontani, eds., *Anthropos: Pensieri, parole e virtù per restare uomini*. Milan: 143–68.
Graziosi, B. and A. Barchiesi. 2020. *Ritorni difficili*. Rome.
Greenwood, E. 2009. 'Re-Rooting the Classical Tradition: New Directions in Black Classicism'. *CRJ* 1: 87–103.
Grévy, J., H. Heyriès, and C. Maltone. 2001. *Garibaldi et garibaldiens en France et en Espagne: Histoire d'une passion pour la démocratie*. Bordeaux.
Guha R. 1983. *Elementary Aspects of Peasant Insurgency in Colonial India*. Calcutta.
Guidi, L., A. Russo, and M. Varriale. 2011. *Il Risorgimento invisibile: Patriote del Mezzogiorno d'Italia*. Naples.
Guthenke, C. 2008. *Placing Modern Greece: The Dynamics of Romantic Hellenism, 1770–1840*. Oxford.
Hall, E. and H. Stead. 2020. *A People's History of Classics: Class and Greco-Roman Antiquity in Britain and Ireland 1689 to 1939*. London.
Hamilton, C. G. 1857. *The Exiles of Italy*. Edinburgh.
Hanink, J. 2021. 'A new path for classics'. *Chronicle of Higher Education*, 21 February; https://www.chronicle.com/article/if-classics-doesnt-change-let-it-burn.
Harney, S. and F. Moten 2013. *The Undercommons: Fugitive Planning and Black Study*. Wivenhoe, New York, and Port Watson.
Harris, L. 2012. 'What Happened to the Motley Crew? James, Oiticica, and the Aesthetic Sociality of Blackness'. In L. Harris, *Experiments in Exile: C. L. R. James, Helio Oiticica, and the Aesthetic Sociality of Blackness*. New York: 17–60.

BIBLIOGRAPHY

Haugen, M. W. 2015. 'Appropriating the Novel: Pietro Chiari's La filosofessa italiana'. *Forum for Modern Language Studies* 51: 212–28.
Heberlein, A. 2021. *On Love and Tyranny: The Life and Politics of Hannah Arendt*. Toronto.
Herrnstein Smith, B. 1983. 'Contingencies of Value'. *Critical Inquiry* 10: 1–35.
Holmes, B. 2020. 'At the End of the Line: On Kairological History'. *Classical Receptions Journal* 12 (1): 62–90.
hooks, b. 1981. *Ain't I a Woman? Black Women and Feminism*. Boston, MA.
hooks, b. 2001. *All about Love*. New York.
Hooper, J. 2015. *The Italians*. London.
Hunter, R. 2012. *Plato and the Traditions of Ancient Literature: The Silent Stream*. New York.
Isabella, M. 2003. 'Italian Exiles and British Politics before and after 1848'. In S. Freitag, ed., *Exiles from European Revolutions: Refugees in Mid-Victorian England*. New York and Oxford: 59–87.
Isnenghi, M. 1997. *Il mito della grande guerra*. Bologna.
Jung C. G. 1928. *Contribution to Analytical Psychology*. London.
Knox, B. 1994. *The Oldest Dead White European Males: And Other Reflections on the Classics*. Reprint New York and London.
Konstan, D. 1994. *Sexual Symmetry: Love in the Ancient Novel and Related Genres*. Princeton, NJ and Chichester.
Kosofsky Sedgwick, E. 1999. *A Dialogue on Love*. Boston, MA.
Kosofsky Sedgwick, E. 2003. *Touching Feeling: Affect, Pedagogy, Performativity*. Durham, NC.
La Regina, S. and A. M. Chiarini. 2016. 'Os dois Narcisos: História de uma tradução inventada'. In L. Settembrini, *Os Neoplatônicos: Novela homoerótica*. São Paulo: 1–4.
Latour, B. 2004. 'Why Has Critique Run out of Steam? From Matters of Fact to Matters of Concern'. *Critical Inquiry* 30 (2): 225–48.
Leitenberg, H. and K. Henning. 1995. 'Sexual Fantasy'. *Psychological Bulletin* 117 (3): 469–96.
Linebaugh, P. and M. Rediker. 2012. *The Many-Headed Hydra: Sailors, Slaves, Commoners, and the Hidden History of the Revolutionary Atlantic*, 2nd ed. London.
Luciano, D. 2011. 'Nostalgia for an Age Yet to Come: *Velvet Goldmine*'s Queer Archive'. In E. L. McCallum and M. Tuhkanen, eds., *Queer Times, Queer Becomings*. Albany: 121–56.
Mack Smith, D. 1994. *Mazzini*. New Haven, CT and London.
Martindale, C. 1993. *Redeeming the Text: Latin Poetry and the Hermeneutics of Reception*. Cambridge and New York.
Marx, K. 2013. *The Eighteenth Brumaire of Louis Napoleon*, trans. D. D. L. Milwaukee.
Mastroroberti, F. 2012. 'Il "codice delle donne"'. *Annali della Facoltà di Giurisprudenza di Taranto* 5: 347–59.
Meriggi, M. 1997. 'Alla ricerca dei padri della patria: Leone Carpi e il "Risorgimento italiano"'. *Mélanges de l'École française de Rome. Italie et Méditerranée* 109: 45–55.

Messbarger, R. 2002. *Representations of Women in Eighteenth-Century Italian Public Discourse*. Toronto.
Minniti, B. 2022. *I Settembrini. Patrioti, letterati, gay e scavezzacollo. Una biografia pop*. Florence.
Murnaghan, S. 2007. 'Review of C. Martindale and R. F. Thomas, "Classics and the Uses of Reception"', Oxford'. *Bryn Mawr Classical Review*, 19 July.
Nails, D. 2002. *The People of Plato: A Prosopography of Plato and Other Socratics*. Indianapolis.
Nay, L. 2014. '"Maschere no": Lo svelarsi dell'io nelle scritture autobiografiche di Luigi Settembrini'. *Studi desanctisiani: rivista internazionale di letteratura, politica e società* 2: 115-28.
Newman, D. B., M. E. Sachs, A. A. Stone, and N. Schwarz. 2020. 'Nostalgia and Well-Being in Daily Life: An Ecological Validity Perspective'. *Journal of Personality and Social Psychology: Personality Processes and Individual Differences* 118: 325-47.
Orrells, D. 2011. *Classical Culture and Modern Masculinity*. Oxford.
Padilla Peralta, D. 2017. 'Slave Religiosity in the Roman Middle Republic'. *Classical Antiquity* 36 (2): 317-69.
Palladino, V., ed. 2010. *I Neoplatonici, l'amore tra uomini è eterno*. By L. Settembrini. Naples.
Papanti, G. 1871. *Catalogo dei novellieri italiani*. Livorno; reprint (2017), ed. E. Mori. Bolzano.
Parente, A. 1998. 'Architettura ed archeologia carceraria: Santo Stefano di Ventotene ed il "Panopticon"'. *Rassegna penitenziaria e criminologica* 1-3: 43-138.
Patriarca, S. 2005. 'Indolence and Regeneration: Tropes and Tensions of Risorgimento Patriotism'. *American Historical Review* 110 (2): 380-408.
Patriarca, S. 2011. 'Italiani/Italiane'. In A. M. Banti, A. Chiavistelli, M. Meriggi, and L. Mannori, eds., *Atlante culturale del Risorgimento: Lessico del linguaggio politico dal Settecento all'Unità*. Rome and Bari: 59-87.
Pedullà, G., ed. 2021. *Racconti del Risorgimento*. Milan.
Pomeroy, S. B. 2013. *Pythagorean Women: Their History and Writings*. Baltimore, MD.
Prezzolini, G. 1921. *Codice della vita italiana*. Florence.
Reeser, T. W. 2015. *Setting Plato Straight: Translating Ancient Sexuality in the Renaissance*. Chicago, IL.
Reidy, D. V. 2005. 'Panizzi, Gladstone, Garibaldi and the Neapolitan Prisoners'. *Electronic British Library Journal*, art. 6.
Riall, L. 2007. *Garibaldi: Invention of a Hero*. New Haven, CT and London.
Riall, L. 2009. *Risorgimento: The History of Italy from Napoleon to Nation State*. Basingstoke.
Riall, L. 2015. 'The Sex Lives of Italian Patriots'. In V. P. Babini, C. Beccalossi, and L. Riall, eds., *Italian Sexualities Uncovered, 1789-1914*. Basingstoke: 37-56.
Rousseau, J. J. 1964a. *Oeuvres Complètes*, ed. B. Gagnebin and M. Raymond, vol. 2. Paris.
Rousseau, J. J. 1964b. *Oeuvres Complètes*, ed. B. Gagnebin and M. Raymond, vol. 3. Paris.
Rousseau, J. J. 1969. *Oeuvres Complètes*, ed. B. Gagnebin and M. Raymond, vol. 4. Paris.

Sahlins, M. 1995. *How 'Natives' Think: About Captain Cook, for Example*. Chicago, IL.
Said, E. W. 1975. *Beginnings: Intention and Method*. Baltimore, MD.
Said, E. W. 1995. *Orientalism: Western Conceptions of the Orient*, 2nd ed. London.
Saïd, S. 1986. 'La *République* de Platon et la communauté des femmes'. *L'Antiquité Classique* 55: 142–62.
Sanrune, C., ed. and trans. 2019. *Los neoplatónicos*. By L. Settembrini. Madrid.
Sarlo, A. and F. Zajczyk. 2012. *Dove batte il cuore delle donne? Voto e partecipazione politica in Italia*. Rome and Bari.
Sconocchia, A. 2019. *I grandi personaggi del Risorgimento: Storie di uomini e donne che hanno contribuito al sogno di un'Italia unita*. Rome.
Sedikides, C., T. Wildschut, J. Arndt, and C. Routledge. 2008. 'Nostalgia: Past, Present, and Future'. *Current Directions in Psychological Science* 17: 304–7.
Settembrini, L. 1879. 'Parole dette il 2 giugno 1861 nel Primo educandato dall'Ispettor generale degli Studi'. In L. Settembrini, *Scritti vari di letteratura, politica, ed arte*, ed. F. Fiorentino, vol. 1. Naples: 1–6.
Settembrini, L. 1879–80. *Scritti vari di letteratura, politica, ed arte*, ed. F. Fiorentino. Naples.
Settembrini, L. 1892. *Ricordanze della mia vita*, ed. F. de Sanctis, 2 vols. Milan.
Settembrini, L. 1934. *Ricordanze della mia vita*, ed. A. Omodeo, 2 vols. Bari.
Settembrini, L. 1961. *Ricordanze della mia vita e scritti autobiografici*, ed. M. Themelly. Milan.
Settembrini, L. 1964. *Lezioni di letteratura italiana*, ed. G. C. Piccoli., 2 vols. Florence.
Settembrini, L. 1969. *Opuscoli politici editi e inediti (1847–1851)*, ed. M. Themelly. Rome.
Settembrini, L. 1971. *Ricordanze e altri scritti*, ed. G. De Rienzo, 2nd ed. Turin.
Settembrini, L., trans. 1988. *Luciano di Samosata: I dialoghi e gli epigrammi*, ed. G. Berettoni. Genoa.
Settembrini, L. 1990. *Lettere ad Adelaide Capece Minutolo e a Raffele Masi*, ed. A. Pessina, Naples.
Settis, S. 2006. *The Future of the Classical*. Trans. A. Cameron. Cambridge, Oxford, Boston, MA, and New York.
Soper, S. C. 2020. 'Southern Italian Prisoners on the Stage of International Politics'. *Journal of Modern Italian Studies* 25 (2): 95–117.
Spaventa, S. 1977. *Lettere a Felicetta*, ed. M. Themelly. Naples.
Sperber, J. 1994. *The European Revolutions, 1848–1851*. Cambridge.
Springer, C. 1987. *The Marble Wilderness: Ruins and Representation in Italian Romanticism, 1775–1850*. Cambridge.
Staël, Madame de. 1998. *Corinne, or Italy*. Oxford.
Stephens, S. A. and Vasunia, P. 2010. *Classics and National Cultures*. Oxford.
Strauss, L. 1959. *What Is Political Philosophy? And Other Studies*. Chicago, IL.
Themelly, M. 1977. *Luigi Settembrini nel centenario della morte*. Naples.
Themelly, M. 1994. 'Tradizione classica e storia nazionale in un trattato inedito di Luigi Settembrini'. *Belfagor* 49: 505–18.
Timpanaro, S. 1965. *Classicismo e illuminismo nell'Ottocento italiano*. Pisa.
Tocci Monaco, S. 1892. *Dieci anni di vita ergastolana sullo scoglio di Santo Stefano: Scritti inediti di Luigi Settembrini e Gennaro Placco*. Corigliano Calabro.

Traina, G. 2023. *I Greci e i Romani ci salveranno dalla barbarie.* Rome and Bari.
Treves, P. 1962. *Lo studio dell'antichità classica nell'Ottocento.* Milan and Naples.
Verri, A. 1793. *Le avventure di Saffo poetessa di Mitilene.* Rome.Villani, P. 2018. 'Luigi Settembrini e l'insegnamento della letteratura a Napoli'. *Studium* 114: 72–81.
Whitmarsh, T. 2011. *Narrative and Identity in the Ancient Greek Novel.* Cambridge.
Zanotti, P. 2005. *Il gay: Dove si racconta come è stata inventata l'identità omosessuale.* Rome.
Zanotti, P. 2006. *Classici dell'omosessualità: L'avventurosa storia di un'utopia.* Milan.
Zanou, K. 2018. *Transnational Patriotism in the Mediterranean, 1800–1850: Stammering the Nation.* Oxford.
Zapperi, R. 2014. 'Thomas Mann und Luigi Settembrini'. *Zeitschrift für Ideengeschichte* 8: 59–72.
Zuckerberg, D. 2018. *Not All Dead White Men. Classics and Misogyny in the Digital Age.* Cambridge.

Index

For the benefit of digital users, indexed terms that span two pages (e.g., 52–53) may, on occasion, appear on only one of those pages.

Aberdeen, Lord 58–9, 63–4, 66–7
Achilles Tatius 124–6
Agresti, Filippo 59–60
AIDS epidemic 143–4
Albanians 65–6, 73–4, 103–5, 138–9
Alciphron 129–30
Alexandrian school of Neoplatonists 120–1
Altimari, Francesco 73 n.55
Amarelli, Vincenzo 38–9
Amazons 103–4
anal sex 4–7, 115–16, 119–20
Anderson, Benedict 80–1
anni di piombo (years of lead) 14
antifascists 10–11, 61
Antonius Diogenes 123–4
Apollo, temple of 41, 156 n.2
Apuleius 123–4, 175 n.5
Argentina 77
Aristaenetus 124, 129–30
"Aristaeus of Megara" 4, 149–50
Aristeides 152 n.13
Aristophanes 116–17, 124–5, 155 n.21, 168 n.8, 171 n.2
Athena 115–16, 153 n.15, 154–5
Athens 41, 100–1, 123, 132–3, 151 n.1, 153nn.15,18, 157 n.6, 162 n.1, 164 n.5, 167 n.1, 176 n.6
Austria 84
authorship, collaborative 25, 56 n.5, 96, 183 n.9
autobiography
  erotic fiction and, parallels between 43–4
  Garibaldi's, Alexandre Dumas' reworking of 81–2
  Italian masculinity, used to redefine 24–5
  revolution and, relationship between 23–4
  Risorgimento literature, importance in 80–1, 90–1
  Settembrini's 55–6, 135–7, 139–40

Baltimore 77–8
Banti, Alberto 80–1
beauty
  divine 121–2
  Greek 103–5
  male and female 151 n.5
  Platonic celebrations of 122
  Settembrini's emphasis on 29, 97, 121–3
Bentham, Jeremy 60–2
Bettini, Sofia 85
bisexuality 42, 117–18, 125–6
Blackness 17–18, 78–9, 94 n.52, 138–9, 145–6
Black feminism 94 n.52, 145–6
Boccaccio 26, 72–3, 103–4, 168 n.10
Bollati, Giulio 91–3
Bologna, University of 86–7
Botzaris, Markos 40–1
Bourbons
  abuse, Settembrini's indictment of 52
  conspiracies against 38, 46, 49, 100–1
  demise of 57
  penal system of 65–6
  revolt against 54–5, 84
British Museum 66–7
Butler, Shane 17 n.39

Cadiz 77–8
Calabria 44–8, 54–5, 64–5, 69, 73–4, 103–4, 138–9
Cantarella, Raffaele 3, 8–12, 19–20, 87, 133–4, 136–7
  Neoplatonism, rejection of 29–30
  Settembrini, wilful misrepresentation of 30–1
Capasso, Mario 87
Carpi, Francesco 60–2
Carretto, Francesco del 50–1, 184
Caserta 40–1, 63
Cassin, Barbara 19, 23
Catanzaro 44–8, 50
Catholics and Catholicism
  devotion 41
  education, Settembrini's 37–9
  hypocrisy 122–3, 150 n.6
  Jesuits 38–9, 42, 88 n.29
  paganism, absorption of 20 n.55, 153 n.15
  revival 29–30
  Settembrini's views on 122–3, 150 n.6, 153 n.15
Cavour, Count Camillo Benso di 75–7, 83–6
Cesarotti, Melchiorre 127–30
Cesena 103–4
Chiari, Pietro 129–30
Chios 103–4
Christian Democrats 11
Christianity, rise and spread of 127, 137 n.3
classics 15–19, 143–4
climate change 28
Collegio di Maddaloni 38–9
colonialism 11–12
communist brigades 10–11
Conoscenti, Domenico 26
Cooper, Brittney 145–6
Copyright Act (1848) 66–7
Cork 78–9
Covid-19 pandemic 144–5
Crimean War 77
Croce, Benedetto 8–10, 8 n.10, 140 n.9

Cuoco, Vincenzo 16 n.36, 92–3, 104–7, 127–8, 131–2

De Leo, Maya 31–2
De Silva, Luigi 89–90, 94, 122–3
Deleuze, Gilles 23
democracy
  Athenian 157 n.6
  Rousseau's view of 108–9
Dioscuri 121–2, 126 n.34, 151–2, 162, 164–5
Dumas, Alexandre 24–5, 81–2, 93–4
Durham 16–17
Durkheim, David Émile 111

Edinburgh Review 59–60, 67
egalitarianism
  love, politics, and sex, in 111, 127, 138–9
  relationships, in 90–1, 94
  sociability, and 108–9
  Settembrini's 17–18, 30, 94, 111, 127, 130–1, 138–40, 144–5
Enlightenment 38, 101–2, 130
equality
  commitment to 30–1
  diversity, and 21
  homosexual relationships, in 118 n.10
  political 30–1
  reciprocity, and 32–3, 118 n.10
eroticism 12, 111
  curriculum in *Neoplatonists, The* 115–16, 125–6
  fantasies and tales 125–7
  fiction 43–4, 114, 149 n.2
  homoeroticism 4–7, 30 n.23, 140–1
  Lucian, import of 138
Erotici greci 129–30
Ethnicity 17–8, 140–1 *see also* Albanians, Calabria, Cuoco, Etruscans, postcolonial theory, race
Etruscans 17–18, 104–5
Eumathius Macrembolites 129–30
exile, Settembrini in 4–7, 43–4, 55–7, 77–8, 87–9

exiles, political 4–7, 38–9, 43–4, 55–9, 77–8, 82, 84, 87–9, 93, 132–5

Fabietti, Ettore 9
fakery, political 47
  literary 4, 61, 106, 127–8, 149–50
fascists 7–11
Faucitano, Raffaella Luigia ("Gigia") 23–5, 43–4, 48–50, 52, 62–3, 94, 99–100
  acumen and courage of 59–60, 75–7
  passport revoked 75–7
  prison visits and smuggling 60, 66, 75
  recollections of 63
  Settembrini, first meeting 43–4
  Settembrini's concern for health of 69–70
  Settembrini's dependence on 69–70, 97–9, 113
  Settembrini's life, crucial role in 56–7
  Settembrini's love of Placco, thoughts on 74
  son, Raffaele, care of 74–5
Faucitano, Salvatore 59–60
feminism 145–6; *see also* suffrage, women
Ferdinand II 54–5
Fermon, Nicole 108–9, 111
Ficino, Marsilio 120–1
Foucault, Michael 60–2
forgery, *see* fakery, translation
Franco, General Francisco 10–11
French Revolution (1799) 7 n.7
French Revolution (1848) 140–1
Freud, Sigmund 91–2, 144

Gallenga, Antonio 93
Garibaldi, Giuseppe 16 n.36, 75–6, 80–8, 93–4
  anticlericalism of 11
  autobiography, Alexandre Dumas' reworking of 81–2
  sex life 85
  Sicilian campaign 85–6

Genoa 74–5, 79, 84
Gide, André 8–10
Gigante, Marcello 99–100, 114, 133
Gioberti, Vincenzo 120–2
Gladstone, William Ewart 23–4, 58, 63–7, 79, 81–2, 92
  anti-revolutionary, monarchic, and imperialist politics of 65
  political prisoners, Neapolitan, denounces harsh treatment of 58–9, 63–4
Graham, Sir James 63–4
Gramsci, Antonio 139 n.5, 145 n.26
Grand Tour 92
Greek
  beauty 103–5
  fiction 43
  heroism 40–1, 103–4
  Italy, communities in 17–18, 73 n.55
  language 24–5
  literature 72–3, 138–9
  love 15, 56
  novels 124–5, 127–30, 151 n.2
  romances 129–30
  texts 106–7, 138–9
  vocabulary 49–50
Greenwood, Emily 138–9
Guacci, Maria Giuseppa 94, 111–12
Güthenke, Constanze 142

Halberstam, Jack 52–3
Haraway, Donna 142–3
Hardwick, Lorna 23
Haugen, Warholm 129–30
Herculaneum papyri 3, 136–7
"hermeneutics of suspicion" 144
Herodotus 152 n.11
Hesiod 158 n.12
heterosexual
  love 31–2, 43–4, 99 n.5, 116–17, 124–5, 138
  marriage, and relationships 72–3, 116–18, 131, 138
  obscenities 72–3

Holland, Lady 71–2
Homer 44–5, 49–50, 152–3, 175–6, 177 n.4, 180 n.5
homosexuality 41, 99–100, 116–17, 125–6, 138
  female, Settembrini on 140–1
  history of 17–18, 114
  homoeroticism 4–7, 30 n.23, 140–1
  homophobia 11–12
  Italian attitudes towards 10–11
  love 31–2, 41, 150 n.8, 152 n.10
  relationships 72–3, 117–18, 118 n.10, 138
  Settembrini's 14, 89–90, 99–100, 118, 122–3, 142–3
Horace 51, 89–90, 92
Humboldt, Alexander von 104
Hunter, Richard 124–5

identity politics 21–2
Illustrated London News 82
imperialism 23–4, 32–3, 65, 68–9, 104–5
imprisonment of Settembrini 24–5, 48–52, 54–66, 68–72, 75, 97
Indoeuropean 18
International Standard Bibliographic Description 66–7
Ireland 78–9
Italy
  Hellenisms 73 n.55
  Italic civilization 104–5
  masculinity in 82–3, 90–1, 93–4, 139–41
  national characteristics 90–1
  republic, establishment of 10–11
  revolutionary movement 10–11
  unification of 52–3, 69
  Young Italy 46–7

Janiculum 8
Jesuits 38–9, 42, 88 n.29
Joughin, Martin 23

Kanaris, Konstantinos 40–1
Kingdom of the Two Sicilies 54, 69, 73 n.55, 103–5

Konstan, David 125–6
Kosofsky Sedgwick, Eve 136, 143–4

Landsdowne, Lord 63–4
Latour, Bruno 28
Lombardy, Spanish rule in 130
London 46, 49, 58–9, 71–2, 75, 89
love
  celebration and worship of beauty, as 121–2
  critical theory, and 143–6
  Greek 15, 56
  heterosexual 31–2, 43–4, 99 n.5, 116–17, 124–6, 138
  homosexual 31–3, 41, 150 n.8, 152 n.10
  marriage and, Settembrini's views on 43–4
  mythical explanation of 124–5
  Platonic 29–30, 119–22, 127–8, 132, 150, 150 n.6, 153–4, 177 n.2
  reciprocal 125–6
  Settembrini and Placco 73–4, 89–90
  symmetry in 21, 48, 116, 124–6
  understanding of 125–6
Lucania earthquake 69
Lucian 8–10, 27, 70–3, 123–5, 131–2, 138–41, 144–5, 152 n.11, 175 n.3
  Amores 125
  Dialogues of the Courtesans 140–1, 180 n.4
  Dialogues of the Dead 175 n.3
  Dialogues of the Gods 175 n.3
  erotic and political import of 138
  On How to Write History 152 n.11
  Philosophers for Sale 134
  Platonism of 144–5
  Settembrini's translation of 70, 73, 131–2, 138–9
  sex between men, writes about 72–3
  True History 123–4
Lucretius 155 n.10

Machiavelli 72–3
Madonna Cia degli Ordelaffi 103–4

Malta 46, 54–5
Manganelli, Giorgio 8 n.10, 12–14, 19–21, 30
Mann, Thomas 8 n.10
Mantua 81–2
Manzoni, Alessandro 130
Marsala 85
Martindale, Charles 18–19
Marx, Karl 7 n.7, 80, 91–2, 111, 144
masculinity
  classical culture, and 17 n.39
  equality and reciprocity, based on 32–3
  Italian 56, 82–3, 90–1, 93–4, 139–41
Masi, Raffaele 26
"Mask, The" (poem) 89–90; *see also* Settembrini, Luigi.
Masuccio 26–7
Mattei, Pasquale 64
Mazzini, Giuseppe 10–11, 16 n.36, 46, 49
Messina, military action against 54–5
Messina, Straits of 85
Middle Passage 78–9, *see also* Blackness
Milan 11–12
"Milesian tales" 125–6, 149–50, 149nn.2,3, 152 n.13
Minniti, Barbara 21 n.57
misogyny 11–12, 111
Montefusco, Vincenzo 71
Muratori, Antonio 93
Murnaghan, Sheila 18–19, 21–2
Museo di San Martino 50
Musolino, Benedetto 46–7
Mussolini, Benito 8–9
Mutiny 78–9

Naples 3–8, 48, 54–5, 58–60, 62, 66–9, 71, 74–5, 85–7
  National Library in 129, 184
  Neapolitan Enlightenment 38
  Neapolitan Republic 38
  University of 44, 87–8
nationalisms, modern 21

Neoplatonism
  "pagan" 121–2
  Settembrini, rejected by 29–30
  term 120–2
Neoplatonists, The 114–35, 149–83
  censorship of 8 n.10
  coded truth-telling in 14
  cover illustration of first edition 13
  erotic curriculum set out in 115–16
  escapism, tendency towards 28
  heterosexual and homosexual relationships in 72–3
  scandal, published as 12
New York 78
Newcastle 75
Nice 84
Nietzsche, Friedrich Wilhelm 144
Nisida, prison at 58–60, 77–8
nostalgia 16–17, 18 n.44, 28, 145–6

oppression 11–12, 17–18, 87–8, 143–4
Orrells, Dan 17 n.39
Orsini, Felice 81–2

paganism
  Catholic absorption of 20 n.55, 153 n.15
  Settembrini's 37–8, 40, 121–2, 121 n.18, 153 n.15
Palatine Anthology 161 n.18
Palermo 85
palimpsest 137
Panathenaic festival 153 n.15, 162 n.1
Panizzi, Antonio 58–9, 66–8, 71–2, 75, 81–2
Panopticon on Santo Stefano 24–5, 38, 55–6, 59–62, 64–6, 69, 71, 75, 79, 88–9, 131–2
  cork model of 62
  deaths, murder, suicides at 65–6
  descriptions of 60–5, 79
  inmates, background of 65–6
  mirror of state, as 65–6
Papal State 85–6
Patriarca, Silvana 91–3

patriarchy 11–12, 112–13
Peel, Robert 58
Pellico, Silvio 81–2
Pertini, Sandro 61
Pessina archive 129
Piedmont 83–4
Piermarini, Emidio 8–10
Placco, Gennaro 73, 79, 89–90, 94
Plater, Emilia 103–4
Plato 29–30, 50–1, 105–6, 111, 120–1, 123–5, 138–9, 144–5
　Atlantis, myth of 123
　gender equality, views on 102–3
　Phaedo 132–5, 137
　Phaedrus 106–7, 133–4, 137
　reading, new ways of 138–9
　Republic, The 42, 102–6, 110–11, 116–17, 123
　Settembrini, influence on 97
　Settembrini's deliberate misquotation of 133–7, 146, 156 n.5
　Settembrini's engagement with 111, 116–17, 123, 137
　Symposium 116–17, 124–6, 155 n.10, 171 n.2
　teachings of 42–3
　Timaeus 123–4
Platonic love 29–30, 119–22, 127–8, 132, 150, 150 n.6, 153–4, 177 n.2
　bravery, compatible with 177 n.2
　concept of 120–1
　nature of 132
Platonic beauty, celebrations of 122
Platonic fiction 97–8
Platonic philosophy 31–2, 120–1
Platonism
　history of 127–8, 130–1
　Lucian's 144–5
Plotinus 120–1, 129
Poerio, Carlo 54–5, 58–60, 63–4, 77–8
political exiles 4–7, 38–9, 43–4, 56–9, 77–9, 82, 84, 87–9, 93, 132–5
political prisoners 24–5, 49–50, 58–9, 75–8, 81–2, 92

politics
　identity 21–2
　revolutionary 25
　Risorgimento 106–7
　sexual 111
Porter, Jim 23
postcolonial theory 24, 62, 91, 139 n.5, *see also* subaltern studies
postmodernism 18–19
"post-truth" politics 19
prison conditions 58–9, 63–5 *see also* Panopticon
prisoners, political 24–5, 49–50, 58–9, 75–8, 81–2, 92
pseudepigrapha, ancient tradition of 123 *see also* fakery
Puoti, Basilio 87–8, 111–12, 127–8
Pythagorean women 105–6

Quattrocento literature 26

race 17–18, 78–9, 94 n.52, 138–9, 145–6, *see also* Blackness, ethnicity, postcolonial theory
Raimondi, Giuseppina 85
reciprocity, sexual 30–2, 118–20, 158–9
relativism 19
Renaissance 120–1
Renaissance Platonism 120–1
revolution, autobiography and, relationship between 23–4
revolutions (1848) 54–5, 80–4, theories of 140–2, *see also* French revolution
Riall, Lucy 11, 80–1, 84–5, 93–4
Risorgimento 19–20, 48, 61, 92–3, 137
　heroes 93–4
　literature, importance of autobiography in 80–1, 90–1
　politics 106–7
　post-war 11
　"Second Risorgimento" 10–11
　women, discourse on 112–13
Rizzoli (publisher) 12

Romans, ancient
  Greece, domination of 127
  imperialism of 68–9, 104–5
  violent subjugators, as 17–18
Rome 16 n.36, 85–6, 104, 124–5
Rousseau, Jean-Jacques 108, 111–12, 124, 129, 140–1
  critique of 101–2
  democracy, view of 108–9
  Discourses 108
  egalitarian sociability, view of 108–9
  Emile 108–9
  misogyny of 111
  Nouvelle Héloïse, La 108–9
  political philosophy 108–9
  political thought 111
  Social Contract 108
  women, on the power and role of 108–10
Russell, Lord John 63–4
Russia 74–5

Sade, Marquis de 92 n.43
Salvini, Matteo 16–17
San Martino, Museum of 62, 71
Santa Maria Apparente prison 97
Santo Stefano 38, 59–65, 75
Schlegel brothers 104
Schleiermacher, Friedrich 121–2
Schwartz, Espérance von 93–4
Scott, Sir Walter 24–5, 49–50
Second World War, end of 10–11
Settembrini, Luigi
  autobiography 55–6, 135–7, 139–40
  arrest and imprisonment 24–5, 48–52, 54–66, 68–72, 75, 97
  beauty, emphasis on 29, 97, 121–3
  Bourbonic abuse, indictment of 52
  Catholic education 37–9
  Catholicism, views on 122–3, 150 n.6, 153 n.15
  classical scholarship 44–5
  classicism, progressive 17–18, 99–100
  conspirator, as 46–8, 100–1
  Dialogue on Women 25–6, 50–1, 97–113, 116–17, 123, 141
  Disquisition on the Life and Works of Lucian 37–8
  egalitarian approach of 17–18, 30, 94, 111, 127, 130–1, 138–40, 144–5
  exile of 4–7, 43–4, 55–7, 77–8, 87–9
  Faucitano, dependence on 69–70, 97–9, 113
  Faucitano, first meeting 43–4
  girls, interest in 41–2
  Gladstone, and 23–4, 63–6
  homosexuality of 14, 89–90, 99–100, 118, 122–3, 142–3
  Lectures on Italian Literature 26, 28–9, 111–12, 120–1, 129, 153 n.15
  legacies of 138–40
  love and marriage, views on 43–4
  Lucian, translation of 70, 73, 131–2, 138–9
  Manganelli, misrepresented by 20–1
  "Mask, The" (poem) 89–90
  Memoirs 37–53
  paganism of 37–8, 40, 121–2, 121 n.18, 153 n.15
  Panopticon, imprisonment 24–5, 60–2, 64–6, 69, 75
  Placco, Gennaro, love for 73–4, 89–90
  Plato, deliberate misquotation of 133–7, 146, 156 n.5
  Plato, engagement with 111, 116–17, 123, 137
  Plato, inspired by 97, 106–7
  Plato, objections to views on heterosexual love found in 116–17
  Platonic fiction, works of 94
  Platonic views 112–13
  political commitments and principles 32–3, 65, 77, 138–9
  professional appointments of 86–8
  Protest of the People of the Two Sicilies 52, 54, 138–9
  Rousseau, views on 109–11
  sex, perspective on 72–3

Settembrini, Luigi (*cont.*)
  sexual fantasy 28
  sexual politics, view of 111
  sexual preferences 47
  smile of 20–1, 135
  symmetry and reciprocity, emphasis on 32–3, 48, 116, 118–20, 139–41, 143
  Three Days in the Chapel 62–3, 79
  women, views on 101–3, 111–13, 142–3
Settembrini, Raffaele 52
  Crimean War service 74–7
  liberation of father and political exiles 78
  Piedmontese merchant navy, refused entry into 75–7
sex and sexuality
  anal 4–7, 115–16, 119–20
  bisexuality 42, 117–18, 125–6
  celebration of 121–2
  communism of sexual partners 116–17
  desire, female, in ancient Greek thought 158 n.12
  education 25, 113, 115
  fantasy 28
  heterosexual love, marriage, and relationships 72–3, 116–18, 131, 138
  history of 137
  homoeroticism 4–7, 30 n.23, 140–1
  identities 21
  nationalist revolution and 21
  politics 111
  reciprocity 30–2, 118–20, 158–9
  symmetry in sexual relationships 124–6
Sicily
  Bourbon rule, revolt against 54–5, 84
  Garibaldi's campaign in 85–6
  liberation of 8
Silva, Luigi De 38–40, 42
social justice 145–6

Socrates 132–5, 137
  execution of 62–3
  gender equality, views on 102–3
  palinode of 133–4, 137
Socrates' Palinode 133–4, 137
Spanish Civil War 10–11
Sparta, women of 103–4
Sperber, Jonathan 80
Staël, Madame de 92, 104
Strato 161 n.18
subaltern studies 24, 59, 62, 101 n.13, 139 n.5, *see also* postcolonial theory
subordination, female 98
Suli 103–4
suffrage 54
  female 109, 112, 140
symmetry
  relationships, in 21, 48, 116, 124–6
  Settembrini's emphasis on 32–3, 48, 116, 118–20, 139–41, 143
Symonds, John Addington 17 n.39

Tacitus 68–9
Teano 85–6
Teiresias, myth of 158 n.12
Thucydides 153 n.15
Torraca, Francesco 8–10
Translation 4, 16, 23, 27, 39, 70–2, 106, 114 n.1, 128–9
Trent, Council of 150 n.6
Trump, Donald 16–17
Turin 75–7
Tuscany, annexation of 84

Undercommons 52–3

Ventotene, island of 75
Venus Callipyge 170 n.1
Venus cult 164 n.5
Verri, Alessandro 129–30
Vicaria prison 55–60, 79, 97, 113
Victor Emmanuel, King 82–6, 93–4
Virgil 92

white supremacy 143–4
women
  homosexuality, female, Settembrini's
    silence on 140–1
  morally superior to men,
    Settembrini's eulogy of women
    as 101
  Risorgimento discourse on
    112–13
  Settembrini's views on 101–3,
    111–13, 142–3
  society, role in 124
  subordination of 98 *see also*
    feminism, suffrage

years of lead 14
Young Italy 46–7
Yugoslavia 10–11